by Carnegie Endowment
for International Peace
a US Based Think Tank

GETTING INDIA BACK ON TRACK

Ideas to
be implemented
in the short run.

CARNEGIE
ENDOWMENT FOR
INTERNATIONAL PEACE

GETTING INDIA BACK ON TRACK

AN ACTION AGENDA FOR REFORM

EDITORS

BIBEK DEBROY
ASHLEY J. TELLIS
REECE TREVOR

FOREWORD BY RATAN N. TATA

Carnegie Endowment for International Peace
1779 Massachusetts Avenue NW
Washington, DC 20036
P+ 202 483 7600
F+ 202 483 1840
CarnegieEndowment.org

The Carnegie Endowment does not take institutional positions on public policy issues; the views represented here are the authors' own and do not necessarily reflect the views of Carnegie, its staff, or its trustees.

To order, contact:
Hopkins Fulfillment Service
P.O. Box 50370
Baltimore, MD 21211-4370
P+ 1 800 537 5487 or 1 410 516 6956
F+ 1 410 516 6998

Cover design by Jocelyn Soly
Composition by Cutting Edge Design
Printed by United Book Press

Library of Congress Cataloging-in-Publication Data

Getting India back on track : an action agenda for reform / Bibek Debroy, Ashley J. Tellis, Reece Trevor, editors.
    pages cm
  Includes bibliographical references and index.
    ISBN 978-0-87003-425-1 (pbk.) -- ISBN 978-0-87003-426-8 (cloth) -- ISBN 978-0-87003-427-5 (electronic) 1. Public administration--India. 2. Administrative agencies--India. 3. India--Social policy. 4. India--Economic policy. 5. India--Politics and government--21st century. 6. India--Economic conditions--21st century. I. Debroy, Bibek, editor of compilation. II. Tellis, Ashley J., editor of compilation.
  JQ231.G44 2014
  330.954--dc23
                                    2014001495

CONTENTS

FOREWORD

RATAN N. TATA

G*etting India Back on Track* comes not a moment too soon. Barely half a decade ago, India's prospects looked exceedingly bright. A dramatic economic boom, with annual growth rates approaching 10 percent, was well under way. Prime Minister Manmohan Singh's government had just concluded a groundbreaking nuclear agreement with the United States, paving the way for a strategic partnership with Washington. It seemed that India's two rounds of economic reforms since 1991 had paid off, and that the country would cement its status as a major economic and political player not only in Asia, but in the world.

Today, these lofty hopes have receded. India's gross domestic product now grows at barely 5 percent per year. This slower pace will undermine the country's expansive development objectives and threaten its deepening relationships with international partners. Protracted approvals and inconsistent policy interpretations are blemishing India's reputation and alienating international investors. If these trends are not arrested, they will short-circuit India's ambitions abroad and at home. Slower growth will also frustrate the ambitions of millions of well-educated young people and dim the hopes of many more without access to the education they need to succeed.

A litany of permissions and clearances stands in the way of many new business enterprises, civil society initiatives, or nonprofit ventures. In an age when it is eminently possible to surmount these structural deficiencies, it is especially perilous to leave them unaddressed. For India to recover its economic dynamism, finding a path forward takes on a new urgency.

The 2014 general elections offer India an opportunity to seriously rethink its policies. The experts brought together in *Getting India Back on Track* represent some of the most incisive policy minds working on India today. They are experts, commentators, and practitioners—and often all three at once. Their individual insights and recommendations have been drawn together and multiplied through the masterful curation of Bibek Debroy, Ashley J. Tellis, and Reece Trevor. It is commendable that this effort has been undertaken by the Carnegie Endowment for International Peace. Carnegie has a rich tradition of scholarly research focused on policy innovation. Its global presence brings insight and ideas from success elsewhere, and its expertise on South Asia is deep and broad.

A national conversation will help to provide a crucible for new ideas and a new commitment to change that could restore India to the path of growth and prosperity. *Getting India Back on Track* should be worthwhile reading, not only for our policymakers, but for every informed person who lives in, works with, comments on, or cares deeply about India's future.

— RATAN N. TATA
Chairman, Tata Trusts
Trustee, Carnegie Endowment for International Peace
April 2014

ACKNOWLEDGMENTS

Getting India Back on Track* originated in a conversation between Bibek Debroy, Jessica T. Mathews, and me in New Delhi last year. Since that original conversation, we profited greatly from further ideas offered by Sunjoy Joshi, K. V. Kamath, Devesh Kapur, Sunil Mittal, Sunil Munjal, Gautam Thapar, Shivnath Thukral, and Milan Vaishnav.

I am deeply grateful, first and foremost, to the contributors of the volume who speedily produced multiple drafts and answered the editors' many queries patiently despite their numerous other commitments. George Perkovich carefully read all the chapters and offered thoughtful suggestions on both presentation and substance. Carnegie's publications team, ably led by Ilonka Oszvald, did a magnificent job in producing this volume on an extraordinarily tight timeline. Marcia Kramer is owed a great debt for her incisive editing, no mean task given the diversity of approaches and voices represented in the volume. Jocelyn Soly designed the wonderful cover and brochures that accompany this book.

For their financial support that made this timely project possible, I am most thankful to the GE Foundation and Karan Bhatia, Ranvir Trehan, and Armeane Choksi. Their generosity enabled this contribution to India's ongoing debates about its future.

Bibek Debroy has been a magnificent colleague, giving generously of his time and his intellectual energy, despite his many other obligations. And Reece Trevor did yeoman's service in shepherding the chapters throughout the editorial process, communicating with both authors and the production staff, and otherwise keeping his fellow editors on task. Without him, Bibek and I would have found this book impossible to produce.

—Ashley J. Tellis
  April 2014

COMPLETING UNFINISHED BUSINESS
FROM THE LONG VIEW TO THE SHORT

ASHLEY J. TELLIS*

The 2014 national elections will be a critical waypoint along the road to realizing India's ambitions of resuscitating economic growth. Opinion survey after opinion survey in the prelude to the polls has suggested a deeply rooted yearning for change. And, in what seems like a conspicuous anomaly when judged against the sweep of India's postindependence history, the electorate at large—both in urban and rural areas—seems seized this time around by the imperative of returning the country to a path of high growth.

India's economic performance was continuously subpar for many decades prior to the 1980s, if not 1991 as well. As long as that was the case, elevated growth sustained for long periods of time was only a dream. But

* The author is deeply grateful to Bibek Debroy, Sunjoy Joshi, Devesh Kapur, and Reece Trevor for their most helpful comments on this chapter.

1

the transformations that have occurred in recent times, beginning with the economic reforms unleashed in the last decade of the last century, have finally given the Indian masses a taste of what structural change, centered on unleashing the energies of a market system, can bring to their everyday lives in terms of both increased wealth and wider economic development. The current explosion of resentment against corruption in India only testifies to the popular desire for better distribution of the nation's economic gains. Such an effort will be doomed to failure if these rewards cannot be produced through continuing growth.

The intense national anxiety in recent years about India's economic slowdown corroborates the proposition that although the voting public may not understand abstruse economics, it has an instinctive sense of when political direction and policy change help sustain or undermine growth. Whatever the balance between the exogenous and the endogenous causes of India's recent economic slowdown may be, there is a widespread conviction in the body politic that the national leadership has failed to steer the nation in a productive direction economically. That leads inexorably to the question of what must be done to recover momentum when the new government takes office.

This volume represents a small effort undertaken by the Carnegie Endowment for International Peace toward answering that question. Obviously, the solutions proffered to such a deceptively simple query can materialize at many levels. After some reflection, the editors of this book concluded that the most useful contribution would consist of relatively short, focused essays that examined key aspects of mainly (though not exclusively) the Indian economy, whose continued reform would be central to accelerating growth. The topics covered, accordingly, range from agriculture and the environment to infrastructure and manufacturing to politico-bureaucratic processes and strategic partnerships abroad. Altogether, the seventeen chapters collected here offer wide-ranging analyses that lead uniformly to specific policy suggestions in each issue area for the consideration of the next government. These recommendations by no means exhaust the totality of the reforms that will be necessary for India's comprehensive transformation over the long term. Rather, they are oriented principally toward what can be achieved in the short term, meaning the life of the 16th Lok Sabha, on the assumption that it will serve a full constitutional term in office.

The conclusions emerging from such a diverse body of analysis are impossible to summarize in any introduction. To the degree that common themes can be culled, the various essays in different ways emphasize the imperatives of continued reform for both economic and strategic reasons; the criticality of returning to the path of high growth and the centrality of markets in the process; the importance of appropriately strengthening key state institutions; the priority of getting the details right for the success of future reforms; and, finally, the necessity of purposive action at the state level, given both the relevant constitutional mandates and the steady shift in power from the central government to the states.

Above all, the essays in this volume consistently look forward, to necessary tasks that are yet to be completed. That very fact, nonetheless, serves as a reminder of how much India's future reforms stem from its grand—but in at least one respect problematic—inheritance. Reviewing that bequest forms the core of this introduction: taking the long, retrospective, view, it highlights the deep roots of the challenges to successful transformation, thus making the necessity for speedy implementation of the recommendations found in the seventeen policy chapters all the more imperative for India's continued success.

THE TRIADIC FOUNDATIONS OF THE INDIAN PROJECT

The Indian national project has undeniably been more successful than was predicted at the time of India's birth as a modern state. When India received its independence in 1947, many skeptics doubted that such a country marked by crushing poverty, bewildering diversities, and weak institutions could long endure. Winston Churchill spoke for the legions of cynics when he plainly declared—long before the British Raj ended in the subcontinent—that India was little other than "an abstraction ... a geographical term. It is no more a united nation than the Equator." Viewed sixty-six years after its founding, the Indian nation has indeed proved the pessimists wrong: not only has the country managed to preserve its national unity, its territorial integrity, and its political autonomy largely unscathed, but it has done so through a historically unprecedented experiment centered on building, as Jawaharlal Nehru told André Malraux, "a just society by just means."

This monumentally ambitious project was erected on a distinctive triadic foundation of liberal democracy, civic nationalism, and socialist economics. These three components were intended to be mutually reinforcing. Together they were meant to fulfill India's dream of becoming a great power in the most comprehensive sense envisioned by the modernists of India's founding generation. That India was a great civilization was to them an evident and acknowledged fact. But transforming this venerable entity into a great power in the contemporary sense—one that would possess the capacity to exert wide influence beyond its own borders—would require India to become the paragon of a new political order.

The success of this order would hinge fundamentally on its ability to produce rapid growth and meaningful development, which would eliminate mass poverty while bringing justice and dignity to millions of socially disenfranchised Indians. These citizens would continue to associate peacefully with their well-to-do countrymen, making decisions about their common future through a system of universal franchise that, whatever outcomes it produced, would be sufficiently respectful of the identities and preferences of the diverse people who made up this new nation. If these accomplishments provided the opportunities for India's millions to flourish and for the Indian state itself to be empowered, the country would undeniably become a true example of political achievement to others. By that very fact it could then lay claim to a seat at the global high tables, where it would participate in making the rules that advanced its vision of a just and peaceful international order.

Liberal Democracy, Holding the Country Together

India's first prime minister, Jawaharlal Nehru, and many others in the postindependence leadership—though, emphatically, not all within this cohort—deeply believed that the combination of liberal democracy, civic nationalism, and socialist economics was essential to successfully building a modern Indian state. That, in turn, was judged to be a prerequisite for mustering both great-power capabilities and wider international approbation. The historical record suggests, however, that those who held these views proved right on only two of the three counts.

Liberal democracy clearly turned out to be the singular glue that has protected India's unity and its territorial integrity. The stunning diversity of

India's primordial nationalisms—whether expressed in language, religion, caste, or even commensality—would have pulled the country apart, as happened in several other postcolonial states, had it not been for the fact that India consciously gave itself a constitutional order that incorporated universal franchise and the rule of law; guaranteed individual rights and a federal system that promulgated separation of powers at the center and limits on the central government's authority over the states; and established recurring elections that tested the strength of contending political parties and endowed them with the privilege of rule for limited periods of time. By adopting such a framework, India enshrined the twin components that mark all real democracies: contestation, or the peaceful struggle for power through an orderly process that confirms the preferences of the polity, and participation, or the right of all adult citizens, irrespective of wealth, gender, religion, or ethnicity, to vote for a government of their choice.

But India went further, much further—and largely for the good. In Nehru's eyes, and in the vision of India's constitution makers, democracy would have been empty if it had been merely procedural, revolving entirely around the system of limited, representative government and its accompanying electoral processes.

Given this belief, the Indian constitution oriented the formal democratic process toward more substantive aims: "to create social, economic and political institutions which will ensure justice and fullness of life to every man and woman," as Nehru framed it in his immortal "Tryst with Destiny" midnight address on the eve of India's independence. This Kantian bedrock in the constitution, centered as it is on inculcating a comprehensive "respect for persons," is what makes the Indian political system not simply democratic but also irreducibly liberal insofar as it holds that the ultimate purpose of governance must be to protect, if not enlarge, the dignity of the human person. Given India's diversities and its social disfigurements, such a vision led ineluctably—and sometimes problematically—to conscious efforts at advancing a conception of secularism grounded on religious tolerance, protecting minority rights, and implementing different forms of affirmative action.

Because liberal democracy, conceived in this expansive sense, was entrenched right from India's founding, it successfully held the country together despite the many competing centrifugal tendencies within: by giving all its citizens an assured "voice" in governance, along with appropriate political and social protections, it freed them from the alternative of having to contemplate secessionism or "exit" from the Indian state as a substitute for their freely bestowed "loyalty."

Despite the odds, therefore, India has survived united—a testament to the consolidating powers of its liberal democracy. And this cohesion has been produced for the most part by peaceful means. In fact, the evidence suggests that the significant episodes of armed uprisings that have occurred in India's postindependence history have materialized mainly when democracy "failed," that is, when representative institutions failed to adequately convey either popular disaffection with the policies of the state or the demand for greater autonomy within the federal system, or when the procedural systems that channeled popular preferences regarding rule were subverted by outside political manipulation.

Civic Nationalism's Vital Success

These formal processes enabling representative rule along with their substantive aims, fundamental to the success of the postindependence project, were boosted further by India's civic nationalism. The ubiquitous familiarity of the Indian identity today often masks the difficulties that went into its making. Until the arrival of the Raj, it was in fact questionable whether the term "Indian" could be used to define the political identity or allegiances of the people residing within the subcontinent. Despite the broad cultural unity of the region, its inhabitants invariably defined themselves by their ethnicity (usually marked by language), their religion (with further reference to caste), or their political membership (as subjects of the local kingdoms they resided in). Often they identified themselves by all three, and sometimes through even more attributes, simultaneously.

The fact that the residents sported multiple identities, then, justified the claim often advanced by British imperialism that India could not be accorded independence because it was not a true "nation." Whatever its underlying motivations, this assertion contained a high degree of truth if the test of nationhood consisted, as it did in modern Europe, of the boundaries of the country coinciding with the spatial limits of the ethnic group residing within.

India's success in building a modern state that defied predictions of its demise derived from its thorough insistence on institutionalizing what was Mahatma Gandhi's greatest bequest to the freedom movement: the construction of a new Indian nation, not by suppressing its many particularities but by incorporating them into a new composite identity that preserved in "marble-cake" fashion all its constituent diversities across ethnic, religious, and racial lines. These diversities, far from being obliterated, acquired salience depending on context but, being enmeshed and free-flowing, they erased the boundaries between the insular and national identities, congealing the latter even as they preserved the former. The modern Indian polity, therefore, emerged not as a nation-state—since, given its myriad diversities, it could not be so—but rather as a *nations*-state. Under the rubric of "unity in diversity," its different ethnic, religious, and racial groups combined to create a novel, multilayered political identity. However confusing that reality may be to the outside world, it is authentically and indisputably Indian.

Some sixty-plus years later, it is clear that this new identity has survived precisely because the self-governing system of rule it has spawned was anchored sturdily in a civic rather than a parochial nationalism. Given its anthropology and its history (including the violent Hindu-Muslim contestation in the period leading up to independence), any parochial nationalism that sought to define what was "Indian" in terms of religion, race, or ethnicity would have exacerbated the country's myriad internal fissures. Creating new, corrosive definitions of insiders and outsiders would have aggravated India's domestic dissensions and the ever-present struggles over economic and social resources to further tear apart the nation brought into being inadvertently through conquest and unification by the Raj and then roused to political consciousness through the nationalist movement led by Mahatma Gandhi.

Recognizing these dangers, India's postindependence leadership eschewed parochial nationalism in favor of civic nationalism where the rights and privileges of being Indian were conceived as arising not from some preexistent modes of belonging—religion, race, or ethnicity—but instead from participation in a collective political endeavor. This common quest, in the words of the Indian constitution's preamble, aimed "to secure to all its citizens: JUSTICE, social, economic and political; LIBERTY of thought, expression, belief, faith and worship; EQUALITY of status and of opportunity; and to promote among them all, FRATERNITY assuring the dignity of the individual and the unity and integrity of the Nation."

The affirmation that Indian democracy would be founded entirely on a shared citizenship centered on upholding liberal principles and participatory institutions rather than religion, race, or ethnicity ensured that the many particularities that might have otherwise divided India were in one fell swoop deprived of any fundamental political meaning. This did not imply that the particularities themselves ceased to exist or that they ceased to provoke contention. Rather, they simply ceased to be privileged attributes that endowed their possessors with either greater rights or natural claims on power—at least as a matter of principle.

The marriage of liberal democracy and civic nationalism thus ensured India's survival as a territorial entity and strengthened its political cohesion over time, an achievement that was not replicated, for example, in Pakistan and in many other postcolonial states. But the success of Indian nationalism since 1947 was not intended to be measured by the brute criterion of physical persistence alone. Whether this endurance contributed toward realizing "justice and fullness of life to every man and woman" was equally at issue. And this ambition, in turn, shaped Nehru's conviction that India's conquest of material poverty would not be achieved through any means other than the third leg of the foundational tripod, socialist economics.

Socialist Economics, the Experiment That Failed

Socialism was beguilingly attractive for many reasons at the time of India's independence. In fact, ever since the Great Depression, socialist ideas increasingly came to be seen as a viable alternative to market capitalism. Furthermore, the visible success of the Soviet Union, which had transformed itself from a feudal society into an industrial economy within the space of a few decades, seemed to prove the superiority of centralized planning and state control over the means of production and distribution sufficiently enough that many newly independent nations in the 1950s voluntarily adopted socialism as the ideology for organizing their own economies.

In early postindependence India, the urgent necessity of quickly overcoming vast poverty made the allure of socialism even more enticing. Its appeal for Nehru, however, derived from more than purely instrumental calculations. He was a Fabian socialist from his early years, and as such his commitment to socialism was based on a deep suspicion of the profit motive that is central to capitalism and his perception of capitalism's intrinsic connection to inequality. He also had a strong conviction that capitalism, imperialism, and colonialism—the last of which he had spent his entire adult life up to that point opposing—were inextricably inter-linked and were the fundamental cause of India's decline since the begin-ning of the modern era.

If the material foundations of the new Indian nation were to be rapidly rebuilt in the aftermath of independence, a socialist reorganization of the Indian economy was thus inevitable so long as Nehru—given his convic-tions—remained at the helm. Given his strong democratic temper, however, Indian socialism would involve neither a violent decapitation of the capitalist classes nor a systematic nationalization of existing capital stocks. In fact, it permitted the existence of a private sector, but unfortu-nately one that would enjoy only restricted opportunities in an economy that would come to be dominated by the state. But because the impera-tives that drove this domination were colored greatly by the desire to make India a conventional great power, Indian socialism took the form of a state-dominated mixed economy oriented toward the acquisition of a heavy industrial base.

At its core lay a systematic effort at centralized planning that was intended not simply to provide strategic direction to the economy but also to increase the share of public investments through the energetic mobiliza-tion of national savings. These savings would be plowed into vast public sector enterprises that would populate the "commanding heights" of the Indian economy. Furthermore, planning entailed systematically regulat-ing the activities of private enterprise in the secondary sector of the economy through comprehensive licensing intended to control the levels and composition of industrial production and prevent the "excessive" con-centration of wealth.

This endeavor unfortunately resulted in the suppression of competition in India's domestic markets with all its pernicious accompanying conse-quences: scarcity, compromised product quality, and higher prices. Moreover, the explicit bias in Indian central planning toward self-reliance resulted in curtailing India's connectivity with international trade. Instead, strategies of "import substitution," aimed at generating increased investment and employment mainly through internal resources (though, in practice, also relying on foreign aid), came to rule the day. The obsession with domesticating high technology and filling the "investment gap" through indigenous resource mobilization, then, ended up preventing the Indian state from emphasizing human capital investments through strengthened private property rights and other direct welfare expenditures that might have straightforwardly assisted the country's indigent population. Finally, the central planners' fixation with mopping up all available domestic resources to support the strategy of directed investment resulted in the creation of a high tax regime. That stifled whatever private initiative survived and, equally problematically, drove the taxable surpluses into the black market beyond the reach of the state. As a result, India's governments could not enjoy the revenue growth required to advance welfare objectives, and the phenomenon of pervasive tax evasion became a legacy with which the nation struggles to this day.

Oddly, the obsession with creating a modern nation through state-dominated planning, investment, and regulation resulted in a dreadful neglect of Indian agriculture and the informal sectors, where the majority of the Indian population found employment at the time of independence. Although Nehru's government in the First Five Year Plan focused on several elements pertaining to agriculture, such as land reforms, irrigation upgrades, and cooperative farming, this focus was quickly displaced by industrialization from the Second Five Year Plan onward. The result, as Ashok Gulati explains in his chapter, "Revamping Agriculture and the Public Distribution System," is that Indian agriculture, which still employs close to half of the population, continues to exhibit weak performance where productivity, innovation, and output are concerned.

The transformation of Indian agriculture—that great base of national employment, especially immediately after independence—actually required the fruits of capitalism for lasting success. The institutionalization of a well-ordered market system for bringing agricultural products to the final consumer would have elicited increased private investments in mechanization, biotechnology, irrigation, and fertilizers. Instead, India embarked on tepid land reforms that served mainly to increase the fragmentation of land holdings. Coupled with the state interventions in food pricing and procurement, these policies have served only to retard the larger transformation of the primary sector of the Indian economy.

The Green Revolution of the 1960s, although making India self-sufficient in foodgrains, actually obscured Indian agriculture's larger problems. By masking the necessity for fundamental market reform, it resulted in the enthronement of an unsustainable production ecology. Today, thanks to subsidies, freebies, and highly regulated agricultural inputs, this production ecology dangerously threatens the public treasury. Furthermore, it has failed to produce the output and productivity gains that the agricultural sector would have otherwise enjoyed under an alternative institutional regime.

Parenthetically, the dominance of the informal sector in India is also a consequence of the restrictions imposed on large enterprises through insidious labor laws. Whatever its causes, however, the low productivity in the informal sector, which is reflected in its pervasively low incomes, implies that the large numbers of individuals employed therein were unable to enjoy the fruits of India's driven effort to grow.

The net result, tragically, was that Nehru's great ambition to "ensure justice and fullness of life to every man and woman" was undermined from the get-go by the relative neglect of the most important sector affecting the lives of most Indians. Worse, the crushing state domination that slowly gathered steam in the remainder of the economy and in national life more generally did not produce sufficient gains overall to justify the policies emerging from the addiction to socialism. These policies produced only meager increases in national output and were perversely accompanied by the growth of a vast bureaucracy that quickly became corrupt and stultifying. Despite the slow incubation of these problems originating ultimately in dirigisme, India's growth during the 1950s was not dismal. The 1960s, however, became a turning point when the commitment to socialism steadily mutated from idealism into a sclerotic instrument of power and patronage. These trends, unfortunately, gathered steam until at least the 1980s, as Nehru's daughter, Indira Gandhi, enthroned the "permit-license raj" as the new face of Indian political economy.

Indira Gandhi took the intrusive control and political manipulation of the Indian economy to heights beyond Nehru's wildest imagination. With her brand of populist socialism came a singular focus on nationalization, extortion from private enterprise for political ends, and expansive promises of state-led redistribution. These endeavors did little to produce the economic transformation her father desired. Instead, they exacerbated the economic and social divides within India and inaugurated the era of questionable entitlements with which the nation struggles to this day. By the end of Gandhi's life, she had achieved the distressing distinction of having managed to firmly enshrine the political decrepitude and economic stagnation that became the hallmarks of Indian socialism—the third element of the defining triad that characterized New Delhi's postindependence project.

By 1980, the sorry results of the Indian socialist experiment were visible for all to see. Many apologists for socialism in India would argue that the country's deplorable economic performance—the 3 percent or so "Hindu rate of growth" chalked up between 1950 and 1980—was still an improvement over the previous one hundred years of the British Raj. During that time, the Indian economy essentially remained stagnant, growing at roughly the same rate as India's population. If India's pre-1980 economic performance is measured relative to the growth chalked up during the Raj, India does appear to be a superlative performer. Even so, it could not transform the lives of its people, whose explosive demographic growth after independence was owed to the falling death rates produced by improved public health and sanitation. When measured against the economic accomplishments in the rest of the world, India's failures were stark and unforgivable. As Arvind Virmani has pointed out in his devastating audit, "The God That Failed":

> In 1950 the welfare of the average Indian was 29 percent of that of the average world citizen. By 1979 it had reduced to 20 percent, or one-fifth, of that of the average world citizen. This means that the world on average was progressing faster than India—not just South Korea, not just east and southeast Asia, but Africa, Latin America and developed countries (all) taken together!
>
> During Nehru's tenure, India's per capita gross domestic product (GDP) at purchasing power parity (PPP) as a

proportion of average world per capita GDP at PPP was reduced by 3 percentage points (or by 11 percent of its previous level). It declined further during the 1965 war and was 23 percent in 1966, when Indira [Gandhi] first came to power. By 1976 [the] welfare of the average Indian slipped further to 21 percent of world levels (thus declining by another 2 percentage points or by 8 percent of its previous level). It remained at the same relative level in 1980.

Per capita income growth data from a different source confirm that Indian economic growth was slower than that of the rest of the world. Between 1960 and 1979 India's per capita GDP grew at an average rate of 1.1 percent per annum compared to an average growth of per capita world GDP of 2.7 percent per annum. Thus, the average Indian's per capita income was falling behind the world by 1.6 percent[age points] per year during this period.[1]

The Indian dalliance with socialism from the moment of its modern founding thus painfully corroborated the aphorism "The road to hell is paved with good intentions." Sadly, it was, and remains to this day, the fatal weakness of the postindependence project and one that the country has struggled to escape from since at least the 1980s. In retrospect, Nehruvian socialism produced two contradictory effects. On one hand, it laid the foundations, however inefficiently, for building a modern industrial state in India, in itself a remarkable achievement. On the other hand, it simultaneously served to stifle native Indian entrepreneurship.

The first element has undergone some change in recent times because resource limitations have constrained the Indian government's ability to pursue high-profile investments of different kinds. The second element, however, persists virulently. Although Indian private enterprise is now freer than ever before, it still struggles in the face of an overbearing state. Instead of creating conditions for its success, the state seems overly focused on extracting societal resources in order to underwrite its populist handouts. More recently, the advocates of these giveaways have sought to legitimize their disbursal under the guise of creating a "rights-based welfare state," where the masses would have unprecedented constitutional claims to such rivalrous and excludable goods as food, education, health, and housing. Forgetting that such private goods can never be distributed as a matter of political "rights"—because their prior production is neither effortless nor can it be assured by a *deus ex machina*—the persistence of such ideational claims only highlights the entrenchment of bankrupt statism in India and the colossal burdens it continues to impose on the nation's productive citizenry. In any event, if all the socialist experiment did was to prevent the country from reaching its economic potential—even though that shortcoming was distressing enough—it might have been forgivable. But its consequences were far more corrosive and sweeping.

CORRODING THE OTHER FOUNDATIONAL PILLARS

To begin with, India's economic failures, which were rooted in the third component of its state- and nation-building endeavor, began to undermine over time the success of the two other foundational pillars, liberal democracy and civic nationalism. That these effects quickly became manifest should not be surprising. The best modern studies on the success of democracy suggest that a high correlation exists between the survival of liberal democracy and national income. India, undoubtedly, bucks the larger trend because its liberal democratic institutions have endured despite its failures to generate the high levels of income that peer developing countries have posted since, say, the 1960s.

Yet, this atypical achievement must not obscure the reality that both India's liberal democracy and its civic nationalism have been disfigured in good measure because of its economic failures. The country's inability to generate high levels of GDP growth, for example, has weakened its ability to raise and maintain an effective state capable of discharging its fundamental obligations of administering law and order (and, increasingly, providing an effective national defense), serving as an impartial instrument of adjudication in the face of competitive social claims, and providing for the economic remediation that is inherent in the liberal vision of its democratic experiment.

Sustained growth is accordingly the chief objective of India's most-needed reforms; Omkar Goswami, for instance, in his chapter, "Generating Employment," in this volume identifies restoring such growth as the single most important step for India to boost employment generation. Moreover, in a situation where the state is still a significant producer and distributor of both private and collective goods, its continuing underperformance has prevented it from being able to satisfy the rising demands of its highly politically conscious populace. Such a situation created the explosive circumstances that led to a suspension of democracy from 1975 to 1977, the Emergency that still remains a blot on India's otherwise storied postindependence record.

Although that episode is unlikely to be repeated anytime soon, India's persistent economic shortcomings have created strong incentives for various constituencies to use the political process to manipulate the patterns of wealth and income distribution for private advantage. The resulting impetus to crony capitalism, then, not only undermines support for a market economy but also brings discredit to the democratic process by spawning a vicious cycle with bitter consequences. The deprived citizenry begins to view "democracy," first and foremost, not as an impartial mechanism for testing collective preferences relating to rule, but rather as a means of hijacking political office in order to control the delivery of rewards. This sad fact is made clear by Devesh Kapur and Milan Vaishnav in their chapter, "Strengthening Rule of Law."

The social remediation undertaken thanks to the liberal character of Indian democracy, then, becomes suspect because it is seen as a misuse of scarce resources—a usurpation by certain constituencies that use politics to remedy their private economic losses—rather than as a collective effort to assist those disadvantaged social groups in becoming effective members of the polity. In such circumstances, the professional politician, in turn, begins to view the organs of the state not as instruments for promoting the common good, but as spoils to be distributed for satisfying various vote banks in order to assure continued electoral success.

Given the persistence of these different perverse phenomena, it is no surprise that cosmopolitan nationalism itself has come under increasing attack by political alternatives in recent decades. These alternatives seek to replace the organic solidarity of citizenship founded on the pursuit of certain ideals with a vision of citizenship based on the protection or promotion of some "national embodiment groups" as the goal of the state. Indian socialism, although constituting only one leg of the nationalist project, has thus served, unfortunately, to weaken the other two, more coruscating, counterparts as well—with damaging consequences for the success of India's "tryst with destiny."

Finally, what made the failures of socialism so destructive was perhaps the fact that, even as the model itself was degenerating and proving unable to deliver on its promises, its hegemony in the Indian worldview remained more or less intact. The great challengers of the socialist program since independence—C. Rajagopalachari, Minoo Masani, N. G. Ranga, and K. M. Munshi, to name but a few—did not have either the political or ideational impact that was their due. This failure of the free-market champions stands in stunning contrast to the protagonists of socialism. They still dominate the Indian polity not only in the political and intellectual classes and the population at large, but also, and however odd it may seem, in business as well. In the case of the latter, however, socialism is often valuable precisely because the superior wealth of the commercial classes permits them to manipulate state policies to their private advantage.

The net result of socialism's intellectual and political dominance in India was that the nation careened toward the betrayal of its promise until it was confronted by a series of crises. Although these debacles first manifested themselves in the 1960s, they reached a boiling point only in 1991. It was in that fateful year that India's nonalignment crumbled with the demise of the Soviet Union and its socialism came apart due to a devastating balance-of-payments crisis. Only then, under the then finance minister Manmohan Singh (at the behest of then prime minister P. V. Narasimha Rao), did India begin to take the first steps toward undoing the economic damage that had been inflicted during the past forty-plus years.

While considerable progress has been made since then, this task is by no means complete. In part, this is because the swing toward introducing market mechanisms after the 1991 crisis was driven principally by pressures of necessity rather than a genuine intellectual conversion to economic liberalism. One continuing challenge to sustaining market reforms, therefore, has been the diminishing enthusiasm for them as their precipitating calamity began to ease.

The ravages of the socialist past are by now widely acknowledged. Still, the absence of an authentic conviction about the indispensability of free markets for successful growth and development implies that it remains difficult to mount a full-fledged defense of "the economics of liberty" in India. Indeed, one need look no further than Rajiv Kumar's analysis in his chapter, "Revisiting Manufacturing Policy," to determine that the vestiges of socialism are in large part responsible for India's woeful business environment. Obviously, a slow rollback of socialist policies has been under way since 1991. But unlike the case in China since 1978, this shift in India has been hesitant, conflicted, and furtive rather than forthright and resolute.

SOCIALISM'S PERILOUS LEGACY

These shortcomings are anchored not merely in ideational failures—although there are plenty on that score. More fundamentally, they are rooted in the fact that socialism has corrupted the deep structure of state-society relations in India, making the task of reform all the more challenging and onerous. This corruption has manifested itself in three ways.

A Paternalistic State

First, Indian socialism created a paternalistic state. The intention of India's founders was not to create a state that would either overwhelm Indian society or alienate the individual. But the sheer magnitude of deprivation in India at the time of independence—and even today—created conditions that made it easy to justify the erection of a paternalistic state. In the initial moments of India's modern nationhood, vast sections of its population were admittedly incapable of exercising effective agency. But India did not make the investments in human capital that might have resuscitated agency in the most impoverished sections of society. Nor did it create the legal and regulatory frameworks that would have permitted market relations among these newly empowered individuals to flourish.

By failing to do so, India lost the opportunity to establish durable foundations for high and sustained economic growth over the long term, a matter of some consequence since most studies of economic success worldwide emphasize the importance of protecting property rights, ensuring security against expropriation, and preserving the sanctity and honest enforcement of contracts as critical to promoting entrepreneurship and investments that lead to rapid growth. Just as importantly, this failure also prevented India from durably remedying what remains one of its biggest structural deficits where economic development is concerned: the low levels of social trust in the Indian polity. Instead of creating institutions that would address these fundamental issues, the early postindependence leadership settled for policy choices that, centering on socialism, enthroned the state as the agent chiefly responsible for generating all productive outcomes.

Thus, India engendered a system of governance that gave the state or various state-run entities free rein over virtually every aspect of its citizens' lives. Through this kind of debilitating domination, which was the logical, even if unintended, consequence of the Indian attempt at controlling economic life, socialism alienated the Indian citizenry from its natural capacities and resourcefulness—the very strengths that had allowed multitudinous communities that were very distant from the centers of rule to survive for hundreds of years—replacing these with a government that became the lifeline of first, rather than last, resort.

Empowerment was thus displaced by entitlement, a preference that appears alive and well to this day, destroying in the process the sense of individual responsibility that is the most far-reaching consequence of dependency on authority and upon which all successful democracy and development subsist. The Indian experience after 1991 has demonstrated that private creativity, initiative, and contribution are far more capable than governmental action in producing desirable economic and societal outcomes. This reality was confirmed even earlier by the millions of unnoticed mitigating actions undertaken by ordinary Indians to overcome their inhospitable circumstances. But large-scale transformation necessarily requires an institutional order that rewards such activities. Surjit Bhalla's chapter, "Dismantling the Welfare State," outlines the argument in favor of replacing the existing misconceived welfare state with just such a framework.

The continuing tragedy of even the post-1991 reforms has been that state entities have resisted, and continue to resist, all attempts to restrain their already pervasive ubiquity. Even the sensible improvements undertaken thus far have served to enhance, rather than to curtail, the presence and power of the state. That fact has been made all too evident in the multiplicity of regulatory institutions that have been spawned in the name of reform. That these institutions are often ill-equipped for their assigned task would have been forgivable if "regulation" had not become the new means by which the deep state has exacted its revenge on the liberalization effort. To the degree that Indian socialism therefore persists in resisting the dismantlement of the paternalistic state, the success of reform becomes all the more precarious.

A Controlling State

Second, Indian socialism created a controlling state. The fundamental material challenge facing the Indian polity in its infancy was the rapid creation of wealth. This achievement would have enabled its huge population to traverse the Maslovian hierarchy of needs from the physiological (the most basic and urgent) to eventual self-actualization (the higher aspirations) as quickly as possible and thus bring meaningful democracy within grasp. The key to creating wealth, or economic development as it came to be called in the postwar era, lies in strengthening private property rights and creating institutions that would safeguard the exercise of those rights. Especially in a country such as India that was predominantly poor, protecting property rights should have been fundamental because it involved recognizing individuals' rights of ownership to themselves and to their labor. But despite ponderous attempts, India failed to enshrine these fundamental rights, and to this day it continues to wrestle with the implications of that failure. Somik Lall and Tara Vishwanath's treatment of land acquisition in their chapter, "Managing Urbanization," taken alongside Barun and Madhumita Mitra's chapter on "Renovating Land Management," in general highlight both the consequences of a weak private property regime and the tensions that emerge when ownership norms threaten to conflict with sustainable development.

The rise of the West has demonstrated that the driving element behind rapid economic development has been the creation of conditions that enable individuals to freely use private property—their goods, land, or labor—to satisfy the demands of others and in so doing to earn the incomes that promote growth. To the degree that such activities occur freely in the marketplace, they also embody an information-carrying function in the form of relative prices. This enables resources to flow into those activities where they are most needed.

On the ideological misapprehension that strengthening property rights would undermine the protection of the poor while stymieing the processes of growth, Indian socialism made it harder for the marginalized to assert their rights. It also undermined the possibilities of rapid growth (which could have otherwise underwritten the justifiable elements of social remediation and the production of collective goods) by replacing markets with highly centralized government planning and control. These twin elements created, among other things, huge state-owned enterprises that were liberated from the obligations of being responsive to their consumers through a functioning market system. Since their outputs were never put to the real tests of either demand or price—because the state regulated the formal economy as a whole to eliminate competition in many critical areas—public sector enterprises could continue to offer unproductive employment to both labor and civil servant managers while continually drawing on the public trough to ensure their survival.

The misplaced emphasis on public sector investments was compounded by other highly interventionist state activities. These included everything from regulating commodity prices to administering vast subsidies. All of them collectively created serious distortions in the market that burdened the Indian treasury, prompted a wasteful misuse of resources, and undermined sustainability across the economy at large.

These systemic problems persist to this day. For instance, Sunjoy Joshi's chapter in this book, "Reforming Energy Policy and Pricing," blames subsidies and other illiberal state interventions for India's massively distorted energy market. The nationalization of Indian banks in 1969 by Indira Gandhi, the prime minister at the time, magnified such problems considerably because control over this segment of the financial sector enabled the state to fund a large gamut of unproductive activities without the discipline otherwise imposed by the market. Thus, it was ironic that these actions, prompted by a desire to alleviate poverty in India, contributed toward perpetuating poverty for far longer than was necessary.

Socialist enterprises, consequently, did not simply crowd out private investment and thwart competition—which was bad enough because the test of economic survival ultimately is a test of efficiency. But they also helped to exacerbate scarcity unnecessarily while concurrently creating a vast set of special interests that became entrenched. The combination of both elements, in turn, contributed toward breeding pervasive corruption. This corruption occurred not simply through the conventional forms of rule circumvention but equally through creating lucrative sinecures that have since become powerful hindrances to reform. Indian socialism's bequest of a controlling state, therefore, produced over time a vast number of economic and bureaucratic entities that existed mainly to protect their monopoly powers, no matter what the costs imposed on stifling private activities or the consequences for perpetuating poverty.

Just as unfortunately, the controlling state that came to dominate the polity at the highest levels also began to manifest itself to the ordinary citizen as the oppressive state. The Indian nation inherited from its British occupiers an army of clerks who laboriously wrote and maintained the copious records necessary to document the health of their imperial possession. When independence came, the colonial masters were ejected but not their bureaucratic ethos: on the contrary, the new government steadily expanded over time the voluminous paperwork that was now demanded of its citizenry for every resource, service, and permission provided by the controlling state. That these bequests were often meager and inadequate did not prevent them from becoming subject to "red tape," the infamous crimson string used by the bureaucracy to secure the countless forms and applications that the hapless public had to submit to receive any benefits from the state. The general scarcity of resources, when coupled with the intricate rules of government business, the burdensome application procedures associated with those regulations, and the discretionary powers of the supervising functionaries all taken together, quickly created a cesspool of corruption. This disfigurement soon became impossible to eradicate. It served only to reinforce the population's helplessness and submission to an intestinal bureaucratic machine that in the eyes of ordinary people was characterized equally by its arrogance and its inefficiency. The controlling state thus simultaneously took a toll of both the Indian economy and Indian democracy.

An Inefficient State

Third, Indian socialism created an inefficient state. Not only was the Indian state inefficient in the sense that it produced goods and services far more wastefully than could be made by private competitors, but it was also structurally inefficient in that it did not discharge the obligations that a state is responsible for of necessity. The genesis of the problem historically, of course, emerged from the socialist predilection for dominating the "commanding heights" of the economy. Once again, the intentions were noble: because the Indian nation was highly constrained initially by shortages of resources and skills, the Indian public sector would take up the mantle of becoming the nation's privileged producer of private goods. This foray would take the Indian state deep into the business of running everything from airlines to hotels to power plants and from extracting natural resources to producing, among other things, cement, fertilizers, steel, wristwatches, and textiles. Across the entire Indian economy—with the exception of agriculture—Indian public enterprises came to have an enduring presence in the production of private goods. Today this presence is manifested most strongly in the defense and financial sectors.

That the performance of Indian public enterprises has varied considerably should not be surprising. That is because the quality of market feedback and internal accountability differs depending on the regulatory environment and the levels of competition permitted in the specific industries. In the defense industry, for instance, where Ravinder Pal Singh, in his chapter on "Building Advanced Defense Technology Capacity" identifies an especially dogmatic commitment to state-run indigenous production, India's achievements are consequently dismal. But then there is the larger question of why the Indian state should have been in the business of producing private goods in the first place. That question has never been satisfactorily answered except on ideological grounds, given that creating a proper investment regime from the very beginning, combined with robust international trading links, would have far more effectively mobilized private capital to produce these products at lower price and better quality. This approach would have simultaneously freed up state resources for investments in those areas where private enterprise is distinctly uncompetitive.

In retrospect, if the state had to focus on producing private goods, India would probably have been better off if its government had concentrated less on tangible products and more on human capital development through education and health care, as both Laveesh Bhandari and A. K. Shiva Kumar counsel in different ways in their respective chapters, "Expanding Education and Skills" and "Confronting Health Challenges." Although these services are ordinarily private goods, they are harder—though not impossible—to produce in a market because of the many disjunctive incentives at play and because they embody some characteristics of quasi-collective goods. In any event, how the state intervenes in these areas is just as important as the fact of its intervention.

Irrespective of how one evaluates the Indian state's fixation on producing private goods, the shortcomings of this strategy could have been overlooked if Indian policymakers had concurrently been attentive to those things that only a state can do: the production of public goods and the creation of strong institutions for effective rule-making, administration, and adjudication. Unfortunately, neither task was satisfactorily performed in India. The provision of public goods remains among the primary duties of the state because, being non-excludable and non-rivalrous items, they are usually underproduced by market arrangements.

Consequently, whether in intangible form (such as law and order, national defense, environmental quality, and public health) or in their tangible manifestations (such as public infrastructure), as Rajiv Lall and Ritu Anand explain in their chapter, "Modernizing Transport Infrastructure," the role of the state in creating these assets is critical. Indian socialism, however, failed to invest in producing such goods at the levels required for speedy growth. This is because the government was diverted by the mirage of promoting heavy industry and the other strategic sectors of the economy. As a result, the critical complementarities that might have enabled private actors to make meaningful contributions to Indian economic growth were sorely lacking. This deficiency magnified the problems arising from the repression of private enterprise.

The second failure was just as debilitating. The failure to invest in institutions that would administer laws, policies, and regulations neutrally, efficiently, and transparently implied that public policies could not be implemented in the manner necessary for either economic growth or effective governance. India inherited a remarkable bureaucratic instrument from the Raj, the Indian Civil Service, the fabled "steel frame," which later mutated into the Indian Administrative Service. After independence, this elite group was supplemented by a few score sister services overseeing everything from the nation's archeology to its zoology.

For an overregulated country, however, the capacity inherent in these bureaucracies remained pathetically small relative to its real needs. The consequences were dire. Tushaar Shah and Shilp Verma's chapter on "Addressing Water Management" offers a telling example of how even specialized bureaucrats are often ill-trained and misguided in their approach, handicapping entire sectors of the Indian economy. Across India's civil services, the quality of the personnel, the professionalism of the institutions, and their supposedly apolitical character has gradually eroded over the years.

As a result, both the administrative and regulatory public service bodies in India are unable to cope with the increasing complexity of India's economy and politics. The transformations in the economy, driven by the recent internal liberalization and the return to international integration after many decades, have presented new and more recondite problems emerging from the complex intersection of market and state, which the generalist bureaucracy has proved ill-equipped to resolve.

The challenges manifested in politics, in contrast, are owed to the growing decentralization of power and the social revolutions occurring throughout India in the face of a slowly expanding market economy that creates its own brand of winners and losers. These forces have intensified the pressures of "demand politics" in historically unprecedented ways, taxing the increasingly heterogeneous quality of the Indian bureaucracy. Because of weaknesses of institutional capacity within the Indian state, the traditional problems of corruption, which originated in socialist scarcity, now encounter the further obstacles of politicization, partiality, and ineptitude. These challenges, unfortunately, have materialized at a time when the Indian bureaucracy itself, its relationship with its political masters, and the conjoint processes of decisionmaking and policy implementation have all grown more complex and unwieldy—a deplorable state of affairs that Bibek Debroy deftly highlights in his chapter, "Correcting the Administrative Deficit."

THE IMPERATIVE FOR COMPREHENSIVE REFORM AND THE PRIORITY OF THE SHORT VIEW

In a nutshell, then, the long view suggests that India's unfortunate fling with socialism resulted in the creation of a mangled state that failed to produce not only growth but its enabling appurtenances as well. Both of these failures then conspired to threaten the success of liberal democracy and civic nationalism, the other, more flourishing, foundations of the postindependence project. Comprehensive reform in India is, accordingly, imperative. And despite whatever a facile analysis may suggest, reform cannot consist of simplistically attempting to replace the state with the market.

Rather, reform requires momentum along three distinct avenues simultaneously: reducing the role and involvement of the state in those areas where it lacks comparative advantage, such as the production of private goods even in what are conventionally viewed as "strategic" sectors of the economy; increasing the contribution and effectiveness of the state through better administrative, regulatory, and adjudicative public institutions as well as more competent creation of public goods, both tangible and intangible; and improving the state's capacity for instrumentally rational public policies by, among other things, subjecting them to market tests to the extent possible. The prospects for Indian success over the secular period thus depend on having both an enlarged, efficient market and an effective, legal-rational state. Ligia Noronha's prescription for "Managing the Environment," her chapter that casts sustainability as a good with economic value to be prioritized by the market and protected by the state, shows that such a model is as achievable as it is necessary.

The reform efforts unleashed immediately after the 1991 crisis represented only the initial steps in undoing the pernicious legacy of forty years of Indian socialism, including its corrosive impact on Indian political life. The early successes of this effort became visible during the first decade of this century, when India chalked up historically unprecedented rates of growth that also had the highly beneficial impact of liberating many Indians from dire poverty. This accomplishment accorded India significant international recognition and gave rise to the hope that the nation was finally on the cusp of the vaunted self-sustaining "takeoff" that had eluded it for decades. As if determined to confirm the wag's old adage that India was eternally doomed to be the country of the future, the last five years proved cruel to India's economic—and reputational—fortunes.

The global financial crisis undoubtedly played a role in India's depressed economic performance. But the plain truth—no matter how much government spokesmen may deny it—is that India faltered because its political leadership failed just when it was most needed. The disastrous bifurcation of power and authority witnessed in New Delhi since 2008 created exactly the conditions that undermined the momentum for further reform and, even more dangerously, provided uncomfortable flashbacks to the heyday of populist socialism with all its attendant detritus. India, however, cannot afford such continued faltering: every day the toxic conditions persist, the more difficult the task of "ensur[ing] justice and fullness of life to every man and woman" will be.

Even more dangerously, while India dawdles without a clear foreign policy vision of the sort that C. Raja Mohan calls for in his chapter, "Rejuvenating Foreign Policy," the world continues to pass it by. India's strategic partners, such as the United States and the key power centers in Europe and Asia, are perplexed by New Delhi's incapacity to cooperate even on issues where it has the greatest stakes. Meanwhile, its competitors, such as Pakistan and China, grow ever more threatening, the former because of its weakness, the latter because of its strength. At a time when India is confronted by the prospect—never before witnessed in its history—of having a genuinely great power appear firmly rooted on its doorstep, the recent Indian failure to successfully balance internally, while continuing to reject external balancing, could prove downright dangerous and imprudent.

If India's most conspicuous failures are still rooted in economic arrangements and political postures that derive their inspiration from various forms of utopianism, the correctives will not materialize in singular or grandiose form. Former governor of New York Mario Cuomo powerfully captured this insight when he declared, "You campaign in poetry. You govern in prose." Reforming India to bring it back on track to the path of high growth—where it can satisfy the material yearnings of its populace, enliven the democratic ideals of its polity, and justify the hopes of its international partners—will remain a complex and involved task that requires what Karl Popper once called "piecemeal social engineering." However animated it may be by the vision of empowering individuals and appropriately strengthening the state, the reforms that advance these aims in the future will be about detail, often involving intricate technical issues. Their beneficial effects will be produced only through aggregation and consistent execution. In other words, it will require the kind of painstaking translation advanced by Ila Patnaik's chapter,

"Maintaining Macroeconomic Stability"—one that transforms the long view into the short view, the one that finally matters.

What also becomes abundantly clear in this volume is that the locus of reform has now shifted decisively from the center to the states. The transformations associated with the first-generation reforms in India, which included the abolition of production quotas, the slow freeing up of internal markets, and the increased openness to international trade, could be unleashed from New Delhi by relatively simple actions, often involving the executive alone. Thanks, in part, to the mandates ensuing from the Indian constitution, many of the most critical follow-on reforms— including those identified in this book and which in general pertain to liberalizing factor markets (in contrast to the first wave, which focused on product markets)—will have to occur through actions at the level of the states. This implies the possibility that future economic liberalization in India will be manifested heterogeneously as the twenty-nine (or more in the future) states pursue different paths to reform at varying pace.

This is just as well because, as the principle of subsidiarity recognizes, social policy is best made at the lowest possible levels of competent authority: in India, this implies, at least for the moment, the myriad states that constitute the Union, although in the future, some kinds of economic decisionmaking could devolve to even lower levels, namely the third tier of governance, which consists of the *panchayats* in rural areas and municipalities in the urban ones. Given India's deep complexities, only a systematic application of the principle of subsidiarity—to begin with, at the state level—would ensure that future reforms stay true to the ambitions of its diverse peoples. While such an approach may risk excessive decentralization, its limitations will be more than compensated for by the gains accruing from the multiple reform laboratories spawned and the competition for success between what are nation-sized entities in most instances. Translating the long view into various short views, then, becomes an interesting endeavor in its own right.

Through its substantive essays, this volume offers ideas about what the short view of economic reform in India going forward entails. Occasioned by the 2014 Indian general election, whose outcome will be pivotal to determining whether India can retrieve its high-growth trajectory, this collection of essays brings together twenty-two distinguished scholars of India to address many different aspects of reform that must be engaged during the life of the next government. The focus of every chapter is thus directed toward explaining what the incoming government must do if India is to regain its economic luster. Toward that end, these analyses are heavily focused on the immediate imperatives of policy. But in each case their recommendations are grounded on a larger explanation of the key challenges in a given policy domain and why they matter for India's economic future.

Obviously, in any collection such as this, many important issues are left unaddressed. It is hoped that these subjects—and those discussed in this book—will be the subject of further scholarly examination and public debate. If this volume, however, reinforces the national urgency of getting India into a more successful groove and stimulates a discussion about how that objective might be realized by the new government, it will have served its purpose. Neither India nor the world—and especially its partners such as the United States—can afford to watch fortune elude New Delhi for another five years.

NOTE

1   Arvind Virmani, "The God That Failed," *Times of India*, November 21, 2013.

RECOMMENDED READING

Sanjaya Baru, *Strategic Consequences of India's Economic Performance* (Hoboken, N.J.: Taylor and Francis, 2013).

Arvind Panagariya, *India: The Emerging Giant* (New York: Oxford University Press, 2008).

Ashutosh Varshney, *Battles Half Won: India's Improbable Democracy* (New Delhi: Penguin, 2013).

CHAPTER 1

MAINTAINING MACROECONOMIC STABILITY

ILA PATNAIK

India's long-term growth potential remains high. The young population is gaining formal education and hands-on training. Gains from internal and international trade are increasing. While elements of the Raj persist, India has largely moved to a market economy. Lately, however, India has been undergoing a sharp downturn. Two years ago the economy generated tremendous optimism. Today, despite the long-term story being intact, widespread pessimism prevails. This has brought a fresh focus upon the policies of macroeconomic stabilization that could dampen business cycles while ensuring that India remains on the path of steady state growth.

Conditions in the economy are daunting. Investment and growth have collapsed, and inflation is in the double digits. Savings have dropped, with households flocking to gold. The fiscal soundness of the government is questioned. What is occurring in the downturn is inevitably related to the events of the boom that preceded it. During the boom years, inappropriate macroeconomic policy spread the seeds of the difficulties seen today, with a faulty fiscal stance and inappropriate monetary policy that produced India's biggest-ever credit boom.

There is a considerable focus on the problems of approvals and legal bottlenecks faced by investment projects, particularly in infrastructure. However, even if clearances are given to projects that have been stalled, they would still face serious obstacles in the financial system. The banks that binged on infrastructure lending during the boom are now not able to finance the next wave of infrastructure investment.

With a large current account deficit, the country needs capital inflows. Yet, the policy framework for capital flows is outdated, with various restrictions on cross-border flows. While India has de facto opened up its capital account, innumerable capital controls remain that do not allow capital to flow in. In 2013, policymakers embarked on a questionable adventure in trying to defend the rupee, an attempt that failed and caused heightened uncertainty. This episode serves as a reminder that macro/finance policy in India today is an idiosyncratic affair that lacks a well understood framework with deep institutional foundations. The country lurches from one crisis to the next.

Global financial markets are likely to remain in turmoil for several years, until the United States returns to normalcy. Until this comes about, international financial markets will experience many shocks. Deep and liquid markets in a country's domestic economy are the essential shock absorbers through which the perilous waters of international financial integration can be navigated. Achieving such deep and liquid markets requires large-scale financial sector reforms, with a complete replacement of the existing regulatory framework.

These developments from 2008 onward have highlighted India's lack of a proper framework for macroeconomic and financial stability. When India was a low-income country with a largely closed current and capital account, it could afford to have the present institutional, legal, and regulatory framework. But there is a large mismatch between the institutional machinery of a developing country and the requirements of a $2 trillion economy. Until India reforms its fiscal, financial, and monetary policy frameworks, macroeconomic and financial uncertainty will only worsen.

WHY IS MACROECONOMIC STABILITY IMPORTANT?

Policymaking in India is often based on the assumption that the economy will follow a linear trend growth rate. This implicitly assumes that the Indian economy does not have business cycles—a continuation of the old socialist thinking, when the government determined the level of investment in the economy, agriculture was a large share of the economy and depended on monsoons, and services production was dominated by the government. When India was a socialist developing country, the sudden downturns that it experienced were due to exogenous shocks such as droughts, oil price shocks, and wars. The economy did not have investment-inventory cycles of the kind seen in all market economies.

These old instincts have not yet been erased, even though India is now a market economy and has graduated from being a developing country to being an emerging market. Both government officials and businesses seem to believe that India is in a world where its economy stays at the trend growth rate with no fluctuations around it. Every cyclical up or down is treated, all too often, as a "new normal" or the new trend growth rate. However, as in the typical emerging economy, India has growth rate cycles around a trend. Emerging economy business cycles are more volatile than those in advanced economies. India's growth swings from 4 percent to 10 percent, which is quite different from what is seen in places like the United States, where the range of values is much more modest.

The most important single issue in Indian economics is that of achieving high and sustained trend growth. If, hypothetically, India is presented with a choice between a high average trend growth rate, with sharp volatility around it, and a low average trend growth rate that is smooth and stable, the former is of course superior. As an example, South Korea went through painful macroeconomic crises in 1997 and 2008. However, South Korea achieved higher trend growth than India, and consequently is now a prosperous country. If avoiding crises were all that was important, India would have been better off than South Korea.

While fluctuations are recognized as not bad in and of themselves, fluctuations of gross domestic product (GDP) matter to the extent to which they can damage trend growth. There are several mechanisms through which high fluctuations hamper trend growth. Events such as financial crises, high inflation, or a fiscal crisis can sometimes create long periods of slow growth. Similarly, if the government intervenes in a knee-jerk manner, setting back the development of markets and price-setting in markets, as has sometimes occurred in India, the resulting distortions can continue to create resource misallocation and prevent the healthy functioning of the market mechanism for a long time. This would have the effect of reducing the long-term steady state growth rate.

- *Financial crises.* In the big booms, investment and credit expand hugely. When the downturn comes, a collapse in the financial system can have an adverse impact on growth. To forestall this, two strategies are required: sound financial regulation and macroeconomic stabilization that reduces the volatility of the business cycle.

- *Price stability.* Macroeconomic stability is synonymous with low and stable inflation. Sustained low inflation goes along with a low interest rate environment and reduced relative price fluctuations. This creates an environment within which the private sector is better able to make projections. The reduced uncertainty encourages long-term investment. In India, low and stable inflation was achieved for only seven years, from 1999 to 2006. Apart from this, inflation has consistently been high and unstable, which adversely affects investment and growth.

- *Inappropriate interventions.* The broad policy environment in India has a low threshold for justifying government intervention in the economy. When economic conditions are difficult, the government tends to engage in more frequent and more distortionary interventions in the economy. But rather than rectify matters, intervention merely generates another channel for trend GDP growth to worsen.

- *Fiscal crises.* In bad times, tax collections are lower and there is greater pressure for populist spending. In the Indian environment of chronic fiscal stress, a business cycle downturn can potentially turn into a damaging fiscal crisis. The state can be crippled in such a crisis for a few years, which would in turn damage trend GDP growth.

This generates another channel through which high GDP growth volatility can reduce trend GDP growth.

Fluctuations are not bad in themselves. While economic policy should focus on achieving high long-run trend growth, it is advantageous for India to create the institutional foundations for macroeconomic and financial stability that will set the stage for such growth. Four elements of reform are needed for macroeconomic stability: fiscal consolidation, financial sector reform, capital account convertibility, and countercyclical monetary policy.

A FRAMEWORK FOR STABILIZATION
Fiscal Consolidation

There is some evidence that at present, India has a pro-cyclical fiscal policy. When the economy does well, tax collections go up and the government finds this is an opportunity to spend more. In bad times, taxes go down and fiscal stress is high. The government then tries to reduce expenditure. This contracts the economy further, thus exacerbating the business cycle downturn. Chronic fiscal stress generates pressure for the government to engineer inflation, which is destabilizing in its own right.

The way forward requires two elements. Fiscal policy must get away from chronic stress into soundness. And fiscal policy must smoothly shift between surpluses in good times and deficits in bad times.

The first issue is fiscal soundness. India needs to graduate out of chronic fiscal distress into a framework of conservative fiscal policy. In good times, it should run a surplus of 2 to 3 percent of GDP (consolidated across the central government and the states), and in bad times, this should turn into a consolidated deficit of a similar magnitude.

The Fiscal Responsibility and Budget Management Act, 2003 (and its amendment in 2012), required the government to bring the fiscal deficit down and keep it at a constant level. This limited the scope of countercyclical fiscal policy. The deficit could not expand in bad times, and the government did not have to generate a surplus in good times. A new arrangement is required under which the government can undertake fiscal expansion during bad times. Under this arrangement, the primary balance would be positive in most years, thus ensuring that in all but a few extreme years, the debt-to-GDP ratio would go down. This adds up to a conservative framework of fiscal policy, one that would offer a measure of safety from the fiscal crisis that always seems to be on India's doorstep.

How can fiscal policy be structured so as to move smoothly from surpluses of 2 to 3 percent of GDP in an expansion to a deficit of 2 to 3 percent of GDP in a downturn? The bulk of this movement should come from automatic stabilizers, or instruments that lead to fiscal expansion during GDP contractions and fiscal contractions during a boom, so that no discretionary actions are required. India has one important stabilizer in the form of the corporate income tax. Programs such as the Mahatma Gandhi National Rural Employment Guarantee Act (NREGA) need to be carefully engineered to ensure that spending goes up in a downturn and goes down in an expansion. The danger at present is that programs like NREGA involve large expenditures that are insensitive to business cycle conditions.

These two lines of thought induce macroeconomic stability in two respects. The ever-present fiscal crisis would subside, and fiscal policy would contribute to reducing business cycle volatility.

Reforming the Regulatory and Legal Framework for Finance

Financial crises are an important source of macroeconomic instability, particularly in emerging markets. India has experienced a diverse array of ailments, including banking distress, international finance crises, bankrupt pension systems, and securities scandals.

A sound framework for financial regulation is required to forestall these problems. This involves six elements:

1. *Consumer protection:* Regulations that are more fair to consumers would reduce risk in the system. They could prevent mis-selling by financial firms and the buildup of risk such as that seen in chit funds and multilevel marketing schemes. Consumer protection would help reduce fraud caused by Ponzi schemes. A two-pronged strategy is needed. First, consumer protection should be the objective of all financial regulation. Regulations need to be written to achieve this

objective, and if they do not, it should be possible to appeal and overturn them. Second, there should be a financial redress agency with a presence in every district of the country, urban and rural. It should have a fast adjudication mechanism in which consumers can file cases conveniently and cases do not take years to solve.

2. *Micro-prudential regulation:* One key element of consumer protection that bears individual mention is micro-prudential regulation, where regulatory agencies force financial firms to reduce the probability of failure. This would help address banking distress, bankrupt pension systems, and securities scandals.

3. *Resolution:* A critical piece of institutional machinery in any financial system is a resolution corporation that identifies distressed financial firms and shuts them down, while protecting the interests of unsophisticated consumers. Such an agency is, at present, lacking in India. This leads to the twin maladies of distressed financial firms growing unchecked and turning into a big problem, and then presenting problems that the government inevitably has to address.

4. *Shock absorbers:* Deep and liquid financial markets are an essential tool for risk absorption. When markets are shallow, shocks generate exaggerated price movements. In addition, when markets are shallow, risk transfer is not possible, and many financial firms end up holding on to excessive risk.

5. *Systemic risk regulation:* A strong database about the overall Indian financial system needs to feed into a sophisticated research program on systemic risk, which leads to concerted action by a council of regulators, the Financial Stability and Development Council.

6. *Regulatory architecture and governance:* A sound regulatory framework needs to be established, without overlaps and gaps, where there is clarity about the objectives of each agency, and where all agencies achieve high performance through strong accountability mechanisms.

All these elements are lacking at present. Hence, the current environment involves heightened risks to the economy. In the absence of this framework, policymakers are repeatedly hijacked by crises and respond to them in an idiosyncratic way. The inconsistent responses of policymakers exacerbate the ex-ante risk as perceived by economic agents.

The Financial Sector Legislative Reforms Commission, chaired by retired justice B. N. Srikrishna, has drafted a proposed Indian Financial Code to replace all existing Indian financial law and solve all these problems. The need of the hour is to translate this draft bill into an Act of Parliament.

Capital Account Convertibility

As emphasized above, achieving macroeconomic stability requires ruling out international financial crisis. This is closely related to the question of capital account liberalization.

India has a complex maze of capital controls. A number of public bodies switch controls on and off based on their views. Various financial sector laws and regulations treat foreign investors differently from Indian investors, with a bias against foreign investors. Today, the framework is so messy that even the government finds it hard to enforce its own rules. The various definitions of foreign direct investment and foreign portfolio investment often lack clarity and legal certainty. The lack of a transparent framework frequently turns away even those investors who want to bring money into India.

These controls have led to a complacent view among many policymakers that India is not vulnerable to the problems of international financial integration. This perspective is incorrect. While a maze of de jure capital controls exists, in practice, economic agents are able to move large sums of money across the border through legal and illegal means. When the rules favor equity but not debt, economic agents relabel transactions as equity. When the rules prohibit cross-border activity, capital is moved through trade misinvoicing.

A strong body of evidence now suggests that despite the de jure restrictions, India is largely a de facto open economy. The controls increase transaction costs and corruption but do not change the ultimate outcome.

As an example, in September 2008, when Lehman Brothers collapsed, disruption of the Indian money market was among the worst of all emerging markets.

It is well known that an emerging market must establish sound frameworks for fiscal, financial, and monetary policy before opening the capital account. In India's case, there is a dangerous accession to de facto openness without laying the commensurate foundations of fiscal, financial, and monetary policy capability.

Shifting from de facto to de jure capital account convertibility would result in two kinds of gains. First, policymakers need to be fully clear of the risks that they are taking; there should be no illusions that India is protected by a wall of capital controls. Second, the rent-seeking, transaction costs, and corruption associated with the present framework would be eliminated.

The difficulties associated with foreign investors in an emerging market are critically related to asymmetric information. An investor in Connecticut who does not know much about Mozambique, for example, is vulnerable to rational herding, sudden stops, and capital flow surges. Because the root cause of the problem is asymmetric information, the solution to the problem lies in a deep engagement with financial globalization. This requires shifting from de facto to de jure openness on the capital account, making it convenient for foreign fund managers to establish operations in India (something that is now blocked by tax law) and creating a conducive environment through which global financial firms acquire organizational capital and human capital pertaining to India.

India is a major emerging market. Once India is de jure open, all large global financial firms will do business in India. People of Indian origin play a leading role in all large global financial firms. Unlike small emerging markets, India has a fair opportunity at overcoming this asymmetric information and thus achieving more knowledgeable foreign investors.

To sum up, India is in perilous territory with a complicated system of capital controls that does not yield safety, that generates an illusion of autarky in the minds of policymakers, and that hinders deep integration with financial globalization. It would be safer if the de jure arrangement were reformed to match the de facto one.

Monetary Policy

A fourth important mechanism through which business cycle volatility can be reduced is countercyclical monetary policy. In good times, interest rates should go up, which cools the economy. In bad times, interest rates should go down, which stimulates the economy. Such monetary policy achieves low and stable inflation.

A properly structured monetary policy framework affects macro-economic stability by providing predictability of future inflation, low fluctuations of inflation, and a force for stabilization. None of these features is visible in India today.

India's consumer price inflation has risen to 10 percent per annum since 2006. The Reserve Bank of India (RBI) chases multiple objectives with multiple instruments. Furthermore, the RBI has neither a clear objective or measure of inflation, nor is it held accountable for inflation. Monetary policy law needs to define the objectives of India's monetary policy, as it does in many advanced and most emerging economies. The law must lay down the instruments of monetary policy. The RBI needs to be made accountable and given independence in order to achieve these objectives.

Decisionmaking on monetary policy in India will become increasingly difficult in the next two years, especially once the U.S. Federal Reserve stops its quantitative easing and U.S. interest rates rise. It is well understood by now that once the capital account is open, a country has to choose between pegging the exchange rate and pursuing an independent monetary policy; it can't do both. If the business cycles in the Indian economy were perfectly aligned with those of the United States, India would not need an independent monetary policy. But if the United States is going to raise rates, India has to make a choice about its de facto open capital account: let the rupee be flexible or peg the rupee to the dollar and tighten along with the United States.

The lack of clear thinking at the RBI is a key source of macroeconomic instability in India. Knee-jerk reactions that focus on only one element of the impact of those policy changes are bound to be troublesome. It was an understanding of these difficulties in monetary policymaking—after many episodes of painful mismanagement that led to years of inflation, recession, stagflation, and large-scale unemployment—that led advanced economies to hand over the task to central banks. They were given independence from government and required to have structures such as monetary policy committees, which allowed informed decisions and a diversity of views. And they were held accountable.

With the Indian economy opening in the past two decades, the difficulties of monetary policymaking have increased. By now, many government committees have suggested that it is time for India to move to a modern framework for monetary policymaking. India needs a central bank with independence and accountability, and with a professional monetary policy committee that decides monetary policy actions using well-defined instruments of policy. The latest of such recommendations is included in the Financial Sector Legislative Reforms Commission's draft law. While it may be very tempting for the government to be able to shape monetary policy at a particular point in time, it needs to understand that such short-term solutions are harmful in the long run. The government will be well served by a framework that provides low and stable inflation. Anchoring expectations on inflation would require not only narrowing the objectives of monetary policy but also bringing in financial sector reforms that can strengthen the currently weak transmission mechanism of monetary policy.

India's aspiration should be to achieve a world where the rupee is a floating currency—with absolutely no government involvement—and consumer price index inflation is reliably within the 4 to 5 percent range (on a year-on-year basis) for decades on end. It will take at least a decade of victory over inflation before the full economic gains come about.

CONCLUSION

Macroeconomic and financial stability in India is suspect, as the institutional machinery for macroeconomics and finance in India is grossly out of touch with the requirements of today's economy. Volatility is an integral part of the market economy and should not be shunned in and of itself. However, extreme fluctuations in macroeconomics and finance can damage long-run trend GDP growth. To address these problems, sound machinery for fiscal and monetary policy needs to be established. Until this is done, India will continue to lurch from one crisis to the next.

The government should take the following steps to improve the policy framework for macroeconomic stability:

1. Enact a fiscal responsibility act that takes business cycles into account and allows for countercyclical fiscal policy. This could mean putting in place rules for keeping the expenditure-to-GDP ratio at a specific level. A task force on the framing of such a law should be put in place right away.

2. The Financial Sector Legislative Reforms Commission has submitted its report and proposed a draft law on how to improve financial regulation and ensure rule of law in the framework for capital controls. The government has started on the following. First, it has started working with regulators to voluntarily adopt sections from the draft. These include provisions relating to better consumer protection, and the process of framing regulations through consultative and transparent procedures. This initiative will have to be followed through and implemented by regulators. Second, the government must undertake a time bound consultation process on the draft and a timeline for completion of this process and table a new bill to Parliament. Finally, for the various new bodies that have been proposed by the commission, the government needs to set up task forces to start the process of design, obtaining office space, IT systems, and recruitment.

3. Countercyclical monetary policy should be achieved through a new monetary policy law to replace the RBI Act, 1934. The new law should clearly define the objective of monetary policy in terms of achieving price stability. This objective should be measurable, and the RBI should be made accountable for it and given the independence and the powers to achieve it. To bring inflationary expectations down, this should be done as soon as possible, as it is one of the easiest among the difficult set of options for achieving macroeconomic stabilization. Yet, it is one where the framework for price stability has to be in place for some time before it can become credible.

CHAPTER 2

DISMANTLING THE WELFARE STATE

SURJIT BHALLA

INTRODUCTION

For any society, two concerns are paramount—economic growth and improvement in the well-being of the poor. Growth is needed to finance redistribution. This redistribution typically takes two forms—productive investment, for example, the financing of infrastructure, expenditures on health and education, and simple transfers of income. This chapter documents the nature and efficacy of such redistribution in India, and whether these redistributive policies have *made* India a welfare state before its time.

The Indian economy is at a crossroads. Just a few years ago, I asked major policymakers if they had anticipated the 2003–2010 GDP growth acceleration, a near doubling of the growth rate to around 8.5 percent per annum. The universal and honest answer was no. Over the past three years I have asked the same policymakers a slight variant of the question: Did you see the great slowdown coming? Again, the same answer.

Let us dispense with the clichéd and false explanation for India's fortunes and misfortunes: that they were, and are, all due to external factors or factors beyond the control of policymakers. The rising worldwide tide lifted India and the rest of the world in the early 2000s, and the post-crisis ebbing tide has left India with the same pre-2003 growth rate of around

5.5 percent per annum. If the 2013–2014 fiscal year yields around 5 percent growth, then the last three years' average growth rate would be the second lowest since the initiation of reforms in 1991. Regarding the influence of global trends, it is useful to compare India's pre-2003 investment rate with that of the 2011–2014 period. The ratio of investment to gross domestic product (GDP) averaged around 20 percent of GDP between 1980 and 2002; since 2002, the average is in the mid-thirties. So, no matter how one looks at the data, the fact remains that India is investing almost twice as much—and obtaining a *lower* GDP growth rate.

Many factors, including policy paralysis and misguided fiscal and monetary policies, are responsible for India's dismal recent growth performance. India has had a sorry record of high fiscal deficits, but it would be wrong to conclude that these are responsible for the Indian malaise. It is the *composition* of these fiscal deficits that is indicative of the problem for the Indian economy. If subsidies are divided into productive and transfers, then the share of the latter has averaged around 3 percent of GDP, approximately double the levels of just a decade ago. With economic growth collapsing, such subsidies are no longer affordable. Furthermore, it may very well be the case that such subsidies are no longer appropriate.

Subsidies and otherwise inefficient policies such as direct transfers that almost beg to be perverted by corruption have been at the heart of the Indian welfare state up to 2013. There are four problems with direct transfer policies in India. First, these policies generate exorbitant leakages and as such do not benefit the targeted poor population. Second, the nature of subsidies—food, employment, fertilizer—has not changed since the mid-1970s, when Indian per capita GDP was $200, despite the fact that per capita GDP now stands around $1,500. Third, India has expanded these subsidies, inappropriate as they were to begin with. Fourth, the recent expansion of subsidies under the United Progressive Alliance (UPA) government post-2004 has been cloaked in the elitist garb of "rights." No other country has done this before or is doing it now. All countries, throughout history, have faced the problem of helping the poor, yet not one has decided to confer rights to food or employment as constitutional acts. While these polices have a seductive appeal, they are even more prone to corruption.

It is important that subsidies meant for the poor reach the poor with a minimum amount of leakage. There are important alternatives to the subsidy schemes practiced in India. Research over the past decade has documented that an important explanation, if not *the* explanation, for malnutrition in India is the absence of proper sanitation (for example, drainage and toilets).[1] If India had implemented a right to toilets rather than a right to food, the poor would have been able to absorb a much larger proportion of the food that was made available to them. And given that the top half of the population already has water and sanitation, the targeting of these projects would have almost exclusively benefited the poor.

As Lenin once asked, "What is to be done?" India today is much transformed from the economy of forty years ago, when the existing food, fertilizer, and employment schemes were first formulated and implemented. It is useful to record that in 1985, just a few years after this formulation, Prime Minister Rajiv Gandhi famously stated that less than 15 percent of allocations meant for the poor actually reached the poor. This statement was based primarily on the experience of the Public Distribution System (PDS) of foodgrains. No other political leader has dared to question PDS in this outright and forthright manner. Indeed, Sonia Gandhi, the chairperson of the Indian National Congress Party, has gone out of her way to comprehensively reject the wisdom and courage of her late husband. Indeed, her view and that of the Congress seem to be that the system has failed and is leaky and corrupt, and yet they conclude that the best way to improve it is to expand it. UPA-II has done just that with an act of parliament that theoretically guarantees two-thirds of the population a right to 5 kilograms of foodgrains a month.

Given these welfare policies, and their likely and possible effects on high inflation and slow growth, a new revised look at India's welfare policies is long overdue. A new vision is required, a vision that demands that the existing welfare programs be discontinued, a vision that requires that India move toward a system where states have greater responsibilities toward implementation and formulation of welfare policies. The Finance Commission correctly worries about, and advocates, the disbursement of funds to the states. All central government expenditures on welfare policies should be allocated as part of the Finance Commission grants—and the states are then free to implement their own food subsidies, their own fertilizer grants, their own employment programs, and their own labor laws. The inevitable future will see greater rights for states, and there is no better time to start implementing it than within months of the swearing-in of the new 2014 government. The evidence for a new approach is over-whelming; only the vision and the will remain lacking.

IT IS NOT POLITICAL ECONOMY—IT IS JUST PURE IDEOLOGY

The past ten years under the UPA-I and UPA-II governments have been noteworthy for their emphasis on rights as a foundation stone for the design of the welfare policies. Policies that ostensibly provide employment and food to the poor are so leaky that less than a fifth of government expenditures targeted to the poor actually reach the poor population. Several of these rights-based policies are unique to India, which in itself raises the question of whether the Indian economy and polity are distinc-tive enough to merit this approach. This overall proposition, and the ideol-ogy behind it, needs to be examined.

Most Indian policymakers behave as if, on average, the country is very poor and that nearly two-thirds of the total population need attention in the form of transfers (that is, food doles) from the government. Most people, and virtually all taxpayers, in India and the world do *not* object to money spent in uplifting the poor and providing them with basic infra-structure and basic services. Expenditures that enhance individual pro-ductivity and increase the incidence of equal opportunity are applauded by most; it is hard to imagine anyone objecting to the provision of roads, water, sanitation, education, and health care to the poor.

It is not redistribution, then, that anybody objects to, but the provi-sion of leaky, corrupt subsidies in the name of the poor. Such subsidies provide little income support for the poor, and their provisioning sub-tracts from the supply of other subsidies that are desperately needed. This fact has relevance for the ongoing and sterile growth-versus-redistribution debate. From the way the debate has been presented by the most promi-nent advocates (including Nobel laureate Amartya Sen, Prime Minister Manmohan Singh, and Sonia Gandhi), it would appear that India spends precious little on redistributing income and indeed should spend more. This is untrue.

A large part of the confusion is in the presentation of facts on taxes and expenditure, unfortunately also indulged in by several economists who should certainly know better. The conventional and politically correct wisdom is that Indian taxation revenue is very low. One often hears the mistaken claim that India collects only 10 percent of its income in the form of taxes when, given its per capita income, it should be collecting nearer to 15 percent.

The confusion arises because India is a large country, and most tax and expenditure data presented by international organizations such as the World Bank and the International Monetary Fund are for the *central* government. In India, the revenue collection is composed of 10–12 percent of GDP in the form of central taxes, around 5–7 percent of GDP in the form of state taxes, and around 4 percent of GDP in the form of non-tax revenue (revenue from such sources as interest payments and disinvestments). The fiscal deficit is around 5 percent at the center and about 3 percent at the state level. This yields taxation levels at 18 percent of GDP and expenditure levels at 30 percent of GDP—one of the largest such levels for countries at India's per capita income levels. Add to this the fact that India has a very small income tax base, with the lowest income taxpayer in the top 20 percent of the population. So neither the poor, nor the emerging middle class, nor half of the middle class pays any income taxes. Also, corporate taxes are paid by the wealthy. So a very large proportion of money spent on redistribution is financed by the "rich" taxpayer. It is not that India taxes too little—the problem is that it spends too much, and spends too much on leaky, corruption-breeding government schemes.

Bad subsidies do not enhance productivity; good subsidies do. And the Congress-led UPA governments have been consistent in their advocacy of the dole as a major supplement to consumption of the bottom half to bottom two-thirds of the population. Never in the history of India—not even under the *Garibi Hatao* (abolish poverty) mantra of Prime Minister Indira Gandhi—were two-thirds of the population considered poor. Indeed, no country in the world sets its own poverty line to contain two-thirds of the population.

Taken together, these facts suggest that India is a welfare state before its time. The composition of expenditures is skewed toward dole subsidies, possibly one of the highest such proportions in the developing world, and certainly so for countries in the per capita zone of $1,000 to $2,000 per year. While targeting data are not available for other countries, the incidence of expenditures meant for the poor is staggeringly low and has been in the 15 to 25 percent zone for the past thirty years. Furthermore, these expenditures have sharply accelerated in the past five years.

There is an alternative economic and political view of India of the last sixty-six years, and the last ten years in particular, than that held by the Congress party. This view holds that poverty, hunger, and malnutrition are problems for which the recommended policies are not only imperfect, but grotesquely wrong. What *does* ail the nation, and particularly the poor, is wastage of available food, bad water, and worse sanitation (the unfortunate Bihar midday meal deaths of schoolchildren in the summer of 2013, for example, were caused not by a lack of food but by bad sanitation). Government expenditures on clean water and sanitation and non-corrupt food delivery in the form of cash transfers will do more to help the poor than any amount of rights-based laws on food and employment.

FACTS ON POVERTY REDUCTION

Regardless of an economy's stage of development or its per capita income, the important concern must be with the poor in society. This is not just an ethical question; it is also an issue about the productivity of the economy, which in turn is heavily dependent on the productivity of its population. So helping the poor become not poor is a win-win proposition for any economy, rich or poor. Depending on its own ethical values and political and economic structure, each country defines what constitutes "poor" according to its own standards. Poverty can be defined in many ways, but broadly the consensus is to define it in income (or consumption) per capita terms.

While there are several instruments of welfare policies, they all share the same basic goal: to provide a minimum level of income support to those who need it. At the extremes, there are two broad approaches to reducing poverty. The first is an indirect approach commonly known as trickle-down growth. This approach or philosophy has as its premise the belief that if economic growth occurs, *and* is broad-based, then all sections of the population will benefit, and perhaps the poor will benefit at a relatively faster pace. At the same time, however, it is possible that because the development process is inherently unequal, the incomes of the poor will

increase at a rate that is lower than average. This prospective reality is the
basic motivation for the direct approach to poverty reduction, more commonly known as the dole approach. It is important that the new administration in India carefully examine the record of the efficacy, in the Indian
context, of both of these polar instruments of welfare policy.

Figure 1 shows the nature of poverty decline in India since 1951 for
two poverty lines, the old Dandekar-Rath poverty line of Rs. 49 per capita
per month in 1973 prices, and the new 25 percent higher Tendulkar
poverty line introduced in 2009.

FIGURE 1. POVERTY IN INDIA, 1951–2012

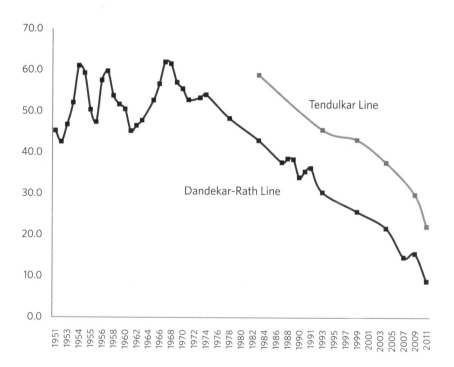

Sources: For data prior to 1982, Gaurav Datt and Martin Ravallion, "Is India's Economic Growth
Leaving the Poor Behind?" *Journal of Economic Perspectives* 16, no. 3 (2002); for subsequent
years, author's computations based on National Sample Survey data. Poverty figures are
according to the mixed recall (30 and 365 days for durables) of consumption items.

Three results stand out. First, "only" 22 percent of the population was poor in 2011–2012, and if the poverty line had not been revised upward by the Tendulkar committee, the poverty level would have been less than 9 percent. This is not to state that the poverty line should not be revised upward, but just to emphasize that poverty in India is low and considerably lower than the two-thirds of the population for whom politically inspired welfare programs are designed. Second, poverty levels stayed stagnant at around 60 percent of the population for the low growth period between 1950 and 1980, but there is a distinct acceleration in the speed of poverty decline post-1980. Third, poverty decline is the steepest during the most recent 8-plus percent per annum GDP growth period from 2003 to 2012.

During both the period of low 5.5 percent per annum growth (1980–2002) and the period of high 8.5 percent growth (2003–2012), direct programs to reduce poverty were in abundance, providing fertilizer, water, power, food, and employment. The major differentiator between the two periods is higher per capita growth.

One additional and somewhat surprising result is that consumption inequality in India has stayed constant for thirty years. This implies that inequality change has had very little positive or negative role to play in the reduction of poverty in India. Indeed, it has marginally improved for the poorest 20 percent; the consumption share of these poorest individuals was 8.9 percent in 1983 and 9.1 percent in both 2009–2010 and 2011–2012. More than 90 percent of the reduction in poverty in India for the thirty-year period 1983–2012 has been due to economic growth; states that grew faster reduced poverty faster; states that grew slower reduced poverty at a lower rate.[2]

NECESSITY AND MAGNITUDE OF DIRECT POVERTY ALLEVIATION SCHEMES

In India, it is evident that too much credibility is given to ideology and not enough to facts on issues pertaining to the poverty industry. The "poverty-industrial complex" is huge, it is well nurtured, and it facilitates corruption. The recently enacted Food Security Bill enlarges, encourages, and endorses this corruption.

There has been a varying pattern of expenditures of the Indian welfare state. Not surprisingly, this pattern has varied with the party in power. Particularly revealing is the pattern of these expenditures since 1998, a period encompassing the two major political regimes of the last seventeen years. Table 1 notes the magnitude of central government spending over the past decade and the nature of "redistributive" subsidies. The subsidies have been divided into two types: good subsidies that enhance individual productivity (roads, education, health expenditures) and bad dole-based subsidies that just transfer income at a point in time and reduce poverty (in the unlikely event that it reaches the poor on a consistent, targeted basis) only at "maintenance" levels.

TABLE 1. GOOD AND BAD GOVERNMENT SPENDING IN INDIA, 1999/2000-2011/2012

	1999-2000	2004-05	2009-10	2011-12
GDP (in 000 crore)	1,952	3,242	6,550	8,354
As % of GDP				
Central government expenditure	15.6	15.6	15.6	15.8
Good Subsidies	**0.81**	**0.86**	**1.19**	**1.52**
Infrastructure	0.27	0.21	0.32	0.42
Education and health	0.54	0.65	0.87	1.10
Bad Subsidies (Dole)	**1.11**	**1.58**	**2.72**	**2.88**
Food and employment	0.66	0.99	1.40	1.25
Fuel and fertilizer	0.45	0.59	1.33	1.63

Source: Government of India, Union Budget and Economic Survey for fiscal years 1999-2000, 2004-2005, 2009-2010, and 2011-2012, available at http://indiabudget.nic.in/budget.asp.

In 2004–2005, good subsidies constituted 0.9 percent of GDP, and bad subsidies were a larger 1.6 percent. In 2011–2012, bad subsidies had reached nearly 3 percent of GDP. Even the Congress party, which has presided over this increase, does not argue that bad subsidies do much to help the poor; regarding food and employment, less than 15 percent of such dole actually reaches the targeted poor. And it is not as if all the 85 percent remainder accrues to the *aam* (common) but not poor *aadmi* (man). A large share (about a quarter) of these expenditures does not reach the rich or poor—it is mostly unaccounted for.[3]

Most countries that undertake transfers endeavor to make sure that the deserving are properly targeted. The world has had considerable experience with various forms of transfers—cash transfers, conditional cash transfers, food stamps—and the record appears to favor cash transfers as the most effective mechanism. But India still lags behind other countries in acknowledging this fact, continuing to debate the merits of such schemes of redistribution. The reason the debate will continue is that powerful interest groups oppose cash transfers because they would substantially decrease (but not eliminate) opportunities for major corruption.

PDS AND NREGA: THE MARQUEE WELFARE SCHEMES OF INDIA

The Food Security Bill is an expansion of the existing Public Distribution System of distributing foodgrains to the poor. But instead of targeting the poor, the law provides subsidized food to two-thirds of the population. It is informative and worthwhile to examine the origins of the foodgrain distribution system.

Unfortunately, there is no more telling example of Kafkaesque economics than the story of foodgrain production and redistribution to the poor in India. The plan started with a desire by the government to deliver food to the poor in the mid-1970s. Cash transfers were not in existence then, and it would be too unfair to expect Indira Gandhi, the prime minister at the time, to have invented cash transfers as a mode of shifting income to the poor. However, two countries—Sri Lanka and the United States—had elaborate food stamp systems in place, and India surely could have followed these success stories. But that would have been too easy a policy to take, and perhaps did not offer enough possibilities of corruption. Because what Indira Gandhi launched—what Sonia Gandhi has expanded via the Food Security Bill—is a system that is likely to challenge any and all programs in India and elsewhere for the number one prize as the most corrupt program ever invented. This is not hyperbole, nor an exaggeration, nor an unsupported assertion. As stated earlier, the late prime minister Rajiv Gandhi reached this conclusion on the basis of his mother's invention of the PDS for foodgrains.

The PDS system was doomed to corruption. Indira Gandhi's government set up the Food Corporation of India (FCI) as the sole buyer and seller of subsidized food for the poor. Rather than buy food on the open market and/or provide direct subsidies to food shops, the government got itself into the act of procuring the food from the farmer at a price that the government itself set (procurement prices), banning the private movement of foodgrains from surplus to deficit states (this draconian policy was removed only in the last decade), storing the food in government silos (buffer stocks), appointing exclusive ration shops to distribute the government-bought foodgrains, and setting up a procedure for eligibility of purchase of foodgrains from government-authorized ration shops.

But this is not all. The state needed "surplus" foodgrains to achieve its lofty ends. So it made provisions for fertilizer subsidies so that farmers could grow more. But fertilizer technology improved, so in order to keep old fertilizer firms in business, the government gave these older, inefficient firms a larger subsidy. Surplus production also required more water, so water subsidies for farmers were introduced. But provision of water required power, so power subsidies were introduced, and, predictably, subsidy expenses exploded.

The consequences of these policies have been unsurprising. For the 2012–2013 fiscal year (the thirty-fifth year of the PDS's operation) half the foodgrains sent from FCI to the ration shops never reached the ration shop. This amounts to some 25 million tons, something not very easy to lose and not accrue to either rich or poor foodgrain consumers. In addition, about 15 million tons of foodgrains (or Rs. 30,000 crore of expenditure) were "lost" due to lack of storage facilities—in other words, the food rots.[4] More likely, this goes to the liquor trade for which rotten grains are a major asset. Notice the singular "beauty" of this leakage—the government writes it off as an expenditure, FCI writes it off as a loss, and the liquor manufacturer writes it off as a cost. Less than 25 percent of the small proportion of food that reaches the ration shop gets to the Tendulkar-level poor.[5] Thus, the broad numbers of PDS corruption are as follows: almost half of the food is "misplaced" between government warehouses and ration shops. An additional fourth is lost in storage. So three-fourths of the food is lost before it even begins to reach the poor. Of the remaining 25 percent, the poor receive less than half. In sum, the poor get less than 10 percent of the food that the government procures in their name. Total expenditure on food subsidies in 2012–2013, the year before the Food Security Bill's introduction, are estimated to be around Rs. 80,000 crore. The poor will receive less than about Rs. 8,000 crore, or about Rs. 320 per person.

Another method of computing the efficacy of the direct policies of government expenditures is to estimate the cost of poverty reduction. The poverty gap is a useful indicator for assessing the efficiency of poverty programs. The gap is defined as the ratio of average per capita consumption of the poor to the poverty line. In 2011–2012, average per capita expenditure of the poor was Rs. 708 per person per month and the poverty line was Rs. 847. With perfect targeting (that is, complete knowledge of who is poor and by how much), a transfer of Rs. 139 per person per month (or Rs. 1,668 a year) would enable the target of zero percent Tendulkar poverty to be reached. In 2011–2012, there were approximately 250 million Tendulkar poor in India. Achievement of zero poverty would require an expenditure of under Rs. 42,000 crore, or less than 0.5 percent of GDP. Admittedly and obviously, perfect targeting is an impossibility, but it does provide a benchmark with which to evaluate policies of poverty alleviation.

The combined operation of the Mahatma Gandhi National Rural Employment Guarantee Act (NREGA) and the PDS system alone incurred an expenditure level of approximately Rs. 100,000 crore in 2011–2012. Fuel and fertilizer subsidies added an additional Rs. 160,000 crore. Total poverty reduction between 2009–2010 and 2011–2012 was about 8 percentage points, and the subsidies allowed a poverty reduction of 4 percentage points for two years, or 45 million individuals per year. Thus the government spent Rs. 260,000 crore to remove 45 million out of poverty. This comes to about Rs. 58,000 a year to bring one person out of poverty. Perfect targeting would involve an expenditure level of Rs. 1,668. The expenditure level of perfect targeting is 2.9 percent of government PDS/ NREGA targeting. Or, in other words, the government spends more than thirty times the expenditure needed to remove poverty—each year.

Would it not be a lot simpler, and considerably more liberal, if the government instituted cash transfers, or at a minimum, delivered food stamps to the poor? Food stamps give the recipient the freedom to buy from whichever grocery store she chooses to buy from. She has the money, provided by the state, to buy food; whether she chooses to buy bread or broccoli is her concern. How can the state get more dictatorial than deciding what food she should buy, and even from what shop? The rest of the world faces identical problems as India, yet other countries face and solve these problems by allowing maximum freedom to the consumer. The world has moved on to cash transfers, but India still debates their worth ad nauseam. This is the development equivalent of debating gravity.

CONCLUSION

An important part of implementing reforms is the recognition that, prior to the UPA governments, partial reform was on its way. The Employment Guarantee schemes that existed were spending less than half of what NREGA ordered, and the different governments were cognizant of the fact that the PDS was both corrupt and unworkable. Sonia Gandhi not only expanded these programs quite significantly, but also made them into expensive "rights." There is a large contingent within and outside UPA that believes that corruption could be reduced by adopting an alternative welfare scheme in the form of conditional cash transfers—a policy that has been endorsed by many countries of the world. If such transfers are fully implemented over the next three years, then the poor, and all Indians, can look forward to considerably lower corruption.

The PDS cannot be disbanded immediately—but certainly a three-year plan is feasible. The Aadhar identification system would also be complete by then. A new redistributive system should be among the first priorities of the new government. And a major part of the new policy must be a large-scale water and sanitation program for India.

NOTES

1   Dean Spears, "The Nutrition Value of Toilets: How Much International Variation in Child Height Can Sanitation Explain," Working Paper, Centre for Development Studies, Delhi School of Economics, December 2012.

2   See Surjit S. Bhalla, "Democracy Growth and Development in India," unpublished paper, prepared for the Centre for Development and Enterprise, Johannesburg, South Africa, July 2013.

3   Ibid.

4   See Surjit S. Bhalla, "Rotting Food—Rotten Arguments," *Indian Express*, September 4, 2013.

5   Surjit S. Bhalla, "The 'Need' and Costs and Alternatives to the Food Security Bill," *Yojana*, January 2014.

CHAPTER 3

REVAMPING AGRICULTURE AND THE PUBLIC DISTRIBUTION SYSTEM

ASHOK GULATI

WHY AGRICULTURE IS CRITICAL

In the Indian economy, where almost half of an average household's expenditures goes toward food and where half of the labor force is engaged in agriculture, one cannot simply wish away the centrality of agriculture just because its contribution to GDP now hovers around 14 percent. That would be an overly narrow viewpoint, and perhaps a misguided one. India's agriculture is responsible for feeding a large and growing population that numbers 1.25 billion today and that is projected to exceed that of China by 2035. But even more importantly, while India focuses on accelerating overall growth, the nature of growth matters a lot for poverty alleviation. The objective of "faster growth with inclusiveness," as elucidated in the Eleventh and Twelfth Five Year Plans, will have little meaning unless agriculture takes a central position in the policy reform agenda. This is because research in the developing world over the past twenty-five years or so has revealed that every percentage point of growth in agriculture is at least two to three times as important in alleviating poverty as the same growth in other sectors. In case of China it was 3.5 times as effective, and in case of Latin American countries, especially Brazil, it was 2.7 times as effective.[1]

It is worth recalling the Chinese experience in this regard. China began its reform process in 1978 primarily with agriculture, dismantling the commune system and liberating price controls to a large extent. As a result, agri-GDP in China grew by 7.1 percent per annum during 1978–1984; with liberalizing prices, farm incomes grew by almost 14 percent per annum. It is this high growth in farm incomes that boosted demand for manufactured goods produced by Town and Village Enterprises, kick-starting the manufacturing revolution in China.[2]

In contrast to the Chinese experience, India started its economic reforms in 1991 with the correction of its exchange rate and rationalizing its trade and industrial policies by reducing industrial protection in a calibrated fashion and to a large extent dismantling the licensing regime for industry. The Indian government gave agriculture only a small dose of liberalization. For example, it opened up exports of rice, wheat, and some other key commodities in 1994, but this policy soon had to be reversed. Export bans were brought back in 1996 as domestic prices started rising. Similarly, on the imports front, the imports of edible oils were relaxed from quantitative restrictions. They were brought under import duties, albeit high ones to start with (65 percent in 1994). The duties were gradually reduced to 15 percent by 1998, but thereafter were raised exponentially to more than 92 percent by April 2001 in the wake of the East Asian crisis and falling commodity prices.[3]

Through it all, agriculture was never brought to the forefront of any direct reform agenda in India. Nevertheless, Indian agriculture did gain indirectly from corrections in the exchange rate and reforms in the trade and manufacturing sector, so that in the initial years (1992–1996), agri-GDP did increase by 4.8 percent per annum and agri-exports accelerated. But for the next ten years, agri-GDP remained below 2.5 percent. It revived to 4.1 percent (revised figure) only in the Eleventh Five Year Plan (2007–2012). It still remains very volatile, falling to 1.4 percent in 2012–2013, and is expected to rebound to 4.6 percent in 2013–2014 (second estimate).

Long-term growth in agri-GDP since the economic reforms began in 1991 has remained at 3.4 percent per annum, well below the targeted growth of 4 percent per annum (see figure 1).

FIGURE 1. GROWTH PERFORMANCE OF OVERALL GDP AND AGRI-GDP

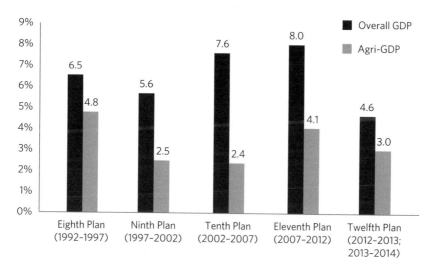

Source: Author's calculations based on data from the Central Statistical Office.

Problems in Indian agriculture have prevented it from achieving sustained growth of more than 4 percent per year. Before prescribing any agenda for revamping Indian agriculture, it is only fair to first see the sector's performance over a longer period and diagnose what could be holding it back from the target growth rate. Accordingly, the chapter first conducts a scoping run of Indian agriculture's performance and then tries to identify constraints to its growth. In this context, one key thing to note is that agriculture is much more comprehensive than just foodgrains. While policy discussions often become cereal-centric, the potential for agri-growth has to come more and more from fruits and vegetables, dairy, eggs, meat, and fish, which together are considered high value agriculture, and where demand pressures mount with rising incomes. That will be followed by an outline of what could be done to raise the growth rate and how such policies might be implemented. The Public Distribution System (PDS), India's food security apparatus, will be viewed in conjunction with the National Food Security Act passed in September 2013, assessing the key challenges it is likely to face and what alternatives could provide food security at lower costs. Finally, the main policy reforms that are needed to put Indian agriculture on a higher growth trajectory will be recapitulated.

LONG-TERM PERFORMANCE, AND WHAT COULD BE HOLDING BACK INDIAN AGRICULTURE

If one looks at the overall performance of agriculture over the past six decades or so, from 1950–1951 to 2012–2013, it looks like a reasonably good success story (see table 1). The production of foodgrains has increased by more than five times, from 50 million tonnes (mt) in 1950–1951 to 259 mt in 2011–2012; production of milk by more than seven times, from 17 mt to 127 mt over the same period; and so on. During this period, the population has increased by a little more than three times, from 361 million to 1.21 billion.[4] What this indicates clearly is that India has been able to produce food faster than its growth in population. The Green Revolution in wheat and rice during the late 1960s and early 1970s, the White Revolution in milk in the 1970s, and the Blue Revolution in fisheries all have contributed to its success story. In the first decade of the 2000s, doubling of production levels of cotton, corn, and Pusa basmati contributed much to boost agri-exports and earn precious foreign exchange. This has made Indian agriculture a net exporter, with exports in 2012–2013 amounting to $41 billion vis-à-vis imports of $20 billion (see figure 2). Interestingly, in 2012–2013, India exported cereals to the tune of 22 mt, a level it had never reached since independence, according to the Commission for Agriculture Costs and Prices *Report on Price Policy for Kharif Crops, 2014–2015*, and perhaps also not in the last three thousand years of written history of India.[5]

TABLE 1. LONG-TERM STRIDES IN INDIAN AGRICULTURE

	1950–1951	1970–1971	1990–1991	2010–2011
Foodgrains Million tonnes	50.8	108.4	176.4	259 (2011–2012)
Milk Million tonnes	17	23 (1973–1974)	53.9	127 (2011–2012)
Fish Million tonnes	0.75	1.75	3.84	8.00 (P)
Eggs Billion number	1.8	7.8 (1973–1974)	21.1	60 (P)
Fruit and vegetables Million tonnes			85	221
Population Millions	361	548	846	1,210

Source: Government of India, Department of Agriculture and Cooperation, *Agricultural Statistics at a Glance* (various issues).

FIGURE 2. INDIA'S EXPORTS AND IMPORTS OF AGRICULTURAL PRODUCTS

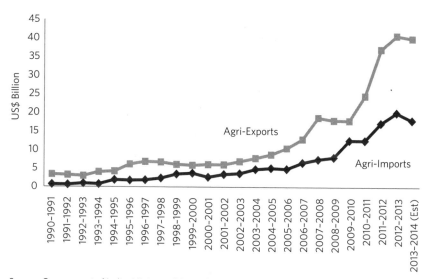

Source: Government of India, Ministry of Agriculture, "Price Policy for Kharif Crops: The Marketing Season 2013–14," Commission for Agricultural Costs and Prices, March 2013.

Not only have grain exports increased significantly, but public agencies have accumulated massive stocks of grain, touching 80 mt in July 2012 and 74 mt in July 2013, historically the highest-ever stocks held by the government (see figure 3).

FIGURE 3. BULGING STOCKS OF GRAINS WITH PUBLIC AGENCIES

Central Pool Stocks as of July 1

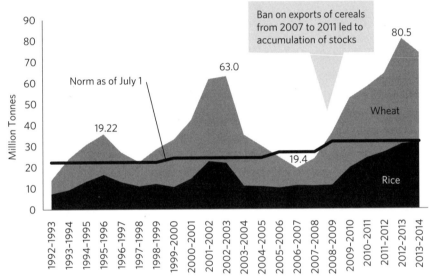

Source: Government of India, Ministry of Agriculture, "Price Policy for Kharif Crops: The Marketing Season 2013-14," Commission for Agricultural Costs and Prices, March 2013.

Notwithstanding these achievements, the fact remains that the overall agri-GDP growth rate has been muted at an average of 3 percent per annum over the past seventeen years (1997–2014), suggesting Indian agriculture's untapped potential.

Normally, growth in any sector is strongly influenced by the investments (capital formation) in that sector and its capital-output ratio. For the Indian economy, the Five Year Plan documents often presume a capital-output ratio of 4:1, that is, by investing four units of capital, one can get one unit of output. Thus, if the overall investments in the economy hover around, say, 30 percent of GDP, then GDP should be growing at around 7.5 percent, presuming all other factors remain largely neutral. Yet GDP growth fluctuates above and below 7.5 percent depending upon factors other than investments. Similarly in agriculture, agri-GDP is influenced by at least three factors: trends in both public and private capital formation in agriculture over multiple years; relative price incentives for agriculture, which are often measured as a ratio of prices of agri-products to prices of manufactured products (loosely referred to as terms of trade between the agriculture and manufacturing sectors); and rainfall.

Looking at agriculture from the point of view of investments in agriculture, it is true that during the 1980s and 1990s, the investments in agriculture hovered largely between 8 to 12 percent of agri-GDP (figure 4). Given that the capital-output ratio in agriculture also hovers around 4:1, it was futile to expect agriculture to perform wonders on the growth front. The average rate of growth in agri-GDP could not be expected to be more than 2.5 to 3 percent, assuming other factors were neutral. However, the situation on the investment front changed during the decade of the 2000s, especially after 2004–2005, and it went all the way up to 20 percent of agri-GDP by the end of 2010. This is surely positive news, and it does show in terms of some revival of agri-GDP growth to 4.1 percent per annum during the Eleventh Five Year Plan (2007–2012).

Another interesting fact about capital formation in agriculture is that the composition of investment sources in agriculture has shifted toward the private sector over the years. Private sector investments in agriculture today account for more than three-fourths of total investments in agriculture, up from about half in 1980–1981 (see figure 4). This is interesting because one would expect that the efficiency of capital under private ownership would be higher than when it is under public ownership. This should also augur well for higher agri-GDP growth rates in the years to come.

The increasing share of private sector investments in agriculture, which is also pushing the overall investments in agriculture, is presumably the result of improving price incentives in agriculture, especially since 2005. The ratio of agri-prices to manufactured prices has substantially improved from almost 1 to 1.4 over the period 2004–2012.[6] This improved price environment in agriculture is attracting substantial investments, which would hopefully accelerate agri-GDP's growth rates.

FIGURE 4. GROSS CAPITAL FORMATION IN INDIAN
AGRICULTURE: CHANGING COMPOSITION BETWEEN
PUBLIC AND PRIVATE SECTOR, AND CHANGES AS
PERCENT OF AGRI-GDP

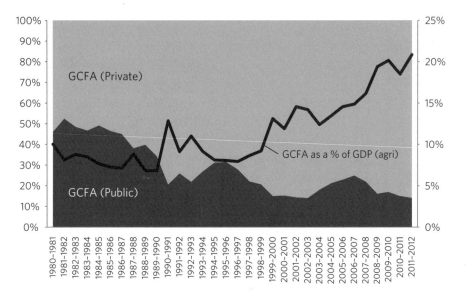

Source: Author's calculations based on data from Government of India, Central Statistics Office.

With all these positive signs—overall production, trade, grain stocks, and investments in agriculture—the picture seems reasonably optimistic, and even rosy at times. But at the same time, one also hears about farmers' suicides and farmers complaining about returns in agriculture not being good enough to keep them in agriculture. Given the size of the country and its diverse agriculture, this situation could also be true in some pockets.

The problem seems to be serious at the consumer end. For the past five years, food price inflation has been at uncomfortably high levels, hovering around double-digit figures. For example, in September 2013, food price inflation was at more than 12 percent (over the previous September), with inflation of food articles at 18 percent, vegetable prices going through the roof at more than 89 percent, protein foods (eggs, meat, and fish) at around 13 percent, and cereals at 13 percent.[7] Over the past few years, inflation in high value products (such as fruits and vegetables, milk, and meat products, which typically have more vitamins and proteins) is much higher than in staples. This indicates a clear trend: that with rising incomes people are spending more on fruits, vegetables, milk and milk products, eggs, meat, and fish. Supplies of these products are lagging behind demand, pushing up their prices. This demonstrates the real dilemma of Indian agriculture: while the policy environment is largely focused on grains for food security concerns, food price inflation is out of gear with high value products leading the charge, although in 2013 even cereal inflation seemed to be getting out of hand. That means people are not getting more nutritious food in the quantities that would be desirable. And it is this policy dilemma that is also holding back overall growth in agriculture. The cereals have an expenditure elasticity of almost zero, meaning that despite people's rising incomes and expenditures, they are not going to eat more cereals on a per capita basis. Instead, the pressure of demand will go to high value products. Domestic demand for cereals will increase largely in line with the rate of growth in population, which is around 1.4 percent per annum. There could be some pressure coming from the animal feed side with rising demand for poultry. So, anything more than, say, 1.7 percent growth in cereals (1.4 percent coming from population growth and roughly 0.3 percent coming from feed demand) will lead to their surpluses that would have to be either exported or accumulated in government stocks. The real growth in agriculture, therefore, has to come from high value products (horticulture, milk, and protein foods). These commodities are perishable in nature and require very fast-moving supply lines to create value. The whole paradigm of India's agriculture policy, from farming to value chains, needs to change if 4 percent growth is to be achieved. And it is here that policies are not very conducive to growth.

POLICIES FROM PLOUGH TO PLATE: TOWARD A DEMAND-DRIVEN APPROACH IN HIGH VALUE PRODUCTS

Given that overall growth of at least 4 percent in agri-GDP cannot come from the grains segment, the government's policy focus must first shift to high value products. Supply chains for the products are currently unduly long and fragmented, leading to large wastages and disproportionate capture of the value by middlemen. This comes at the expense of producers, who get a lower price, and consumers, who pay a higher price. This situation must change. To create value, supply lines need to be compressed in order to connect farmers directly to organized processors, retailers, and exporters. Only by making these value chains more efficient can farmers and consumers get a better deal than is the case today. Changing the supply lines would also help tame the high inflationary pressures on these commodities.

It may be recalled that this is what was done under Operation Flood, which turned India into the world's largest milk producer, through the Amul model, where milk was first aggregated at the village level from all farmers, even small and marginal holders; then chilled in villages and transported to homogenizing and pasteurizing plants through refrigerated trucks; and finally distributed to retail outlets in mega cities. This ensured that farmers get a good share of the consumers' rupee while consumers also got the milk at a reasonable price. A similar approach, at a similar or even bigger scale, needs to be adopted for fruits and vegetables (vitamins segment) and for eggs, meat, and fish (protein segment). The processing of milk and milk products also needs to be scaled up; despite Operation Flood and the White Revolution, India still processes less than 20 percent of its milk production through the organized sector, which means there is a huge untapped potential for business in milk and gains to farmers and consumers.

These compressed and efficient value chains are not feasible without changes in policy, new institutional structures, and large investments in logistics, processing, and organized retailing. The private sector can do much of this, provided the policy environment creates ample space for it and incentivizes it to move in that direction. So far the gap in policy and what is needed on the ground to build efficient value chains is large, and unless that is reduced, India will keep suffering from low growth in agriculture, high wastages of fresh produce, and lower and more volatile prices for farmers and higher prices for consumers. So what needs to be done?

First, the Agriculture Produce Marketing Committee (APMC) Act needs to be amended by de-listing fruits and vegetables, which would allow farmers to sell to anyone inside or outside the APMC markets. That would imply that any buyer can buy directly from the farmers without paying any market (*mandi*) fee or commissions to the commission agents (*artihas*). This amendment has been overdue for more than a decade, and reforms in this area are going in circles. The central government says it is a state subject, but the states have their own political compulsions and do only minor tweaking, which is of little use. A simple way to get it done is to make the allocations under the National Horticulture Mission to different states conditional subject to reforms in the APMC Act. Even that, however, is not enough to build efficient value chains.

Second, streamlining supply chains and making them efficient requires institutional innovations and major investments in terms of aggregating produce from smallholders, cleaning, washing and drying, grading and packaging, bar-coding for traceability, as well as cold storage and movement via refrigerated vans to the shelves of organized retailers. Organized retailers will be interested in streamlining the back-end operations only if they have full freedom to scale up their operations in the front end. Foreign direct investment policy on organized multi-brand retail has run into rough weather without taking off in any serious manner. Domestic players, too, are not very gung-ho on this, having seen the myriad problems in dealing with fresh commodities and dealing with a multitude of small farmers. Normally, in organized retail, handling fresh produce and sourcing directly from small and marginal farmers is the last bastion to conquer as it is the most difficult. Eighty to ninety percent of produce in organized food retail is processed. So, first attention must be paid to scale up the food processing activity and to connect farmers to food processors.

Thus, the third policy change needed is to treat food processing as a priority sector and remove food processing from the list of small-scale industry reservation, which limits the investment and scale of operations in these units. (For example, groundnut and mustard processing oil plants are still reserved for small-scale industry.) Large-scale modern plants, with economies of scale, are what is needed to add value to agriculture, reduce massive wastages, and provide a better deal to farmers and consumers. Given how expensive food is for most Indians, this must be the country's next sunrise industry. But for this to happen, reforms are needed on two fronts: (a) taxes and commissions on food articles need to be brought to zero or at most less than 5 percent, and also taxes on processed food must be kept at less than 5 percent to bolster that industry; and (b) farmers need to be organized in clusters, known as Farmer Producer Organizations, to create economies of scale at the farmer level. Given that the average farm size in India is just 1.16 hectares, the challenge is to incentivize large-scale organized processing and retail to work with fragmented farms.[8] The transaction costs of working with millions of farmers are high, which need to be underwritten by the government to promote inclusiveness in business, besides efficiency. A public-private partnership model can be developed to help the industry invest at the back end to streamline value chains that are efficient, competitive, and inclusive.

Fourth, massive reforms are needed to get the markets right for staple cereals. This is a policy issue since it is related to the National Food Security Act (NFSA) of 2013, and because it involves public procurement, stocking, and distribution at large scale. Without massive reforms, there is every likelihood of having large efficiency losses, which may outweigh the welfare gains that NFSA is meant to achieve.

THE NFSA, LEAKY PDS, AND THE OPTION OF CONDITIONAL CASH TRANSFERS

The NFSA basically provides 5 kilograms of cereals per capita per month at highly subsidized rates (Rs. 3, 2, and 1 per kilogram for rice, wheat, and coarse cereals, respectively) to 67 percent of the population. These issue prices are frozen for at least the next three years. The NFSA relies on the public distribution system to do this. India's other major nutrition programs include its mid-day school meal scheme and some cash compensation for lactating mothers. All these packages amount to roughly 62 million tonnes of grains to be distributed every year through the Public Distribution System, costing the national treasury roughly Rs. 130,000 crore.[9] The NFSA also addresses the need to invest more in storage, in agriculture to ensure high production, in logistics to carry food to various places, and so on. These investments are needed, on top of the Rs. 130,000 crore expenditure as a food subsidy, to stabilize the food production, store the procured grains in proper godowns, and move them efficiently across the country where grains are needed for distribution. If one includes these additional investments and the fact that the procurement prices of cereals are likely to rise every year as production costs go up while issue prices remain fixed, the real cost of the NFSA is likely to be much higher. A crude estimate by the Commission for Agriculture Costs and Prices is more than Rs. 200,000 crore annually, if India is serious about implementing the

NFSA.[10] If this is not achieved—a likely possibility—the country will simply muddle through food security, and even after a number of years, economic access to food will remain a challenge for millions of Indians.

It may also be noted that average cereal consumption, as per the National Sample Survey Office (NSSO) consumption survey of 2011, is 10.7 kilograms per capita per month (weighted average of rural and urban).[11] This implies that even for cereals, people will have to rely on open markets for more than half of their consumption needs. So what the state agencies do with procurement, stocking, and distribution of food through PDS will have repercussions on the open market prices.

The biggest challenge of the NFSA is to fix the high leakages of food—the amount that due to inefficiencies or corruption never reaches the intended beneficiaries, of the existing PDS even when it is released from government stocks. The author's estimates, based on the consumption data of withdrawals from PDS in 2009 reported in NSSO's consumption survey and quantities released through PDS, show a leakage rate of 40 percent at the national level. At the state level, it varies from state to state with the highest rates in Bihar (71 percent), West Bengal (69 percent), Assam (67 percent), Rajasthan (67 percent), Punjab (65 percent), and Uttar Pradesh (59 percent) and almost zero in Tamil Nadu and Chhattisgarh (see figure 5). Of course, these ratios can change from year to year, and one hopes that the overall leakage decreases as time goes on, but given the weak governance in the system, the chances of significant improvement remain low.

Even if one hopes to reduce these leakages in due course by computerizing the whole system, the high taxes and levies on grains imposed by certain states will persist. In Punjab, for instance, these can amount to as much as 14.5 percent. Similar taxes in Andhra Pradesh, Haryana, and Odisha exceed 10 percent. Should these states raise these taxes to, say, 20 percent—and there is nothing stopping them from doing so—the matter will only grow more dire. Also, one should note that in many states with surplus commodities (Punjab, Andhra Pradesh, Haryana, Chhattisgarh, and Madhya Pradesh), almost 70 to 90 percent of market arrivals of wheat and common rice are being procured by state agencies, leading to a de facto state takeover of the cereal trade. The state agencies are inherently high cost. Under such a situation, the hurried launching of the NFSA without fixing the leaky bucket and rationalizing various taxes remains an open issue for debate.

FIGURE 5. LEAKAGES FROM THE PDS (2009) (PERCENTAGE)

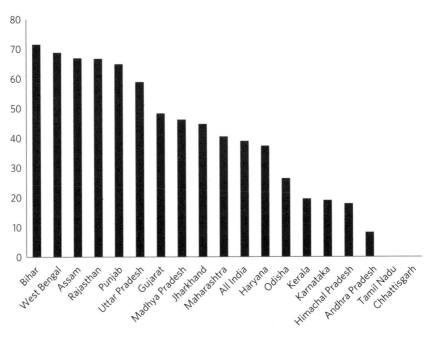

Source: Author's calculations based on data from the National Sample Survey Office and Food
Corporation of India.

So the big question in regard to distribution of food remains: how can one achieve economic access to food more efficiently? And the answer is simple: switch the policy from one of physical handling of grains by state agencies to one of conditional cash transfers based on India's Unique Identification Authority using the Aadhar scheme. Because this would require fingerprints of all those drawing benefits from the government and would deposit the cash benefits directly in their accounts, the leakages can be dramatically reduced. Furthermore, such an approach would not mess up the grain markets. The economic logic behind this suggested approach is simple: it uses an income policy to achieve equity ends and does not manipulate price policy.

The best international practices, from Brazil to Mexico to the Philippines—and now even Pakistan—have adopted conditional cash transfers, while India is stuck with mammoth handling of grains, leading to large efficiency losses. It is not too late to change, and it will be still advisable to introduce cash transfers to at least 51 cities with populations greater than one million that have ample financial infrastructure, and then extend it to farmers, giving an option to deficit states to receive payment in cash or physical quantities. India is too large a country to have just one model for the whole country. It must innovate and bring efficiency in public expenditure if it is to alleviate poverty and extend true food security to its people. Such a move would release pressure on public agencies, reduce leakages, not disturb the grain markets, and hopefully bring greater efficiency. The government would need to keep critical reserves of only 15–20 million tonnes against any possible drought—much less than the 80 million tonnes it had on hand in July 2012. This would also help reduce and stabilize prices of staples in the open market, thus giving a big relief to food inflation. Moving to cash transfers would allow the natural process of diversification in agriculture toward high value products, augment farmers' incomes, and allow consumers to consume better and more nutritious food. All of these amount to a win-win situation for the government as well as for the people, and at a much lower cost than under the current system.

CONCLUSION

To recapitulate the reforms indicated above, and some others, which can help put agriculture on a higher growth path, augment farmers' incomes, and also control price inflation benefiting consumers, the following would be helpful:

- De-list fruits and vegetables from the APMC Act; link funding under the National Horticulture Mission with reforms in marketing on this aspect; free up organized retailing (including foreign direct investment); put food processing on a priority list; and encourage food processors and organized retailers to streamline and build back-end operations with Farmer Producer Organizations under public-private partnership.

- Open up the land-lease markets to let the economically viable size of the holdings emerge in line with the needs of organized processors and retailers. This would also facilitate better utilization of capital on farms.

• Amend the Essential Commodities Act and allow the private sector to build storage and stock grain. The only requirement should be that those having large stocks, say more than 10,000 tonnes, should keep the government informed about their stock levels on a quarterly basis. Furthermore, the government should encourage a negotiable warehouse receipt system with a due regulatory framework in place. All of these steps will go a long way to get the markets right and take the pressure off of the government.

• Gradually switch from the physical distribution of grains at highly subsidized rates to conditional cash transfers, starting with 51 cities with more than a million population and extending the policy change to farmers. This is in line with best international practices and would save large resources.

• Switch input subsidies on fertilizers, power, water, and credit to investment subsidies and cash transfers directly to farmers, while fully lifting controls on fertilizer and other input markets and prices.

NOTES

1   World Bank, *World Development Report 2008: Agriculture for Development* (Washington, D.C.: International Bank for Reconstruction and Development/World Bank, 2007).

2   Ashok Gulati and Shenggen Fan, "The Dragon and the Elephant: Learning From Agricultural and Rural Reforms in China and India," International Food Policy Research Institute, Issue Brief 49, July 2008, www.ifpri.org/sites/default/files/pubs/pubs/ib/ib49.pdf.

3   Ashok Gulati and Ashok Vishandass, "Trade and Food Security: A Case Study of Edible Oils in India," in *Regional Trade Agreements and Food Security in Asia* (Bangkok: Food and Agriculture Organization of the United Nations, 2012).

4   Government of India, Ministry of Agriculture, "Table 2.1: Selected Economic and Social Indicators," in *Agriculture at a Glance 2013*, Directorate of Economics and Statistics, December 2013, http://eands.dacnet.nic.in/Publication12-12-2013/Agricultureat%20a%20Glance2013/page24-89.pdf.

5   Government of India, Ministry of Agriculture, "Price Policy for Kharif Crops: The Marketing Season 2013–14," Commission for Agricultural Costs and Prices, March 2013.

6   Government of India, Ministry of Finance, "Table 5.4: Index Numbers of Wholesale Prices—Relative Prices of Manufactured and Agricultural Products," in *Economic Survey 2012–13* (New Delhi: Government of India, 2013), http://indiabudget.nic.in/budget2013-2014/es2012-13/estat1.pdf.

7   "Wholesale Price Index September 2013," ICRA Research Services, October 2013, www.icra.in/Files/ticker/ICRA%20WPI%20Sep%202013.pdf.

8   Government of India, National Informatics Centre, "Agricultural Census 2010–11: Average Size of Holding by Class Size," Agricultural Census Data Base, http://agcensus.dacnet.nic.in/natt1table4.aspx.

9   "World Food Programme Can Help India Plug Leakage in PDS: KV Thomas," *Economic Times*, November 21, 2013, http://articles.economictimes.indiatimes.com/2013-11-21/news/44327071_1_food-security-bill-wfp-kv-thomas.

10 Ashok Gulati et al., "National Food Security Bill: Challenges and Options," Commission for Agricultural Costs and Prices, Discussion Paper no. 2, December 2012, http://cacp.dacnet.nic.in/NFSB.pdf.

11 Government of India, Ministry of Statistics and Programme Implementation, "Table 1R: Monthly per Capita Quantity and Value of Consumption for Each State/UT and Sector: Food Items," *Household Consumption of Various Goods and Services in India*, National Sample Survey Office, Report no. 541 (February 2012), A145, http://mospi.nic.in/mospi_new/upload/nss_report_541.pdf.

CHAPTER 4

REVISITING MANUFACTURING POLICY

RAJIV KUMAR

THE CONTEXT: THE STATE OF MANUFACTURING IN INDIA

Manufacturing is in trouble in India. The share of the manufacturing sector in the country's GDP reached 16 percent in 2006–2007, then stagnated for the next few years and declined since 2010–2011 (table 1). Even at its highest level, about 18 percent of GDP in the late 1980s, the manufacturing sector's share in India's GDP has been far below that in other Asian economies such as Thailand (36 percent), South Korea (31 percent), China (30 percent), and Taiwan (30 percent). With a gross value addition of $226 billion, India's manufacturing sector looks tiny when compared with China's at $1.9 trillion. Consequently, its share of global manufacturing is a mere 2.2 percent, compared with China's 18.9 percent.[1] Employment in absolute terms has declined in the formal manufacturing sector from 55 million in 2004–2005 (12.2 percent of India's overall employment) to 50 million in 2010 (10.5 percent) (table 2).[2] The share of manufactured exports in India's total exports has also declined, from 74 percent in 1991 to about 61 percent in 2011–2012. This chapter argues that India's development model is responsible for stymieing manufacturing sector growth.

TABLE 1. MANUFACTURING'S SHARE OF GDP, 1993/1994–2012/2013

1993-1994	14.6%
1994-1995	15.2%
1995-1996	16.4%
1996-1997	16.6%
1997-1998	15.9%
1998-1999	15.4%
1999-2000	15.1%
2000-2001	15.5%
2001-2002	15.0%
2002-2003	15.4%
2003-2004	15.2%
2004-2005	15.3%
2005-2006	15.3%
2006-2007	16.0%
2007-2008	16.1%
2008-2009	15.8%
2009-2010	16.2%
2010-2011	16.2%
2011-2012	15.7%
2012-2013	15.1%

Source: Reserve Bank of India.

TABLE 2. SECTOR-WISE SHARE IN TOTAL EMPLOYMENT

	1999-2000	2004-2005	2009-2010
Agriculture	59.9%	56.6%	52.9%
Manufacturing	11.1%	12.2%	10.5%
Non-Manufacturing	5.3%	6.5%	12.2%
Services	23.7%	24.7%	24.4%

Source: Government of India, Planning Commission.

But more worryingly, the rate of growth of the manufacturing sector has been consistently declining since January 2010 (figure 1). This has now culminated in an actual shrinking of the value addition in the sector, with the growth rate plunging into negative territory in the first quarters of both 2012–2013 and 2013–2014. In the absence of a well-conceived policy response, it can be reasonably concluded that the manufacturing sector in India is either already in a major crisis or will soon descend into one.

FIGURE 1. QUARTER-WISE GROWTH IN THE MANUFACTURING SECTOR

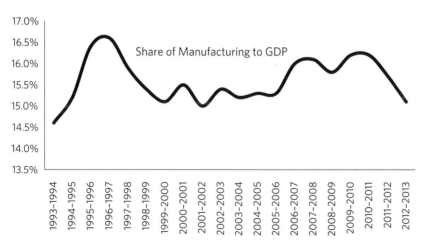

Source: Reserve Bank of India.

Indian manufacturing's relatively poor performance has come about despite several government attempts to improve its fortunes. These included the creation of the National Manufacturing Competitiveness Council in 2004 and the New Manufacturing Policy announced in September 2011. Both of these initiatives have the explicit objective of improving the sector's global competitiveness and raising its share of GDP to an ambitious 25 percent by 2025. Yet, in the subsequent period, the sector's share of GDP has continued to stagnate, and its growth performance has significantly weakened over the past two years.

The manufacturing sector is marked by extensive and deep dualism—gaps between the formal and informal economies—in virtually every subsector, most clearly pronounced in final consumer products. This dualism is reflected across all aspects—wages, productivity, technological capabilities, working conditions—and creates capacity fragmentation, a relative absence of economies of scale and scope that makes the sector globally uncompetitive. The presence of a large number of "informal sector producers" also leads to a lack of quality consciousness and a general lack of attention to attracting and nurturing high-quality human skills, a phenomenon that Indian commentators often label as the sector's *chalta hai* culture.[3]

A disturbing feature that has emerged over the past ten years has been the slow but steady exit of established manufacturers. Many of them have switched to importing the same line of products from China and other sources, rather than carrying on with manufacturing activity within the country.[4] This has happened as a result of an increasingly difficult environment for manufacturing in the country. The recently passed Land Acquisition, Rehabilitation, and Resettlement (LARR) Bill, which has raised rural land prices by a minimum factor of four and mandated a very complicated and time-consuming acquisition procedure, is most likely to greatly accelerate this process of de-industrialization in India. Given that India needs to find new jobs for at least 1 million new entrants to the workforce every month for the next fifteen years (180 million over the next fifteen years, according to the Twelfth Five Year Plan), this prospect of a shrinking manufacturing sector should be a cause for extreme concern.[5]

By all accounts, manufacturing sector growth will have to keep pace with the overall GDP growth rate in the foreseeable future in order to generate the required number of jobs and for India to meet its development targets of rapid, inclusive, and sustainable growth. In Uttar Pradesh, Bihar, Punjab, Odisha, Rajasthan, and Madhya Pradesh, the growth rate should be even higher for them to achieve the same share of manufacturing in their state GDP as is the average level in the country overall. This will require an urgent, radical, and sustained reform effort.

WHAT HAS GONE WRONG?

The manufacturing sector suffers from multiple challenges, a majority of which are policy-induced. There are, however, a few for which the industry itself is responsible. Given that all discussions on the problems and challenges begin (and also end) with pointing a long finger at the government, it may be useful to take a more novel approach to what plagues the sector by looking at some constraints that have resulted from the Indian industry's self-induced weakness.

Challenges That Can Be Addressed by Industry

First, Indian industry continues to face an acute skill shortage. The sector laments this problem but does not even attempt to emulate the information technology (IT) and other services sectors, which have tried to tackle this with large-scale in-house training programs. Second, the Indian private sector has been unable or unwilling to adopt effective forms of collective action for either demanding and enforcing government accountability or finding solutions for collective problems. Third, there is no attempt at self-regulation by the industry against corrupt practices by its own members. This results in negative public perception, minimal credibility with the government, and an increasing level of judicial intervention. Fourth, Indian small and medium enterprises (SMEs) do not receive money owed to them from their larger buyers, a far cry from the nurturing such companies enjoy in Japan and South Korea. It is reported that if Indian SMEs received their payments on time, their profitability could go up by 25 percent.[6] Fifth, and finally, it can be said with a reasonable degree of confidence that Indian industry is in large parts cartelized. The direct implication is a great deal of resistance to enter into price competition to try to keep return per unit of output as high as possible.[7] This is inimical to the long-term interests of the manufacturing sector as it prevents the industry from achieving economies of scale and becoming globally competitive. All five of these weaknesses can and should be addressed by the industry itself if it hopes to improve its competitiveness and also its credibility in the eyes of policymakers and consumers.

CHALLENGES THAT ARISE FROM GOVERNMENT POLICIES

The challenges caused, directly or indirectly, by government policies are rather well known and repeatedly discussed in the literature over the years. They can be grouped under five headings: a difficult business environment; labor deployment rigidity and legacy issues related to labor; an extensive infrastructure deficit that affects the economy, especially the manufacturing sector; costs of time overruns and uncertainty in getting environment clearances and in land acquisition; and the high cost—when it's even available—of commercial bank credit, especially for SMEs.

Difficult Business Environment

India ranked 132 out of the 185 countries in the World Bank's Doing Business survey in 2013. The ranking has declined in recent years, signifying a relative worsening of the business environment. According to the official data, nearly 70 clearances are required annually for businesses to be opened and continue in operation. In addition, more than 100 returns have to be filed in one year.[8] The greatest cost of these procedures and processes falls on SMEs, where the proprietor has to bear the entire compliance burden. This has also become the source of extensive rent seeking and corruption. More crucially, such a business environment, combined with retroactive changes in tax demands, creates a great deal of uncertainty, which is anathema for investment. Another, more fundamental, challenge faced by manufacturers, especially SMEs, is the weak or nonexistent protection against extortion, protection rackets, and outright organized crime operations. While not openly discussed, these illegal activities are quite pervasive.[9]

Labor Deployment Rigidities

In the context of labor market conditions, Indian manufacturing has suffered in the past from the twin constraints of militant and competitive trade unionism and a plethora of labor legislation. In recent years, competitive and militant unionism has ostensibly weakened. Nevertheless, it is still present in major industrial centers, and its infrequent but violent demonstration discourages foreign investors and induces others to keep employment to a minimum. India has nearly fifty laws, either at the central or state level, that in one way or the other affect labor conditions in India.[10] Consequently, hardly any enterprise can claim to be in total compliance with the legal provisions governing labor conditions. It would not be unfair to say that this dysfunctional legal framework is perhaps the principal reason for the slow growth of large-scale and globally competitive manufacturing in India.

Infrastructure Deficit

India's infrastructure deficit in comparison to other economies is best captured by the summary statistics that India's per capita commercial energy consumption is about 760 kilowatt-hours (kWh), while that of China is nearly 3,000 kWh and that of the United States is 12,000 kWh. Peak power deficit in India is estimated at 7–8 percent, and industry is not insulated from the resultant power cuts that are common across the country. A significant majority of large manufacturing units have to put up 100 percent power backup capacities, which raises capital costs and also costs 40–50 percent more than electricity consumed from the grid. As a result of the infrastructure deficit, Indian industry across the board bears a significantly higher price for infrastructure services and utilities than their global competitors.[11]

Regulatory Delays and Lack of Transparency

Over time, a rather complex regulatory structure has been established in India to deal with land acquisition and change of land use, protection of natural forests, and safeguarding of the environment. The situation has become increasingly time-consuming, opaque, and unpredictable over the years, especially during the past ten years under the rule of the United Progressive Alliance. According to one survey, there are in all (counting both the central and state governments) 1,240 regulations that apply to the industrial sector.[12] This is far too severe a compliance requirement, especially for SMEs.

High Cost and Non-Availability of Commercial Bank Credit

Normally, manufacturers in India face real capital costs (nominal lending charges minus inflation) exceeding 4–5 percent compared with the 1–2 percent costs for their global competitors.[13] This has been mitigated recently, with the government permitting external commercial borrowing of up to 200 percent of a company's net worth. But this measure has helped only the very large manufacturing units, and even for them the foreign exchange risk raises the real cost of capital. It is reported that in a survey, more than two-thirds of SMEs preferred not to utilize commercial bank credit because of the long and complicated processing times and large volume of collateral demanded by banks. The owners preferred to secure credit from the informal markets at higher rates but with less onerous conditions that did not leave them personally vulnerable. This defeats the avowed aim of the government's selective credit control policy that requires banks to earmark 10 percent of their credit to SMEs.

WHAT IS TO BE DONE

Self-Help by Industry

Industry could help make things better by implementing some steps that are in its direct control and do not require any policy intervention. Private companies are just beginning to tackle the skills shortages by adopting about 110 industrial training institutes. These have achieved mixed success depending upon the private sector's relative control over curriculum and management. The training institutes can be expanded much further, and industry would do well to take the initiative in collaborating with vocational skill providers in growing capacities, designing curricula, and offering assured placements.[14] This could be supplemented with a large-scale internship program that does not principally depend upon government funds for its implementation. In general, Indian industry has to recognize the value of positive externalities that emerge from their individual actions and not focus exclusively on private returns. This is a major weakness that has to be overcome.

Indian firms also would benefit greatly by empowering their chambers and associations to take collective action on their behalf in demanding and enforcing accountability for delivery of public services in a time-bound manner and with acceptable quality. This would require three conditions. First, that industry associations be given autonomy and not be seen as having been captured by and serving the interests of a few corporate honchos. Second, that industry associations not accept government grants and that they guard their independence vis-à-vis the government. Third, that individual members not undercut the efforts of the associations and chambers by directly interacting with policymakers for individual gains and signaling the acceptance of lower-than-expected delivery of public services and government accountability.

Collective action by industry will be tenable if and only if it is seen as credible and legitimate by the government and civil society. To achieve credibility, industry will have to improve its record of self-regulation and of identifying "bad apples" within its ranks. This will also allow the industry to effectively counter and change its public image from that of a collection of "robber barons" or "crony capitalists" to one that plays by the rules and observes corporate governance and ethical norms.

Fourth, large businesses must adopt a nurturing attitude toward their suppliers, which invariably belong to the MSME category of micro, small, and medium enterprises. This has been done all over the world and also very successfully by some Indian companies. Furthermore, better relations between large business and their suppliers will help to reduce the existing dualism in the manufacturing sector and modernize the country's informal or unorganized manufacturing sector. While government policies can also help, industry must recognize its own critical role in bringing about this much-needed change.

Fifth, if Indian companies are serious about attaining global competitiveness, they should substantially increase their research and development expenditures. As for government encouragement of R&D, fiscal incentives should be switched from input-based to outcome-based criteria and then made far more attractive.[15]

Sixth, it is time that Indian industry, of its own accord, disbands the thousands of sector and subsector associations whose ostensible raison d'être of negotiating fiscal concessions and securing licenses from the government is increasingly irrelevant in the post-liberalization period.

The Government's Agenda for Policy Reforms

There are at present two quite distinct schools of opinion on the government's policy reform priorities. The first school believes that the structural conditions that have emerged over the past six and a half decades of populist democracy and the recent information explosion do not permit the growth of mass manufacturing in India. By putting a statutory floor under both the price of labor and land, the political process has effectively raised the cost of both labor (skilled and unskilled) and land, the two principal factors of production for manufacturing. Moreover, the complicated resettlement and rehabilitation (R&R) provisions enshrined in the LARR make land procurement even by private industry a most cumbersome and time-consuming process. In addition to the relatively higher costs of labor and land, this school argues that the new generation of workers, being more educated and IT savvy than earlier generations, will not accept low-productivity shop floor jobs, an essential component of mass manufacturing. It can be surmised that if these structural conditions and policy regime are accepted as the given operating framework for Indian manufacturing firms, India should give up trying to enter mass manufacturing at this stage.

Instead, this school of opinion holds that the government should increasingly focus its promotion policies on "sunrise industries"—sectors that use frontline technologies, require highly skilled labor, and are design- and technology-intensive. This form of specialized manufacturing can be met by stand-alone, high-tech, relatively small-scale firms that focus on innovation. Policy in this case should be directed to hugely scaling up the numbers of such high-tech firms and connecting them to a public sector science and technology establishment, which is given additional resources and encouraged to work together with private entrepreneurs.[16] The policy focus would be to create and sustain a learning environment for businesses; India could emulate the Japanese and South Korean example where private firms, government science and technology agencies (including those involved in defense R&D), and technology institutes can come together to produce large-scale product and process innovations, which can then be commercialized by dynamic Indian entrepreneurs.

This is a seductive model for the future of India's manufacturing sector, especially if one accepts the existence of structural conditions that are inimical to mass manufacturing. The factors that make this model somewhat infeasible are low R&D orientation of the Indian industry and also of the public sector agencies, as reflected in India's comparatively low R&D expenditures; low technology absorptive capacity of the large mass of manufacturing firms in the informal sector; the absence of a culture of collaboration among government agencies and the private sector; the relative scarcity of high-grade skills reflected in the low rate of patent activity in India; the low penetration of broadband connectivity and Internet access, which has reached only 10 percent of the population in 2012; and, finally, the weak governance capability and negative environment in the government, which has deteriorated even further during the past ten years. This condition does not encourage any innovation and risk-taking by government officials and therefore virtually precludes their ability to collaborate with private firms. These weaknesses are quite critical and may prevent a successful implementation of this model.

Alternative Policy Approach

The alternative approach for policy reforms—which represents the better and more desirable way forward—is not to accept the high cost of labor and land as given. Instead, this approach takes as given that the large majority of entrants to the workforce will continue to be semiskilled and willing to accept productive jobs in the formal manufacturing sector (though not in the unorganized sector, where working conditions are abysmal and productivity and income levels fall below the expectations of a relatively more educated workforce). This will require government policy to be directed toward the more conventional form of intervention.

Land Costs. These costs can be kept at acceptable levels by using the land already acquired by industrial development corporations of various states (for example, it is reported that Maharashtra Industrial Development Corporation owns land amounting to more than a million square meters) for new manufacturing capacities; increasing the floor area-to-space ratio, thereby effectively expanding the supply of land in urban areas and bringing down the prices; releasing the vast stock of land owned by government departments, defense, public sector enterprises, and port trusts and allocating them for manufacturing capacities; and amending the LARR to remove the R&R requirement for private purchase of land irrespective of the size of the land purchased and also doing away with the ban on acqui-sition of agricultural land, as is currently stipulated in the law.

Labor Conditions. It is pointless to argue for the removal of Article 35A in Chapter V of the Industrial Disputes Act and give employers permission to hire and fire; this is a non-starter in the present Indian context. Instead, other ways have to be found for achieving the desired level of flexibility in labor deployment. The proposal in the New Manufacturing Policy for the creation of a "resource pool" to retrain retrenched workers and teach them new skills and for giving them unemployment security for a minimum period while they undergo this training is well worth considering for application even outside the National Investment and Manufacturing Zones. This could provide the necessary flexibility for employers while ensuring income security to the workers.

MSMEs will benefit greatly if the existing plethora of labor laws, num-bering more than fifty, is rationalized and reduced to four or five compre-hensive laws that take care of workers' minimum wages; minimally acceptable working conditions, with special focus on proper conditions for female employees; social security in case of demise, injury, or unemploy-ment; workers' welfare in terms of medical, maternity, and related condi-tions; and post-retirement benefits for both regular and contract employees. Such a modernization of labor laws is long overdue.

It is important to formalize the system of contract labor by mandating equal wages and welfare measures for them (or even a slightly higher ter-minal benefit) in lieu of the workers' voluntarily accepting short tenures for their employment.

Provision of reasonable workers' housing has been a common feature in industrialized economies all over the world and over centuries. This is not yet the norm in India. Government and employers must work together to improve the living conditions of laborers, especially migrants, on an urgent basis. Doing so will improve productivity, reduce turnover, and in effect bring down labor costs.

Business Environment. Five measures can improve the business environ-ment almost immediately. First, as suggested by the World Bank, is to introduce a combined application form in place of the existing forms prescribed under any applicable laws, rules, orders, and instructions for obtaining the required clearances.[17]

Second is to introduce a system of common return that will dispense with the need to submit multiple returns with different frequency. This common return would replace most of the more than one hundred returns currently in use.[18]

Third is to drastically reduce the time taken for starting and exiting a business. For starting a business, a time limit of three days should be implemented across the country, as is reportedly already being achieved in Gujarat. The average time taken for exiting a business, according to the World Bank's Doing Business survey, is at present a horrendous ten years. This surely can be brought down to less than a year by establishing special tribunals or fast-tracking the adjudication process in labor courts.

Fourth is to give serious consideration to shifting to a system of self-certification rather than annual clearance by designated inspectors. This will greatly reduce the compliance burden, especially for SMEs, where it is borne by the owner-entrepreneur.

Finally, there are other procedures, such as the single window for applications, acquisition of income tax, and sales tax registration numbers, in which there now is a very wide range of performance across states. The central government can encourage states to replicate the best practices that are already in place in other states. This in itself will bring about a great deal of improvement in the business environment in the country.

The considerable delays and uncertainty caused by regulatory procedures and processes can be reduced by putting in place a clear time-bound process for all regulatory clearances. With all its lacunae and potentially adverse impact on industrialization in the country, LARR lays down a clear procedure for land acquisition. A similar approach should be adopted for all other regulatory clearance—forests, environment, security, and so on. An IT-enabled clearance process will greatly reduce the regulatory burden on manufacturing units.

To lower costs of commercial credit, the government should increase competition in the banking sector by granting fresh licenses on a more regular basis. The government could license some private sector banks to specifically cater to the needs of the MSMEs. This will increase competition for the Small Industries Development Bank of India (SIDBI) and also create a specialized cadre of credit officers who would be better equipped to evaluate risks and opportunities in the MSME sector, which can emerge as the main driver for manufacturing sector expansion in the country.

CONCLUSION

India needs a rapidly growing manufacturing sector both to meet its rising demand for industrial products and even more so for absorbing the one million per month new entrants to the workforce. This will require that the current slowdown in the sector be decisively reversed and the sector be put on a path of sustained rapid growth—higher growth than the overall rate of GDP growth. This requires both industry and government (central and states) to implement a reform agenda together. This agenda would in essence increase competition, reduce the extent of dualism in the manufacturing sector, make the regulatory process more transparent, and reduce the compliance burden.

The two approaches toward the future of manufacturing in India, discussed above, are not necessarily conflicting. They can co-exist. Expanding islands of innovation and high-technology firms can co-exist with a manufacturing sector in which the size of the informal sector is constantly being reduced and in which productivity and technology levels converge within the same industry. The separate category of SMEs should be retained for some time, if only to achieve a greater technological and productivity convergence within each sector and nurture the more employment-intensive segments of the manufacturing sector. The reforms necessary for the manufacturing sector expansion must be undertaken urgently. For if the country is to achieve its strategic and development objectives, it cannot afford to have a shrinking manufacturing sector.

NOTES

1 Government of India, Planning Commission, *Twelfth Five Year Plan* (New Delhi: SAGE Publishers, 2013), vol. II, 52.

2 It had increased by 25 percent from 44 million to 55 percent between 1999 and 2005. See *Twelfth Five Year Plan*, 51.

3 While difficult to precisely render in English, *chalta hai* expresses a tolerance for a merely "good enough" result, often bordering on irresponsibility in a business context.

4 See Rajiv Kumar, *Many Futures of India* (New Delhi: Academic Press, 2010).

5 For more on the topic of India's future employment needs, see chapter 6.

6 Pankaj Chandra, lecture at the Lal Bahadur Shastri National Academy for Administration (Bangalore, October 7, 2013).

7 The recent decisions of the newly established Competition Commission of India, which has imposed severe penalties on some industries to discourage cartelization, are testimony to the existence of cartels in Indian industry. But so far this may have touched only the proverbial tip of the iceberg. There are thousands of sector industry associations (as opposed to national or umbrella industry organizations) with extremely narrow sector mandates whose raison d'être is to lobby the government either for fiscal concessions or against import protection and perhaps to keep prices at levels that will allow the most inefficient to remain operational.

8 Government of India, Department of Commerce & Industry, "Annex to Press Note 2: National Manufacturing Policy," 2011, http://dipp.nic.in/English/policies/National_Manufacturing_Policy_25October2011.pdf.

9 It also affects large industry, but the costs are more easily absorbed and managed.

10 Some of these laws are: Trade Unions Act, 1926; Industrial Employment (Standing Orders) Act, 1946; Industrial Disputes Act, 1947; Factories Act, 1948; Minimum Wages Act, 1948; Contract Labour (Regulation and Abolition) Act, 1970; Payment of Wages Act, 1936; Payment of Gratuity Act, 1972; Employees' State Insurance Act, 1948; Provident Funds Act, 1952; Maternity Benefits Act, 1961; Employees' Compensation Act, 1952; and Contract Labour (Regulation & Abolition) Act, 1970.

11 For an additional discussion of the energy sector and these statistics, see chapter 12.

12 S. Tripathi, lecture at the Lal Bahadur Shastri National Academy for Administration (Bangalore, October 7, 2013).

13 Under the prevailing interest rate regime, manufacturing units, especially the SMEs, which do not have access to external commercial borrowing, get commercial bank credit at about 13–14 percent, while the wholesale inflation is around 5–6 percent and retail inflation is 9 percent. This yields a real cost of capital of at least 4–5 percent.

14 Some beginning is being made with the formation of Sector Skills Council and Industry Knowledge Hubs. But overall the industry can be far more proactive in this area, given the critical nature of this constraint.

15 Currently, the incentives are based on the expenditure incurred by the corporation on R&D activities. This can be changed to rewarding them far more handsomely on the basis of actual outcomes such as patents registered or new designs and innovation breakthroughs.

16   As, for example, successfully achieved by the National Chemical Laboratory, Pune, while under the stewardship of Professor R. M. Mashelkar and reported quite widely in the publications of the Council of Scientific and Industrial Research (CSIR), the apex body for managing science and technology establishments in the government of India.

17   Some of the clearances that can be affected through CAF are: Provincial Registration Certificate for SSI Unit; Land/Shed Allotment/Allotment of Government Land/ Conversion of Agricultural Land/Change of Land Use; Consent for Establishment (Water); Consent for Establishment (Air); Permission for Site to Situate Factory; Permission to Construct Factory Building; Approval of Factory Building Plans; Permission to Construct Factory Building; Permission to Erect Building—Town Planning/Approval of Building Plan; Fire Prevention; Power Supply; Water Supply; Provincial Registration—Sales Tax; Registration—CST; Registration—Entry Tax; Registration—Profession Tax; Enrollment—Profession Tax; Registration & Grant of License—CIF&B; Consent for Operation (Air); Consent for Operation (Water); Treatment of Hazardous Wastes Registration & Use of Boilers; Notice for Mining Operations; Registration—Central Excise.

18   This has again been recommended by the World Bank and merits serious consideration. Some of the examples of returns that can be replaced by this common return are as follows: Factories Rules; Contract Labor (Regulation & Abolition) Rules; Minimum Wages Rules; Payment of Wages Rules; Payment of Bonus Rules; Shops & Establishment Rules; Motor Transport Workers Rules; Maternity Benefit Rules; Sales Tax, VAT Rules; Central Sales Tax Rules; Entry Tax Rules; State Tax on Professions, Trades, Callings, and Employment Rules.

CHAPTER 5

GENERATING EMPLOYMENT

OMKAR GOSWAMI

I t is perhaps best to start with stating a principle that is so basic as to approximate a truism: when the growth of national income slows down, so, too, does that of employment. Quite often, the speed of decline of the latter overshadows the former.

This is important given India's dramatic fall in real GDP growth over nine quarters. Figure 1 and table 1 show this very clearly.

FIGURE 1. INDIA, REAL GDP GROWTH

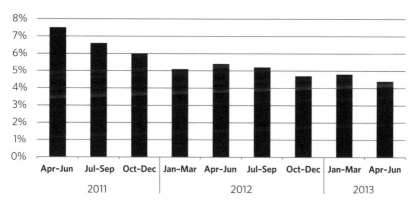

Source: Government of India, Central Statistical Organization, National Account Statistics.

TABLE 1. SECTOR-WISE GROWTH OVER NINE QUARTERS

Rate of Growth (%)	2011			2012				2013	
	Apr–Jun	Jul–Sep	Oct–Dec	Jan–Mar	Apr–Jun	Jul–Sep	Oct–Dec	Jan–Mar	Apr–Jun
Agriculture, Forestry, and Fishing	5.4	3.2	4.1	2.0	2.9	1.7	1.8	1.4	2.7
Mining and Quarrying	-0.4	-5.3	-2.6	5.2	0.4	1.7	-0.7	-3.1	-2.8
Manufacturing	7.4	3.1	0.7	0.1	-1.0	0.1	2.5	2.6	-1.2
Electricity, Gas, and Water Supply	6.6	8.4	7.7	3.5	6.2	3.2	4.5	2.8	3.7
Construction	3.8	6.5	6.9	5.1	7.0	3.1	2.9	4.4	2.8
Trade, Hotels, Transport, and Communications	9.6	7.0	6.9	5.1	6.1	6.8	6.4	6.2	3.9
Finance, Insurance, Real Estate, and Business Services	11.6	12.3	11.4	11.3	9.3	8.3	7.8	9.1	8.9
Community, Social, and Personal Services	3.5	6.5	6.8	6.8	8.9	8.4	5.6	4.0	9.4
GDP at Factor Cost	**7.5**	**6.5**	**6.0**	**5.1**	**5.4**	**5.2**	**4.7**	**4.8**	**4.4**

Note: Growth compared to same quarter of the previous year.

Source: Government of India, Central Statistical Organization, National Account Statistics.

In nine consecutive quarters, India's real GDP growth has shrunk by 3.1 percentage points, from 7.5 percent in April–June 2011 to 4.4 percent in April–June 2013. The decline has been particularly sharp in manufacturing, with growth dropping by 8.6 points, from 7.4 percent in April–June 2011 to –1.2 percent in April–June 2013. Construction has also taken a significant hit, down from the heady double digits of four years ago to 7 percent in April–June 2012, and then to 2.8 percent a year later. Similarly deflated are trade, hotels, transport, and communications

—falling from 9.6 percent in April–June 2011 to 6.1 percent a year later, followed by 3.9 percent in April–June 2013.

It is all too easy to blame the extended global economic crisis since the fall of Lehman Brothers in September 2008 as the prime cause of this sharp decline in India's growth, as many spokesmen for the Indian National Congress and the United Progressive Alliance (UPA) government have done. No doubt, some of the downturn reflects global conditions. However, much of the blame for poor economic performance over the last few years lies at the door of the central government in power—on account of its consistent lack of focus on major economic issues and a general absence of governance despite having a greater parliamentary majority than before.

The faults of the UPA-II government in Delhi, while legion over the past four years, are not to be enumerated here. Instead, the objective is to evaluate the prospects of increasing employment in the years to come and to suggest policy changes that might aid such a process. In doing so, two things need to recognized: how the falling growth rate has affected employment, and the size of the problem that future governments will have to grapple with.

HOW BAD IS IT?

Job loss has dominated India's headlines in recent months and years. For instance, an *India Today* cover feature in the fall of 2013 stated that job losses in fiscal year 2013–2014 would be around 500,000.[1] The *Economic Times*, similarly, ran a story focusing on the slowdown in urban employment.[2]

The Planning Commission has also posted disturbing figures. Between fiscal years 1999–2000 and 2004–2005, employment across various sectors increased significantly by almost 61 million, to a total of 457.5 million. Since then, however, employment growth has dramatically slowed: between 2004–2005 and 2009–2010, it increased by merely 2.7 million, to reach a total of 460 million. The largest absolute decline in employment in the five years leading up to 2009–2010 was in agriculture—by 15.7 million people, 6 percent of the number employed in 2004–2005. The second-worst crunch was in manufacturing—down by 7.2 million people, or almost 13 percent of those employed in 2004–2005.[3]

The decline is worrisome enough. More disconcerting is the sharp fall in employment elasticity, the percentage change in employment for each percentage change in value added. For all sectors taken together, the employment elasticity has slumped from 0.44 in 1999–2000 to 2004–2005 to 0.01 in 2004–2005 to 2009–2010. Simply stated, in the first period, a 1 percent increase in value added led to 0.44 percent growth in employment; in the second period, it was virtually zero.

In some sectors, the decline in employment elasticity has been truly alarming. Manufacturing has seen a fall from 0.76 in the first period to −0.31 in the second; thus, growth in value added has occurred in a milieu of an absolute decline in manufacturing employment. So, too, was the case for agriculture: down from 0.84 to −0.42. And, what is probably most disturbing given its share of GDP, the employment elasticity in services has slumped from 0.45 to −0.01.[4]

It seems clear that commercial entities, especially in the unorganized and non-factory sectors, have been reducing their labor complement in the face of a serious growth slowdown. Though much smaller in size in the labor market, the organized factory sector has not had a decline in employment, if one were to go by the numbers given in the *Annual Survey of Industries* (ASI). Between 1999–2000 and 2004–2005, the number of workers in approximately 136,000 factories increased by 5 percent, and then by an additional 39 percent between 2004–2005 and 2009–2010, in over 159,000 factories.[5] However, there is little doubt that the rate of growth of factory employment—be it of those legally recognized as workmen or workmen plus other employees—has been significantly lower than that of value added. While this is obviously a positive from the point of view of growing labor productivity, the fact remains that additional employment demand in factories is getting muted.

Broadly speaking, therefore, the story runs as follows. Employment demand is slowing down quite significantly across the country. This is true of both the organized and the unorganized sectors. There are two complementary causes. The first relates to a rapid slowdown in growth across the economy that is not only reducing demand for labor but is also contributing to retrenchment, wherever possible. The second relates to a general substitution away from labor in favor of productivity-enhancing capital, exacerbated by the falling relative price of capital compared to that of labor. This is certainly the case in manufacturing, and it is also true for many organizations in the services sector.

But just as falling, even negative, growth has significantly reduced the demand for labor across sectors, so, too, will a phase of sustained high growth bring back the need for additional employment. As we shall see, regulatory changes can help, but only at the margin. The panacea for employment ills in India is a phase of sustained growth of 7 percent to 7.5 percent per year over a ten-year period. Whether the country and its states have the governing capacity to make that happen is a matter of debate. But if the average growth rate hovers around 4.5 percent to 5 percent per annum, India will never generate a demand for labor even vaguely in line with its future supply.

THE SIZE OF TOMORROW'S PROBLEM

This sets the stage for the second issue: the challenge that India faces in generating adequate employment over the next three decades. To appreciate this, it is useful to examine population growth and additions to the workforce over five-year periods.

The population data used in this analysis are the medium variant estimates obtained from the Population Division of the United Nations Department of Economic and Social Affairs for every five years from 2010 to 2040.[6] These are given in terms of females, males, and total. The 68th round of the National Sample Survey (NSS), conducted for 2011–2012 and based on a sample of 101,724 households in rural and urban India, gives the ratio of workers to the population of men and women.[7] This is called the worker population ratio, or WPR, which is used to estimate the size of tomorrow's problem.

Two WPR variants are considered: (1) WPR1 remains fixed at the rate estimated by the NSS in 2011–2012 to 2040, and (2) WPR2, in which after 2015, the male WPR rises by 2.5 percent every five years, while the female WPR rises by 5 percent (the latter's higher rate of change is due to the much lower current female WPR). Multiplying the two sets of WPRs with the relevant population statistics gives a reasonable estimate of the numbers of men and women who might be in the job market up to 2040. Table 2 and figures 2 and 3 present these figures.[8]

TABLE 2. GENERATING EMPLOYMENT UP TO 2040

	2010	2015	2020	2025	2030	2035	2040
Male Population (millions)	624	663	699	732	760	784	803
Female Population (millions)	582	620	655	687	716	741	763
Scenario 1: Fixed WPR (WPR1)							
Male WPR	0.544	0.544	0.544	0.544	0.544	0.544	0.544
Female WPR	0.219	0.219	0.219	0.219	0.219	0.219	0.219
Male Workers (millions)	339	361	380	398	414	426	437
Female Workers (millions)	127	136	143	150	157	162	167
Total Workers (millions)	**467**	**496**	**523**	**548**	**570**	**589**	**604**
Extra Jobs Needed (millions)		**30**	**27**	**25**	**22**	**18**	**15**
Scenario 2: Rising WPR (WPR2)							
Male WPR	0.544	0.544	0.558	0.572	0.586	0.600	0.615
Female WPR	0.219	0.219	0.230	0.241	0.254	0.266	0.280
Male Workers (millions)	339	361	390	418	445	471	494
Female Workers (millions)	127	136	151	166	182	197	213
Total Workers (millions)	**467**	**496**	**540**	**584**	**627**	**668**	**707**
Extra Jobs Needed (millions)		**30**	**44**	**44**	**43**	**41**	**39**

Source: United Nations, Department of Economic and Social Affairs, Population Division; and
    Government of India, Ministry of Statistics, National Sample Survey (NSS), 68th Round,
    2011–2012.

FIGURE 2. ESTIMATED NUMBER OF WORKERS (MILLIONS)

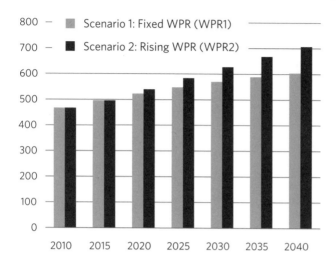

Source: United Nations, Department of Economic and Social Affairs, Population Division; and
    Government of India, Ministry of Statistics, National Sample Survey (NSS), 68th Round,
    2011–2012.

FIGURE 3. EXTRA JOBS NEEDED (MILLIONS)

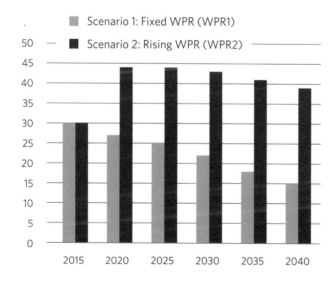

Source: United Nations, Department of Economic and Social Affairs, Population Division; and
    Government of India, Ministry of Statistics, National Sample Survey (NSS), 68th Round,
    2011–2012.

The situation looks grim even in the case of the fixed WPR. According to the evidence, an additional 30 million jobs need to be created between 2010 and 2015—which will certainly not happen given the depressed state of the economy and the fact that only 2.7 million extra jobs came into being between 2004–2005 and 2009–2010. As it stands today, India has neither the growth nor the required institutional flexibility to create 6 million extra jobs per year up to 2015 and a bit over 5 million per year from 2015 to 2025.

Things get worse under scenario 2, which incorporates the more realistic assumption that, armed with better education, the percentage of men and women joining the labor force will be higher than before. Hence, both the labor force participation rate and the WPR will rise—less for men and more for women.

This rise in WPR is modest, but the absolute numbers are dramatically larger. Under scenario 2, India will need to find 44 million additional jobs between 2015 and 2020 at an annual rate of just under 9 million, compared with a bit over 5 million per year with the fixed WPR of scenario 1.

These numbers claim no exactitude. Instead, they set the stage in terms of broad orders of magnitude. The data underscore the urgent need to create much wider employment in the years ahead. The question is, "What needs to be done?"

THE ROAD AHEAD

Despite the existence of certain laws that prevent unfettered entry and exit of labor in the organized sector, the fact of the matter is that India has reasonable labor market flexibility. For one, the vast unorganized sector, which accounts for more than 90 percent of India's 470 million workers or thereabouts, has absolutely no entry or exit barriers. Moreover, the legal constraints that allegedly prevent extra hiring in the organized sector—such as sections 25(N) and 25(O) of the Industrial Disputes Act, 1947, or provisions of the Contract Labour (Regulation and Abolition) Act, 1970—are often overstated.

As an example, it is worth focusing on what most commentators consider to be the most recalcitrant group of workers and employees in India: the 20 million or so who work for the government, including state-owned public sector enterprises (PSEs). In 1992, the government of India intro-duced the National Renewal Fund, which was used mainly to finance voluntary retirement schemes for PSE employees. The extent of surplus labor was huge. In 1992–1993, 55 centrally owned sick PSEs had an esti-mated 84,283 surplus staff. Of these, almost half were in nationalized textile and jute mills.[9] Between April 1992 and June 1994, 70,826 workers from these PSEs took voluntary retirement under schemes offered by man-agement; of those, 38,363, or 54 percent, were from the cotton textile and jute mills.[10] By August 1997, an additional 146,663 workers were volun-tarily separated.[11]

No doubt, creating legal flexibility can help. But not as much as stated by those who believe that the "freedom to fire" is a prime driver of labor market reforms without which India can never hope to achieve signifi-cantly higher employment. Facts bear this out. Today, even in the orga-nized sector, which has considerable labor law oversight, there is enough scope for hiring workers and keeping them beyond the pale of becoming legally "permanent"; likewise, there are no barriers to reducing the labor complement, provided there is a fair termination agreement. The barriers to additional employment lie elsewhere.

Simply stated, it is generally untrue that more people are not being hired because of a fear that they can't be made to leave in difficult times. They are not being hired because of an environment that is increasingly cramping the country's growth potential.

As an example, consider construction—a sector that has a great deal of de facto flexibility in the use of workers. It has an employment elastic-ity of 1.54, meaning that a 1 percent increase in value added generates 1.54 percent growth in employment. Even in 2009–2010, it accounted for more than 56 million workers, or 12 percent of total employment of the country across all sectors. Within the sector, a major driver of employ-ment is the construction of roads and highways. The National Highways Development Program is slated to construct 47,476 km of highways. As of July 2013, only 42 percent had been built out into four or six lanes; an additional 25 percent was under implementation. The remaining 33 percent, or 15,748 km, has not even been awarded for construction.[12] The pace is dismal: around 8 km per day (kmd) versus the target rate of 20 kmd—itself modest by South or Central Asian standards. Why so?

Because successful bidders are overleveraged and do not secure adequate funding on time, coupled with a "pro-people" stance in many state governments that creates expensive barriers to acquiring the land needed for widening highways. The result is a reduction in construction growth from double digits to 2.8 percent in April–June 2013, and with it less incremental demand for labor.

There are 76,818 km of national highways in India. If the government were sufficiently serious about creating growth-enhancing infrastructure, it would prioritize the four- or six-laning of every kilometer and work on completing this task at the rate of at least 25 km per day. This would immediately create a huge demand for workers throughout India and help increase gainful employment while improving much-needed infrastructure.

What is true for highways also holds for the telecom industry. On February 2, 2012, the Supreme Court of India canceled 122 mobile telecom licenses awarded under the dispensation of the then-telecom minister A. Raja, allegedly on account of rigging to generate below market prices. Since then, it has been impossible for the Telecom Regulatory Authority of India and the department of telecommunications to allot additional licenses and spectrum—thus slowing down the growth of mobile telephony in India. The sector is also employment-intensive. Its slowdown has reduced the potential for creating additional jobs in urban as well as up-country India.

There is a long list of sectors that have slowed down on account of lower growth as well as judiciary and regulatory overreach. Bans imposed by the Supreme Court in Goa, Karnataka, and Odisha have a played a major role in reducing iron ore output from almost 210 million metric tons in 2010–2011 to 136 million metric tons in 2012–2013, and with it a possible loss of some 200,000 direct jobs.[13] This sector had an employment elasticity of 0.82.

A severe crunch in the life insurance business after September 2010— when the Insurance Regulatory and Development Authority constrained life insurance companies from selling unit-linked plans—has led to a massive reduction in business and, with it, a major downsizing of the industry. Here, too, employment elasticity was high at 1.24; with a major shrinking of top-line and escalation of losses, there has been widespread unemployment of insurance agents and support staff.

Before moving on to some recommendations, it is useful to touch upon three other issues relating to labor markets. The first is important and relates to skills issues in the labor market. The skills that will be needed across many segments of industry and services over the next two decades are woefully short in supply. At present, this is especially acute in computing, information technology, telecom services, logistics, modern retail, engineering, nursing, and other sectors. Ruling governments will likely be tempted to bridge these gaps by setting up more state-financed vocational training institutes. These should be resisted, however, because recent history shows that most of them have not taken off. Instead, the country will necessarily have to rely on private training institutions and on-the-job learning. In some sectors, private training schools have been quite successful—the hospitality industry is a notable example. So, too, in nursing. One hopes that sufficient skills deficits in specific sectors will create enough excess demand to generate the setting up of "fit-for-purpose" training institutes, which will need to be supplemented by on-the-job training. It is a serious challenge, one that will remain so in the foreseeable future. It is unlikely to be dealt with by the government, but possibly by the private sector.

The second issue relates to geographical mismatch between labor supply and demand. It exists in large measure, but it is not a problem. Labor in India is far more mobile than commonly believed. In the last quarter of the nineteenth century, the rural poor of several districts of Bihar and Eastern Uttar Pradesh (then the United Provinces) went as indentured laborers to Durban, Mauritius, and Trinidad. The same districts supplied workers for the cotton textile mills in Mumbai and Ahmedabad and the jute mills of Kolkata. Today, every large city in India and each major factory town is populated by workers—be they plumbers, bricklayers, glaziers, weavers, construction workers, taxi drivers, nurses, hotel and restaurant staff, or all manner of unskilled and semiskilled labor—from other parts of the land. Their savings are sent back by postal money orders to their families in rural villages. The better-off parts of India employ vast numbers of people from the worse-off parts, and their savings increase the purchasing power of families living in the poorer catchment areas. The geographical mismatch exists. But it is hardly a problem because of massive labor mobility.

The third issue is the impact of the Mahatma Gandhi National Rural Employment Guarantee Act (NREGA) scheme, which aims to enhance livelihood security in rural India by providing at least one hundred days of guaranteed wage employment in a financial year to every household whose adult members volunteer for unskilled manual work. Despite leakages, the NREGA scheme has certainly raised rural incomes across India, particularly in the backward districts. It has also tended to raise daily wages—in rural India and among unskilled migrant labor in urban India. While employers point to the NREGA wages as yet another hurdle to creating their preferred utopia of a seamlessly flexible and sufficiently cheap labor market, it is not anywhere near as significant a problem as it is made out to be. The ability to absorb extra workers in the coming decades will not be deleteriously determined by NREGA. It will depend on overall economic growth—or the lack of it.

This brings to the fore a set of recommendations for the new government that takes over after the 2014 general elections.

- The new government needs to focus on getting 7.5 percent GDP growth back to the region. This is an absolute must if India is to entertain the slightest hope of getting jobs for an additional 27 million people between 2015 and 2020 under the relatively modest scenario of WPR1—let alone the extra 44 million who might need jobs under WPR2.

- The new government has to come up with reforms that can substantially grow the more employment-intensive sectors which, outside agriculture, are: manufacturing; mining and quarrying; construction; transport, storage, and communications; education; health; and real estate. For instance, the kind of restrictions that have hampered the growth of mining need to be reviewed and removed. It is perfectly possible today to conduct environmentally sensible mining. To ban or severely restrict mining altogether, as has been done by court decisions, will harm not only the sector but also employment growth. Similarly, additional telecommunications spectrum space must be allotted, and the mobile network needs to expand. Raja's act needed censure and punishment. But what should come next?

- Industries—be these in manufacturing, utilities, or infrastructure—have to get access to land to build factories, power plants, and highways. While proponents will argue that the Right to Fair Compensation and Transparency in Land Acquisition, Rehabilitation and Resettlement Act, which was passed in August 2013, rectifies serious imbalances against those who were compelled to give up land, the fact is that it will significantly increase the cost of securing land for nonagricultural use. The cost—both price and procedural delays concomitant to the new law—can seriously alter project economics to a point where infrastructure work may be abandoned. The new government might need to look at the law and make amendments that, at the very least, reduce procedural delays.

I am intentionally not making a case to abolish labor legislation such as sections 25(N) and 25(0) of the Industrial Disputes Act, 1947, or the Contract Labour (Regulation and Abolition) Act, 1970. History has repeatedly shown that these are politically impossible to repeal, and therefore no government will raise such an issue in Parliament. In any event, as suggested earlier, these do not matter anymore. For one, 90 percent of employment is in the unorganized sector, which is beyond the reach of such laws. For another, there is sufficient flexibility in organized manufacturing to keep demand for labor relatively elastic. The last thing anyone wants in this era of "reforms by stealth"—which has become the leitmotif of reforms, if any—is to behave like a bull in a china shop.

Moreover, the political and economic case for labor market reforms has to be built in terms of creating additional employment. The rhetoric has to say that in order to generate the demographic dividends that will define higher growth and greater purchasing power for the vast majority of the nation, India needs to create gainful additional employment for anywhere between 30 million and 44 million citizens between 2015 and 2020. This cannot be done by government spending alone. It needs growing investment from the private sector—investment that will create jobs and generate growth. India, therefore, needs everything at its disposal to create a better investment climate, backed up by laws, regulations, and procedures that organically encourage job creation. That—and not the case for frictionless firing—is the basis of labor market reforms.

If India develops this rhetoric and puts it to practice under the wider rubric of nation building, there can be optimism that additional employment, accompanied by a more sensible and flexible labor market, may be achieved. Hopefully, this language of reforms will come into play, as it occasionally has in the past—and with it, the space for greater employment.

NOTES

1   M. G. Arun, "Will You Be Fired Next?" *India Today*, September 9, 2013, http://indiatoday.intoday.in/story/job-crunch-hits-indian-markets-will-you-be-fired-next/1/304612.html.

2   Bibek Debroy, "The 47 Million Urban Story," *Economic Times*, September 8, 2013, 20.

3   Government of India, Planning Commission, "Employment Across Various Sectors (in millions), Employment Elasticity, CAGR and Share of Employment and GVA: 1999–2000, 2004–2005, 2009–2010," April 22, 2013, www.planningcommission.nic.in/data/datatable/2504/databook_84.pdf. The data are based on the 61st round (2004–2005) and 66th round (2009–2010) of the National Sample Survey Organisation (NSSO), under the Ministry of Statistics and Programme Implementation.

4   Ibid.

5   Government of India, Ministry of Statistics and Programme Implementation, *Annual Survey of Industries, 2010–11*, Table 1: Annual Series for Principal Characteristics, December 31, 2012, http://mospi.nic.in/Mospi_New/upload/asi/asi_result_2010_11_tab1_31dec12.pdf.

6   United Nations Department of Economic and Social Affairs, Population Division, "World Population Prospects: The 2012 Revision" database, http://esa.un.org/unpd/wpp/unpp/panel_population.htm.

7   Government of India, Ministry of Statistics and Programme Implementation, "Key Indicators of Employment and Unemployment in India, 2011–12," June 2012.

8   It is important to realize that by using the WPR, this analysis is consciously understating the problem. Had it used the labor force participation ratio, i.e., the ratio of labor force to the population, the number of people in the job market would have been higher by an additional 2.5 percent.

9   V. R. S. Cowlagi, "The National Renewal Fund: Promise, Performance and Prospects," *Vikalpa* 19, no. 4, 7.

10 Ibid., 9–10.

11 Government of India, Planning Commission, *Ninth Five Year Plan*, vol. 2, ch. 5, paragraph 5.8.

12 "NHDP and Other NHAI Projects," National Highways Authority of India, September 30, 2013, www.nhai.org/WHATITIS.asp.

13 "200,000 Iron Miners Jobless as Curbs Bite," *Hindustan Times*, August 4, 2013, www.hindustantimes.com/StoryPage/Print/1103281.aspx.

CHAPTER 6

EXPANDING EDUCATION AND SKILLS

LAVEESH BHANDARI[*]

INTRODUCTION

It is well known that for India to achieve sustained all-around progress, formal education and skills-based training must be made accessible to the masses. That they currently do not have such access is not surprising, given the general inability of the Indian state to either provide these services or create an environment where the private sector could step in. A host of reasons lies behind this failure.

The requirements for a good learning environment change as children grow. In the initial years, it has more to do with strengthening core enabling powers. In later classes, the matching function becomes more important so that adolescents may pursue the knowledge and skills that are in line with their talents and interests. At the higher levels, specialization becomes more critical; the need there is to expose students to a finer but deeper set of issues of importance in their area of interest. And in each of these stages, quality is critical, though in different ways.

*   I am grateful to Suryakant Thakur and Sumita Kale for their assistance with the data and their critiques of previous drafts of this chapter. I would also like to thank the editors of this volume, Bibek Debroy, Ashley J. Tellis, and Reece Trevor. All errors contained herein are mine. I can be reached at laveesh@indicus.net.

It is not that education has never been accorded adequate importance in India. The writings of the founding fathers—including Mahatma Gandhi, Rabindranath Tagore, Maulana Azad, Ambedkar, and even the spiritual torchbearers of modern India such as Vivekananda and Sri Aurobindo—stressed that education would form the core of India's "tryst with destiny," as Jawaharlal Nehru would have put it. Almost all of them suggested ways by which a new generation of Indians could be educated in a liberal and scientific environment where modern society was built on traditional strengths, one supplementing but not substituting for the other, and where education was deeply connected to the needs of people. But somehow, independent India could not build on the richness of this philosophical tradition, or on the depth of its populace's respect for education. This history seems to have been lost in the current debate, mired in the more mundane issues of access and quality defined in terms of enrollment numbers and teacher-student ratios.

While independent India retained the largely colonial superstructure of primary, secondary, and tertiary education, the emphasis on improving access by improving quality has gone by the wayside. Consequently access, quality, and outcomes all are far lower than what anyone would have desired.[1] What the Indian government needs to do is to change its educational policy orientation from access to quality, from infrastructure to services, and from inputs to outcomes in terms of a happier and more productive workforce.

To better understand the direction and method of change, we first investigate the current status of educational achievement to help extrapolate the key issues and points where India needs to focus in the future. Unlike in many other countries, a large proportion of schooling and tertiary education in India occurs in private institutions; this is briefly discussed in the next section. The following section lays out the institutional structure that governs education delivery in India. This understanding of status, roles, and institutions then enables the derivation of specific instruments of change that are possible at the level of the central government, which is discussed in the next section, followed by a conclusion.

CURRENT STATUS

Every decade India has succeeded in putting an additional 20–25 million children into primary schools up to grade V; its record in upper primary (grades VI to VIII) is not as good. Large numbers of students drop out during adolescence (typically in the upper primary level), and the gender gap also increases dramatically at this stage. Most of those students who are able to cross this barrier go on to secondary school. Even so, of those who reached secondary school, most used to drop out. Thus higher education, by process of elimination, was accessed by only a small share of students (about a third in the 1991–2001 decade). However, this pattern changed over the subsequent decade (2001–2011), with the number of students in the tertiary level increasing threefold (table 1).

TABLE 1. ENROLLMENT ACROSS EDUCATION LEVELS (MILLIONS)

	1951	1961	1971	1981	1991	2001	2011
Primary (classes I–V)	19.2	35.0	57.0	73.8	97.4	113.8	135.3
Upper Primary (VI–VIII)	3.1	6.7	13.3	20.7	35.6	42.8	62.0
Higher & Senior Secondary (IX–XII)	1.5	3.4	7.6	11.0	20.4	27.6	51.2
University and Above	0.4	0.9	3.3	4.8	4.9	8.6	26.7

Note: 2011 numbers are provisional.
Source: Government of India, Ministry of Human Resource Development, "Educational Statistics—At a Glance," 2012, http://mhrd.gov.in/sites/upload_files/mhrd/files/EAG_2012.pdf.

Dropouts are only one outcome of bad quality. Poor learning outcomes, low employability of graduates, low productivity, and consequent low wages constitute another set of outcomes. The problem, then, is not as much one of access as one of quality—and all of these negative outcomes can be traced directly to that inherent flaw of bad quality in Indian education.

A deeper vision for education in India would need to first spell out and prioritize the qualitative aspects of education, placing content and pedagogy at the core of its foundations across all three tiers—primary, secondary, and tertiary.

First consider the primary level (grades I to VIII). Focusing on qualitative aspects and joyful learning would involve making schooling useful and enjoyable for children rather than creating infrastructure and mindless accessibility. The provision of better content and committed teaching in line with the requirements of children in the primary grades is needed to improve learning outcomes at this level.

Secondary schooling (grades IX to XII) suffers from a lack of adequate choice in terms of schools, courses, and content, which contributes to the high dropout levels. But low employability and poor returns on the investment (in terms of income) suggest that serious quality issues exist here as well. Private schooling, which already accounts for the bulk of secondary schooling in India, suffers from the same flaw. Sooner or later private school students have to conform to government-mandated coursework either in the form of board-overseen examinations in grades X and XII or largely government-driven structures of tertiary and professional education.

At the tertiary level, formal vocational training had been limited in scale and scope, but significant movement has occurred in this space over the past decade, essentially in the private domain. Still needed are improved quality of delivery, monitoring, and nationally mandated standards. In the case of university education, the problem is not so much the quantity of institutions but the quality of the educational services being delivered.

It should be noted that memorization of content has become the norm across the educational hierarchy, especially at the tertiary level. The sole objective of students has been reduced to obtaining high marks on state-mandated examinations or on entrance examinations to state-run professional institutions. That kind of "learning" may help gain entry into higher education institutions, but it comes at the cost of employability. What is required is a movement away from examinations that encourage rote learning; instead, greater application of mind and skills needs to be fostered. Institutions therefore should be encouraged to respond, through internal flexibility and through competition, to market conditions to better prepare students for greater employability, productivity, and incomes.

Absent a regime where the quality of educational services can be improved at all levels, greater budgetary allocations would be wasted in terms of educational outcomes. Once such a regime is in place—where quality is important and returns to education are high—it will be easier for democratic governments to make greater allocations, and those allocations will have a meaningful impact.

THE PRIVATE AND THE PUBLIC

Various studies have shown that the performance of children in private schools tends to be better than that of those in public schools.[2] In tandem, arguments are increasing for enabling school choice through some form of education vouchers that parents can redeem in either public or private schools.

But the issue is not one of private versus public. First, the fact that private schools provide better learning outcomes does not imply that policy initiatives to improve public schooling should not be taken. In fact, they go hand in hand; better quality delivery in public institutions would force private entities to further improve. Second, even though learning outcomes may be better in private schools, they are not that much better, or else leakage from public schools to private schools would have occurred faster. Third, the private sector becomes more important at the higher grade levels, but dropout rates remain consistent even at those levels.

TABLE 2. PERCENT DISTRIBUTION OF PRIVATE
AND PUBLIC SCHOOLS IN INDIA

	Government		Private		
	State/ Central	Local	Aided by Gov't	Un- aided	**Total**
Intermediate/Senior Secondary Schools	34.0	0.9	27.4	37.7	70,770
High/Secondary Schools	31.3	8.5	24.0	36.2	128,370
Upper Primary Schools	60.8	16.5	9.9	12.7	432,737
Primary Schools	54.8	29.0	8.9	7.3	721,816
Pre-Primary	47.9	26.0	3.9	22.3	68,413
All Schools	53.2	21.8	11.2	13.8	1,422,106

Source: Government of India, Ministry of Human Resource Development, Bureau of Planning, Monitoring and Statistics, "Statistics of School Education, 2011–12," 2012, http://mhrd.gov.in/sites/upload_files/mhrd/files/SES-School_201011_0.pdf.

As is apparent from table 2, secondary schooling in India is currently delivered primarily by private schools. Some of these are aided by the government, but most are not. All these schools are not-for-profit entities and mostly run by private charities. However, the problem of secondary education (and, frankly, of any education in India) is not that of public delivery but of poor design.

This poor design percolates across all types of institutions, including the regulatory regime overseeing education delivery in India. In the case of secondary schooling, providing choice cost-effectively requires large schools, and that in turn requires large numbers of students. It matters not if this is done in the private sector or in the public domain—what is critical is that delivery of teaching and vocational skill training be properly overseen. The issue, therefore, is more about choice—oversight by the right stakeholders, with the power to replace teachers, a voice in determining course content, the monitoring and enforcement of quality, and regulation of schools—than it is about public versus private. What is most important is that this choice be provided to students and the community (and not the bureaucrats) in all domains of learning—schools, teachers, and curriculum.

Clearly, there is a need for a set of reforms addressing a very specific set of issues at each tier of the educational hierarchy. How can this be done? Which part of the government should do this? What tools can it use? Before attempting to answer such questions, we need to briefly delineate the institutional structure that governs delivery of educational services in India.

INSTITUTIONAL MECHANISMS

As per the Indian constitution, the power to legislate, regulate, and affect educational services is divided between the central and state governments (the Union and State lists, respectively). Some areas are shared by the two (Concurrent List); in case of a conflict, the central government has overriding powers. Education, including vocational education, is in the Concurrent List, and consequently both the central government and the states fund, regulate, and deliver educational services. And the Union List assigns the determination standards for higher educational institutions exclusively to the central government (though the states can incorporate and also regulate universities).

In practice the central government is quite empowered to change the institutions governing education in India, but a large component of delivery rests with the states. Multiple regulatory institutions set up by the central government mandate and monitor standards; the All India Council for Technical Education, for instance, and the University Grants Commission provide regulatory oversight and funding to central universities. The National Assessment Accreditation Council, an autonomous body set up by the central government, monitors and accredits universities. Schooling is typically provided by the state and local governments as well as private entities, though the central government does run a few schools. The quality of educational services in schools is mandated and overseen by national or state education boards. However, through its Sarva Shiksha Abhiyan (SSA) universal education scheme, the central government requires the state government to contribute only 50 percent of the funding for primary schooling until grade V, with the remaining 50 percent covered by the central government. The central government can directly influence the educational policies that state governments have to follow. This is because central government funding is subject to the state governments' meeting certain conditions, including on such issues as infrastructure and teacher quality.

All things considered, the central government is very well placed to effect change in the educational ecosystem. It can do so by changing laws (Concurrent List), funding (through centralized schemes), mandating rules (through conditional transfers), and monitoring and regulation (through elements in the Union List). The next section discusses the specific problem at each stage, and what the central government can do.

ADDRESSING POOR EDUCATIONAL OUTCOMES

Experts and policymakers have suggested numerous changes to improve India's educational sector; our focus will be on those that relate to quality, particularly those actions that can be taken soon yet have long-term and deep impact.

Primary Schooling (Grades I to V) and Upper Primary (Grades VI to VIII)

The Primary Problem

Enrollment rates in primary schools in India are in the vicinity of 95 percent. In large measure that success is due to the SSA's putting primary school infrastructure close to every village, as well as the midday meal scheme that feeds all children who attend primary school. As one progresses up the grades, however, the number of dropouts increases and gender imbalances do, too. Poor learning, bad teaching methods, puberty and safety considerations for female students, and the distance between children's homes and upper primary schools are typically blamed for this. Not surprisingly, only a small proportion of students make it to secondary school and above.

A child is in school when the benefit-cost trade-off of attending school leads to substantial net benefits. One can achieve this by providing schools close to home and offering free meals in school. But much greater impact is possible if the benefit side is addressed. Typically, outcomes from primary schooling—employability and productivity—have been low in India, and much lower than those of individuals who achieve higher levels of education.[3] And given that returns are also quite uncertain and in the distant future, not sending a child to school makes economic sense (table 3).

Why are returns to primary schooling so low in India? Many believe that it has to do with the poor quality of teaching, but that is only one problem. Course content has an important role to play. At the primary level, the objective is to teach arithmetic, reading, and writing to a large group of children. And even this limited objective has had modest achievements, as data from the comprehensive surveys by the Annual Status of Education Report Center have repeatedly shown.[4] Recent data since the implementation of the Right to Education Act that came into force in 2010 show that there is a fall in learning outcomes, as the objective is now more to ensure that children remain in school, as opposed to providing good-quality education. The net result is that students will find it difficult to continue at the higher levels, and if they *don't* drop out, there will not be that much of a gain in employability, productivity, and incomes.

TABLE 3. PERCENTAGE DIFFERENCE IN INCOME FROM THOSE WHO ARE ILLITERATE

(After correcting for all other factors that affect incomes)

Education Completion Levels	Impact on Income Compared to Illiterates	Percentage Difference in Likelihood of Employment From Illiterates
Primary Schools (I–V)	31.0	1.5
Middle School (VI–VIII)	45.5	2.5
High School (IX–X)	71.1	3.4
Higher Secondary (XI–XII)	89.8	3.3
Tech. Educ./Diploma	137.0	3.8
Graduate	136.3	4.2
Professional Degree	171.8	5.1
Postgraduate and Above	190.0	5.1

Source: Laveesh Bhandari and Mridusmita Bordoloi, "Income Differentials and Returns to Education," *Economic and Political Weekly* 41, no. 36, September 9, 2006.

There is another element that needs to be appreciated: most income-earning opportunities in India have been in the self-employed, daily wage employment, and unorganized domains. None of these opportunities necessarily requires formal learning as a precondition for entry. Productivity and wages would be higher among those workers who have greater understanding and experience in working with the tools of the trade. Merely having a school certificate without such abilities would, at best, have a marginal impact. India needs to introduce as a necessary objective and as tools of primary education joyful leaning methods such as handicrafts, drawing, and music. These should not be add-on extracurricular activities, but a core part of the curriculum. This is no different from the vision that the leaders of the independence movement held for India.

The second, much-discussed part is the issue of poor delivery. It is well known that a large proportion of primary school teachers are absent, the teaching methods are poor, materials are missing, classroom infrastructure is poor, and schools are far from where the students live. All of these factors make children's access to teaching difficult and costly, and consequently learning outcomes are low.

These issues are themselves the result of a deeper underlying flaw: the absence of a partnership among the state, parents, and community in planning, monitoring, and enforcing delivery of quality education. Given the weakness of the Indian state in enforcing the right service delivery environment, it will need to ensure that those who have the right set of incentives can do the job that the bureaucracy cannot. And the local community and parents are just the right set to pull this off. Oversight by the community should not be too difficult—it indeed occurs in many countries, and is also enshrined in the Indian constitution via the 73rd and 74th Amendments. As has been repeatedly stressed, simply using the term "community participation" does not do the job. The mechanism of community and parental control over the teacher and content needs to be spelled out; the fact that it is not spelled out in the Right to Education Act is a key failure of that legislation.

The Solution

The central government can achieve community and parental control without resorting to any legal or constitutional reforms. The norms specified in the SSA can be changed to ensure greater community control via only a few changes: teacher continuation in the primary school is cleared by the parent-teacher association (PTA) and the *gram panchayat* (a village-level governing body) on an annual basis; the PTA and the *gram panchayat* can appoint new teachers out of their own funds if they so desire; and the PTA and *gram panchayat* would have the power to design the curriculum for at least one study period of 40 minutes every day.

Secondary (Grades IX to X) and Higher Secondary (Grades XI to XII) Education

The Problem

While primary schooling is all about making basic content accessible, enjoyable, and useful for children, the higher classes need to build on that foundation by allowing students greater latitude to choose subjects and areas in which they are interested. But this choice is currently limited in India. The net result is that even if students are interested and able to continue into higher classes, they can pursue only what is available, not what they desire or may be good at.

Under the SSA, every village needs to have a primary school within a kilometer of the village in rural areas, and the Right to Education Act extended this requirement to apply to upper primary schools as well. This makes it easy for a child to get to school. In addition, all government-run primary schools provide the midday meal to all students at this level (recently extended to all upper primary schools as well). But neither of these norms applies to secondary schools. Consequently, higher classes lack the incentive of a free meal and a school close by, while poor teaching quality, bad infrastructure, and the lack of choice described above combine to produce powerful disincentives. Moreover, vocational training options are limited generally and are rarely available in secondary schools.

These problems are to be expected. In a regime where centralized monitoring and quality enforcement are difficult, putting more funds into the system is unlikely to achieve much. Given that course and content choice is costly to achieve and further worsens the monitoring and enforcement problem, the current system will not be able to scale up without compromising on the quality of delivery. India therefore needs a solution that proactively addresses these issues.

The Solution

There is one solution that can, in one go, address all of these issues. Large secondary schools need to be located in centralized locations, with children bused from their village or habitation in the morning and dropped off in the afternoon. Since, by design, the student body would be large, it would be possible to provide enough options in terms of courses and vocational training. Moreover, busing would eliminate the safety issue that adolescent girls currently face in getting to school. Large schools also make it easier to monitor teaching and teachers, as that can be partly done by peers. Arguably the coeducational environment helps reduce gender biases right from early ages, and this could have an additional positive impact.

The secondary schools can be either in the public, private, or government-aided domain; significantly, parents and communities should be able to choose among different schools in the vicinity. By introducing choice, the state would necessarily support the new focus on quality of education and not simply the old values of infrastructure and proximity.

This would need to be a multidimensional program involving infrastructure creation in the form of large secondary schools, expansion and improvement in the quality of service (education) delivery, and a universal transport mechanism. The expenses for this scheme would need to be primarily borne by the central government (as is the case with the SSA). Each state would need to meet certain implementation norms and also co-allocate some share of the funds. But the implementation itself would be done by the state government, as is the norm for primary schooling.

Vocational and Tertiary Education

The Problem

Enrollment in vocational and tertiary education has been rising rapidly over the past few years, as table 4 demonstrates. India today boasts the second-largest number of students in the tertiary sector. Tertiary enrollment stood at 26.6 million in 2011–2012, growing at about 14.5 percent annually since 2005, as opposed to 31.3 million growing at 7.2 percent for China and 21 million growing at 3.3 percent for the United States. This growth is naturally a result of increasing enrollment in both degree and professional courses, as well as post–school diploma programs, many of which are vocational. Universities and many of the professional training institutions in India have also ramped up capacities in recent times. That is partly as a consequence of meeting promises related to increased reservation for underprivileged groups,[5] and partly as a supply response to rapidly increasing demand. As mentioned previously, both the central and state governments can give permission to form universities in the public or private domain. Of these, a few state governments have been quite active, but even the central government has boosted its creation of new institutions and added seats within existing ones.

TABLE 4. ENROLLMENT IN HIGHER EDUCATION

	Under-graduate enrollment	Post-graduate enrollment	Doctoral	Post-School Diploma	Post-graduate Diploma	Total
UNITS						
2007–2008	11,063,827	1,514,115	76,227	849,689	87,953	13,591,811
2008–2009	11,814,457	1,577,162	78,388	1,099,127	107,020	14,676,154
2009–2010	13,872,870	1,833,507	92,211	1,407,406	89,092	17,295,086
2011–2012	19,837,580	2,704,412	90,658	3,694,002	120,864	26,447,516
PERCENT						
2007–2008	81	11	1	6	1	100
2008–2009	81	11	1	7	1	100
2009–2010	80	11	1	8	1	100
2011–2012	75	10	0	14	1	100

Note: 2011–2012 numbers are provisional.
Source: Government of India, Ministry of Human Resources Development, "Statistics of Higher and Technical Education," 2012, http://mhrd.gov.in/AISHE2011-12P.pdf.

Three key elements work across both vocational and tertiary education:

- Entry by private entities is allowed, though for-profit private enterprises are limited to the vocational category. That in itself is not a problem; however, the norms governing entry are poorly specified and not monitored adequately. As a consequence, many of the new entities have been able to enter even though they are incapable of providing quality services (though it can be argued that this is also the case for the older ones, including those in the public sector).

- The quality of monitoring and regulation is extremely poor. Consequently, both the private and public sectors are inadequate in their provision of the bulk of tertiary education and vocational training. Even where minimum standards are specified, they are not monitored, and therefore not enforced, affecting the quality of delivery.[6]

- A few institutions provide somewhat better services; these institutions are difficult to enter and require either passing the dedicated entrance exams with a high rank or getting extremely high marks in the board exams at the end of grade XII. The net result is that adolescents and youths spend an inordinately large proportion of time studying for that additional mark or score, at the cost of other activities. Overall quality of learning suffers since the importance of scoring higher marks outweighs all other considerations. This, paradoxically, exacerbates the unemployability problem.

The net result of all of the above is that not only is delivery poor, but the employability of graduates is compromised. Merely increasing the supply of education is not enough. Policymakers must promote conditions—either through regulation or through market forces—in which the quality of education services is at the core of the higher education agenda as well, just as it needs to be at the primary and secondary levels.

The Solution in Tertiary Education

The National Knowledge Commission has studied the problem of tertiary education in great detail and suggested a set of reforms that the central government can undertake. Other studies as well have recommended a range of important changes.[7]

The central government can achieve much by improving regulation and competition:

- First, an independent regulatory authority for higher education should be created that can function at arm's length from the government and resist takeover by stakeholders.

- Second, the key problem with competition is the inability of students to assess courses and colleges, and this lack of credible information prevents students from comparing educational institutions. A universal national rating mechanism for all tertiary education can be a critical enabler of informed choice by students and at the same time foster healthy competition. Such a rating system would also need to cover universities and colleges, vocational training institutions, and diploma and certificate granting institutions; it would need to rate the courses and institutions that are offering them.[8]

Many observers have called for an overarching education regulator, but a nationally recognized universal educational rating system has more immediate and arguably stronger benefits. First, rating is the first step to accreditation and also benefits regulatory oversight. Second, it improves choice by ill-informed students (most of them being first generation graduates). Third, a universal rating mechanism can be instituted far more quickly than universally applicable accreditation systems and regulatory mechanisms. Fourth, market forces will automatically generate conditions for improved quality, which is more in line with the needs of the economy.

CONCLUDING NOTE: OVERHAULING INDIA'S EDUCATION REGIME

The absence of an overall vision is the primary flaw of the education regime in India today. This has resulted in a poor appreciation of the quality of education. Weaknesses related to the allocation of resources, design, and implementation are simply outputs of this missing vision. And poor learning outcomes, absentee teachers, large numbers of educated unemployed, and low employability, not to mention high suicide rates among youths around exam times, are all the outcome of this inherent flaw.

India needs to have a vision for its children and youth, and this vision needs to be enshrined properly in a synchronized design of oversight mechanisms either through the community, through choice and markets, or through specialist regulatory institutions. A focus on quality is the centerpiece of the desired changes, with the type of changes required differing across different levels of education.

At the primary and upper primary levels, improved quality can best be achieved through greater community and parental involvement in overseeing delivery and content. At the secondary level, quality and choice would best be achieved by increasing school size and implementing busing programs. At the tertiary level, the best chances for success lie with improved rating and certification—and its recognition across the country—as well as improved regulation of college education. All of these, at all three levels, are possible through action by the central government, and none requires any changes in the laws.

Undoubtedly, greater budgetary allocations would be required, but these should not be the primary vehicle of a general education enhancement program. Rather, greater public expenditures would be a facilitating action, necessary but concomitant with a thorough overhaul of India's educational regime.

NOTES

1   The recently promulgated Right to Education law is no different in that it mandates "a right to compulsory education" in schools with very specific infrastructure benchmarks. At the same time, it mentions community participation but does not mandate it. Local elected bodies such as *panchayats* still do not have significant control over teachers, teaching, or content. Effectively, the block- and district-level officials of the state governments continue to exercise such control.

2   Sonalde Desai et al., "Private Schooling in India: A New Educational Landscape," India Human Development Survey, Working Paper no. 11, National Council of Applied Economic Research and University of Maryland, 2008.

3   Laveesh Bhandari and Mridusmita Bordoloi, "Income Differentials and Returns to Education," *Economic and Political Weekly* 41, no. 36, September 9, 2006.

4   See ASER Centre, *Annual Status of Education Report (Rural) 2012* (New Delhi: ASER Centre, 2013), www.pratham.org/file/ASER-2012report.pdf.

5   Some 27 percent of all seats in higher education in India have been set aside for the group labeled as "other backward castes" since 2008. This is in addition to the constitutionally mandated 15 percent reserved for even more underprivileged groups labeled as "scheduled castes" and 7.5 percent for "scheduled tribes."

6   Pawan Agarwal, "Higher Education in India: The Need for Change," Working Paper no. 180, Indian Council for Research on International Economic Relations, June 2006, www.icrier.org/publication/working_papers_180.html.

7   Ibid.

8   All institutions would first need to be classified in a standard manner (similar to the Carnegie Classification, but developed specifically for Indian institutions), and then rated on multiple dimensions on an annual basis within their respective classes.

CHAPTER 7

CONFRONTING HEALTH CHALLENGES

A. K. SHIVA KUMAR

INTRODUCTION

India has recorded several gains in health since independence in 1947. Life expectancy at birth has risen to sixty-five years today, up from thirty-two years in 1950. The infant mortality rate has come down from 129 deaths per 1,000 live births in 1971 to 42 in 2012.[1] Smallpox and guinea worm have been eradicated, the spread of HIV/AIDS has been contained, and the World Health Organization is expected to declare India polio-free this year. Yet, India's achievements in health are far from impressive. High rates of infectious diseases, reproductive and child health problems, as well as nutritional deficiencies coexist with a large and growing burden of chronic diseases. Both the infant mortality rate and the maternal mortality rate remain high.[2] Almost half of children under five years of age are stunted, 43 percent are underweight, and 20 percent are reported to be affected by wasting. Nearly 70 percent of children ages 6–59 months are anemic.[3] The neglect of women's health in particular is striking. More than half (55 percent) of Indian women are anemic. More than one-third (36 percent) of women ages 15–49 in India have a body mass index below 18.5, indicating chronic nutritional deficiency.[4] At the same time, cardiovascular disease has become a major cause of morbidity and mortality among adults. High rates of tobacco consumption contribute significantly to mortality from cardiovascular diseases, cancer, and tuberculosis. More than a million deaths annually are attributed to smoking alone. Close to 65 million Indians have been diagnosed with diabetes.[5] In addition, several aspects of disability, mental illnesses, and occupational health and safety remain neglected by both government and society.

Confronting these challenges—and many others detailed below—requires that India's next central government take meaningful steps to ensure universal health coverage. Four key action steps are necessary to achieve this goal. First, the government must embrace the idea of tax-funded universal coverage, as opposed to contributory or subsidized private insurance schemes. Second, it must incentivize preventive care by setting up more robust primary care facilities, especially in underserved rural areas. Third, it must pursue meaningful public-private partnerships with trustworthy private actors; this step should be undergirded by a better national regulatory framework established by the central government. Fourth, the central government should work with state governments, which can function as laboratories that experiment with different kinds of health coverage schemes that could be adapted to work on a national level. To enable any and all of these steps, India must double the share of its funding for public health programs to at least 2.5 percent of GDP. Financed by general taxation, the additional resources should be used to strengthen the delivery of primary health care, improve the quality of services, and promote more equitable access, especially to poor and marginalized communities.

THE EXTENT OF THE PROBLEM

We find that health outcomes in India are far from equitable. Differences in morbidity, mortality, and nutritional status linked to differences in socioeconomic status, caste, class, gender, and geography persist. Levels of undernutrition and child mortality are typically higher in rural areas than in urban areas, and among socially disadvantaged communities. The infant mortality rate for urban India is 28 deaths per 1,000 live births, versus 46 per 1,000 in rural India.[6] The under-five mortality rate among children born to communities classified as Scheduled Tribes is 15 percent higher than the national average.[7] Similarly, nearly 25 percent of children born to parents in the bottom wealth quintile are severely malnourished, compared with 5 percent born to parents in the top wealth quintile.[8] Girls face a particularly acute survival disadvantage. For instance, in the 2000s, the risk of dying between ages 1 and 5 was more than 75 percent higher for girls than for boys.[9]

It is a little-known and sad fact that health conditions in India are similar in some respects, and even worse in others, to those prevailing in sub-Saharan Africa. India, as one would expect, does better on mortality indicators than sub-Saharan Africa (which has had to face a huge burden of HIV/AIDS infections). However, there are many similarities in the reach of primary health care. For instance, the proportion of children immunized against diphtheria, pertussis, and tetanus is 71 percent in sub-Saharan Africa and 72 percent in India. Similarly, the proportion of institutional births is identical: 47 percent in both India and sub-Saharan Africa. On other measures, India fares much worse in child undernutrition than sub-Saharan Africa. Close to 43 percent of children under five in India are moderately or severely underweight; the proportion in sub-Saharan Africa is 21 percent. Similarly, compared with the 12 percent of babies who are born with low birth weight in sub-Saharan Africa, the share in India is much higher at 28 percent.[10]

India's health performance is particularly disappointing because today it has fallen behind Bangladesh and Nepal on many health indicators, despite a higher per capita income and two decades of rapid economic growth (see table 1).

TABLE 1. SELECTED HEALTH INDICATORS, INDIA AND OTHER SOUTH ASIAN COUNTRIES

	India	Bangladesh	Bhutan	Maldives	Nepal	Pakistan	Sri Lanka
Per capita gross national income (Purchasing Power Parity international dollars) **2012**	3,910	2,030	6,200	7,560	1,470	2,880	6,030
Life expectancy at birth (years) **2011**	65	69	67	77	69	65	75
Infant mortality rate (per 1,000 live births) **2011**	47	37	42	9	39	59	11
Under-5 mortality rate (per 1,000 live births) **2011**	61	46	54	11	48	72	12
Proportion of underweight children (moderate and severe) **2007–2011**	43	36	13	13	29	32	21
Use of improved sanitation facilities (%) **2010**	34	56	44	97	31	48	92
Immunization coverage (%): **DPT3 2011**	72	96	95	96	92	80	99

Source: United Nations Children's Fund, *The State of the World's Children 2013: Children With Disabilities* (New York: UNICEF, 2013), www.unicef.org/sowc2013/statistics.html.

The health status of Indians remains poor even though today they have access to a wide range of allopathic as well as various non-allopathic systems of medicine, including ayurveda, yoga, unani, siddha, and home-opathy (collectively referred to as Ayush) from both the public and private sectors. The foundation of the government's health care system rests on a three-tier structure. Health subcenters in villages act as the first point of contact and take care of essential health needs, including treatment of minor ailments, family planning, nutrition, immunization, and diarrheal control. The second tier consists of primary health centers, which serve as a referral unit for subcenters and provide integrated promotive, preventive, and curative health care. The third tier is made up of community health centers, 30-bed hospitals that serve as a referral unit for primary health centers. In addition, around 8,000 hospitals function as the secondary tier for health care for the rural population and as the primary tier for the urban population. Some of them offer world-class allopathic services at highly affordable prices. The private sector in health is highly fragmented. At one end are "quacks," private health practitioners with little medical knowledge or formal training. At the other end are top-rated private hospitals that cater to both Indians and foreigners who can afford to pay for often expensive care. Between these two extremes, other private providers range from small private clinics to hospitals, some for-profit entities and some not-for-profit.

Though public expenditures on health are shared by both the central and state governments (with the center contributing 36 percent), health is a state subject under the constitution. This makes state governments responsible for the provision and delivery of health services.

States' performance remains mixed. Kerala and Tamil Nadu are among the good performers, while Madhya Pradesh and Uttar Pradesh fall in the category of poor performers. To illustrate, in 2012, the infant mortality rate was 56 per 1,000 live births in Uttar Pradesh and 58 in Madhya Pradesh, as against 21 in Tamil Nadu and 12 in Kerala.[11] Similarly, there is a thirteen-year life expectancy differential among women between those living in Kerala and the two states of Uttar Pradesh and Madhya Pradesh.[12]

Generally speaking, states with better health outcomes have a higher level of human development, including greater per capita incomes, higher levels of educational attainment, and better physical and social infrastructure. For instance, in 2007–2008, 87 percent of primary health centers in Tamil Nadu and 97 percent in Kerala enjoyed regular power supply, compared with 12 percent in Uttar Pradesh and 20 percent in Madhya Pradesh.[13] Moreover, the political leadership in states such as Kerala and Tamil Nadu has ensured sustained investments in health and education, prioritized the provision of public services, and introduced policies to break deep-rooted caste and social hierarchies. Equally striking about Kerala and Tamil Nadu (unlike in Madhya Pradesh and Uttar Pradesh) is the relatively better status of women reflected not only in the higher levels of educational attainment but also in greater public visibility and participation in society. Kerala and Tamil Nadu have also established an efficient primary health care system, unlike Uttar Pradesh and Madhya Pradesh. For instance, in 2007–2008, 97 percent of primary health centers in Kerala and 95 percent in Tamil Nadu had cold chain equipment, compared with only 49 percent in Madhya Pradesh and 21 percent in Uttar Pradesh. Kerala and Tamil Nadu have roughly one public hospital bed for a population of 1,200–1,400, versus one hospital bed for 3,400–5,700 in Madhya Pradesh and Uttar Pradesh.[14] The proportion of fully immunized children ages 12–23 months in 2009—82 percent in Kerala and 77 percent in Tamil Nadu—far exceeded the proportions of 41 percent in Uttar Pradesh and 43 percent in Madhya Pradesh.[15] Part of the mixed outcomes in health can be explained by the wide variations that exist in the levels of per capita public spending on health. In 2009–2010, for example, the annual per capita public expenditure on health in Tamil Nadu and Kerala was around Rs. 580, compared with Rs. 312 in Madhya Pradesh and Rs. 372 in Uttar Pradesh.[16] Additionally, overall governance and the health administration systems are far more efficient in Tamil Nadu and Kerala than in Madhya Pradesh and Uttar Pradesh.

THE ROOTS OF THE PROBLEM

Several factors account for India's poor health outcomes. With few exceptions, neither the central nor state governments have assigned high priority to health. Despite the increase in real annual per capita public expenditure on health from Rs. 256 in 2004–2005 to Rs. 484 in 2011–2012, India's levels of public health spending are low compared with those of other countries. In per capita terms adjusted for purchasing power, the Indian public expenditure on health is $43, versus $85 in Sri Lanka, $240 in

China, and \$265 in Thailand.[17] Moreover, public expenditure on health accounts for only around 1.2 percent of GDP, which is among the lowest in the world and has remained at this level for over a decade. Public expenditure on health, in contrast, is around 1.5 percent of GDP in Sri Lanka, 2.7 percent in China, and 3 percent in Thailand. India's low public health expenditure has had several consequences. First and foremost, the financial burden of private out-of-pocket spending on health—69 percent of total health expenditures—is among the highest in the world and much more than in Thailand (25 percent), China (44 percent), and Sri Lanka (55 percent).[18] Millions are driven into poverty every year as a result of having to meet such large medical expenses out of limited private incomes. More than 40 percent of Indians who are hospitalized are reported to either borrow money or sell assets to pay for their care, and close to 25 percent of those who are hospitalized fall into poverty.[19]

Almost every country in the world that has achieved universal health coverage or is working toward it has done so through the public assurance of comprehensive quality primary health care for all. Though treatment is nearly free in India (except for a small user fee), only 22 percent of the population in rural areas and 19 percent in urban areas access government facilities for outpatient care. Even for inpatient care, only around 42 percent of Indians in rural areas and 38 percent in urban areas utilize government facilities.[20] Although in many rural areas and also in several urban settings, the public sector is often the only source of any credible medical care, underfunding has produced insufficient reach and poor quality of public provision. Most government facilities tend to be understaffed, underresourced, and poorly managed. The better ones tend to be overcrowded. The Twelfth Five Year Plan (2012–2017) document points to a severe shortage of doctors, nurses, and auxiliary nurse-midwives. For example, in 2007, there were only 45 doctors per 100,000 population, far short of the target of 85 per 100,000. Similarly, there were only 75 nurses and auxiliary nurse-midwives per 100,000 population; the desirable number is 255.[21] The overall shortage is exacerbated by a wide geographical variation in availability across the country. Rural areas are especially poorly served. Other reasons Indians give for the poor utilization of government facilities include distant locations, inconvenient timing, high absenteeism of staff, and the insensitive attitude of many health workers.

The government's own analysis has repeatedly pointed to gaps in staffing and infrastructure especially at the primary health care level, preoccupation with the promotion of curative and clinical services through city-based hospitals, the reluctance of doctors and paramedical staff to serve in rural areas, and poor referral services. High attrition and inadequate replacement resulting from the lack of transparent and effective human resource policies have contributed to poor quality and poor performance. With few exceptions, most state governments have not created a professional cadre of public health specialists. There is less than optimal use of available resources due in part to the mismatch between personnel and infrastructure; suboptimal inter-sectoral coordination; lack of continuing education and skill upgrading of personnel; the preponderance of technology-centric disease-specific intervention; and the absence of effective processes of monitoring, evaluation, and feedback. Also, not having specialized information and knowledge on health needs makes it virtually impossible to draw up community-specific or even design area-specific plans and strategies.[22]

Government's failure to provide good quality health care services has led to a rapid expansion of the private sector. From 8 percent in 1947, the private sector today accounts for 93 percent of all hospitals, 64 percent of all beds, and 80–85 percent of all doctors. The consequences of such excessive reliance on an unregulated private sector are well documented. Large informational asymmetry (where the profit-oriented doctor can "cheat" the patient by prescribing unnecessary medicines or unwanted treatment) renders private markets in health care grossly inefficient. Further inefficiencies are generated by the "public goods" nature of health care stemming from the interdependences involved. The private sector in health remains unevenly distributed, highly fragmented, and unregulated. While some qualified private providers offer good quality services at affordable prices, costs in general tend to be unreasonably high. A majority of Indians, especially in rural areas, are at the mercy of quacks. Reportedly, many self-declared "doctors" have not even completed their schooling and have picked up their skills by working as assistants to pharmacists or doctors. Even within the formal private sector, given the virtual absence of regulations, overdiagnosis and overtreatment are common, as is faulty treatment. Many private practitioners indulge in malpractice by selling substandard and even counterfeit medicines, prescribing unnecessary drugs and tests, receiving commissions for referrals, requiring unnecessary hospital admissions, and manipulating the length of stay.

The government of India has taken several steps over the past nine years to improve the provision of health services. These include, notably, the launch of the National Rural Health Mission in 2005 and the announcement of the National Urban Health Mission in 2013. More specifically, the central government has introduced the Janani Suraksha Yojana scheme, which offers cash incentives to those who give birth in institutions; the Janani-Shishu Suraksha Karyakram, which guarantees free antenatal and postnatal treatment for infants in public health facilities; and the Rashtriya Bal Suraksha Karyakram, which guarantees child health screening and early intervention services as well as free patient transport. Funding from the central government has helped augment human resources, particularly with the recruitment of some 800,000 Accredited Social Health Activists in villages, nearly 160,000 health workers from 2005 to 2013, and an increase in medical college openings by 54 percent and postgraduate medical openings by 74 percent between 2009 and 2013.[23] Some state governments have introduced a cadre of public health professionals, streamlined the procurement of drugs, and started offering free diagnostics and medicines in public sector facilities.

TOWARD UNIVERSAL COVERAGE

Looking ahead, over the coming five to ten years, many specific actions are needed to accelerate much-needed progress in health.

First, Indian society, including both the central and state governments as well as the influential middle class, should more firmly embrace the concept of universal health coverage. The principal approach of the government so far has been to provide—as far as possible, however limited it may be—universal access to free primary health care; rely on insurance mechanisms to offer cashless secondary and tertiary care to the poor and to a small set of privileged government employees; and leave the rest of the population to buy health care in the private market. This has perpetuated a fragmented, inefficient, iniquitous, and expensive system of health care. Only recently has the central government called for expanding the reach of health care and working toward the long-term objective of establishing a system of universal health coverage in the country. The Report of the High Level Expert Group on Universal Health Coverage set up by the Planning Commission defines universal health coverage as: "Ensuring equitable access for all Indian citizens, resident in any part of the country, regardless of income level, social status, gender, caste or religion, to affordable, accountable, appropriate health services of assured quality (promotive, preventive, curative, and rehabilitative) . . . to individuals and populations, with the government being the guarantor and enabler, although not necessarily the only provider, of health and related services."[24]

Universal health coverage ought to be primarily tax-funded. Contributory options are unlikely to yield substantive revenue, given that close to 93 percent of India's workforce is engaged in the informal sector. User fees, however small, at the point of service provision ought to be done away with, in keeping with the growing evidence from across the world that such fees, by and large, tend to be inefficient, inadequate, and iniquitous. Much more public discussion on specifics is needed to build a national consensus and coalition of support for the idea of universal coverage.

Policymakers should realize that neither private health care, even if properly subsidized, nor commercial health insurance subsidized by the state can meet the challenge of universal health coverage. The interests of providers, consumers, and insurance companies are simply not aligned to maximize returns to consumers. Serious incentive-incompatibility problems arise when insurance companies deny use, medical practitioners induce demand or encourage overuse, and patients themselves misuse the facility (commonly referred to as the "moral hazard" problem).

Available evidence from across the world points out that insurance schemes incentivize tertiary care, and neglect primary and preventive care, especially when they cover only hospitalization costs. As a result, it is also not clear whether improved health can be counted as one of the real benefits of commercial health insurance schemes. High administrative costs tend to reduce considerably the amount that can be devoted to health care per se out of the premiums paid. Commercial health insurance schemes have also not been found to be financially sustainable. Cost escalations are commonly reported, and, in some instances, there has been a paradoxical rise in out-of-pocket payments as well. Finally, there is overwhelming evidence to suggest that commercial insurance schemes suffer from a lack of oversight to check medical malpractice.

Second, both the central and state governments should thus give top priority to ensuring the basics of state-provided primary health care services, including early management of health problems, and better quality of care. Strengthening primary health care delivery by ensuring the basics such as universal immunization can greatly reduce morbidity, lower the costs of curative care, and reduce specialist (and often expensive) tertiary care. Investing in primary health care is also likely to yield more equitable outcomes with substantial benefits accruing to poor and disadvantaged groups.

Third, opportunities exist—and many new ones are opening up—for partnerships with the more credible segments of the private sector in promoting health in areas such as public health education and training, technology applications, information processing, management, and provision of curative care. Recognizing the massive need for expanding the reach of health care services and the fiscal constraints that governments face, the central and state governments need to evolve new and innovative ways of engaging the private sector especially in the provision of tertiary care. At the same time, the government needs to put in place a national health regulatory and development framework for improving the quality (through, for instance, the registration of all health practitioners), performance, equity, efficiency, and accountability of health care delivery across the country. A regulatory authority entrusted with these functions should specify legal and regulatory norms for facilities, staff, quality and rationality of services, and costs. It should put out standard treatment guidelines for public and private providers, frame a patients' charter of rights, engage with professional associations and civil society, and establish a regular audit system.

Fourth, the fundamental requirement and challenge facing India is for the central and state governments to step up public expenditures on health. To a large extent, deficiencies in health financing are both a cause of and an exacerbating factor in the challenges of health inequity, inadequate availability, unequal access, poor quality, and costly services. Public spending on health in India has continued to hover around 1.2 percent of GDP for close to a decade. This needs to be stepped up to 2.5 or even 3 percent of GDP over the next five years in keeping with the commitments made by the prime minister and the president of India. In keeping with such a thrust, it is important to earmark a significant proportion of public spending to cover the provision of primary health care.

State governments have the primary responsibility for delivering on health. And today, close to two-thirds of public expenditures on health are incurred by state governments. Though its financial contribution is relatively small, the central government has considerable room for effectively leveraging its resources for health. New and flexible mechanisms of transferring financial resources to state governments must be introduced to improve health outcomes. It is important to revisit center-state financing arrangements to equalize the large variations in the levels of public expenditures across Indian states as a way to offset the general inability of many states to mobilize resources for health. For greater flexibility, the central government should ensure better integration of disease control and other programs; revisit essential requirements; and motivate state governments through core, program, and outcome conditionalities.

State governments will need to customize strategies to meet the health needs of different groups and communities. Adopting a uniform policy is unlikely to yield the desired health outcomes in a country with enormously varying contexts and health conditions. Separate strategies need to be worked out for addressing the health needs of the urban poor, tribal communities, and those living in mountainous regions of the northeast. Similarly, integrated strategies will need to be developed for addressing a range of health-related concerns that have not yet been fully addressed. State governments should also draw up blueprints for universal health coverage and begin experimenting and innovating with pilot programs. Learning by doing is the only way forward to paving the way for a healthy India. In the ultimate analysis, strong political commitment and effective stewardship are desperately needed if India is serious about improving the health of its citizens.

RECOMMENDED READING

K. Srinath Reddy et al., "Towards Achievement of Universal Health Care in India by 2020: A Call to Action," *Lancet* 377 (February 26, 2011): 760–68.

A. K. Shiva Kumar et al., "Financing Health Care for All: Challenges and Opportunities," *Lancet* 377 (February 19, 2011): 668–79.

NOTES

1   Government of India, Ministry of Home Affairs, Office of the Registrar General & Census Commissioner, Vital Statistics Division, *SRS Bulletin* 48 (2) (September 2013), www.censusindia.gov.in/vital_statistics/SRS_Bulletins/SRS_Bulletin-September_2013.pdf.

2   Government of India, Ministry of Home Affairs, Office of the Registrar General and Census Commissioner, "A Presentation on Maternal Mortality Levels (2010–12)," July 7, 2011, www.censusindia.gov.in/vital_statistics/SRS_Bulletins/MMR_release_070711.pdf.

3   Institute for Population Sciences and Macro International, *National Family Health Survey* (NFHS-3), 2005–06: India, vol. 1 (2007), www.measuredhs.com/pubs/pdf/FRIND3/00FrontMatter00.pdf.

4   Ibid.

5   International Diabetes Federation, *IDF Diabetes Atlas*, 6th edition (2013), 118, www.idf.org/sites/default/files/EN_6E_Atlas_Full_0.pdf.

6   Office of the Registrar General and Census Commissioner, Vital Statistics Division, *SRS Bulletin*.

7   Institute for Population Sciences and Macro International, *National Family Health Survey* (NFHS-3).

8   Ibid.

9   United Nations Department of Economic and Social Affairs, Population Division, *Sex Differentials in Childhood Mortality*, United Nations Publication ST/ESA/SER.A/314 (2011), www.un.org/esa/population/publications/SexDifChildMort/SexDifferentialsChildhoodMortality.pdf.

10 United Nations Children's Fund, *The State of the World's Children 2013: Children With Disabilities* (New York: UNICEF, 2013), www.unicef.org/sowc2013/statistics.html.

11 Vital Statistics Division, *SRS Bulletin*.

12 Government of India, Office of the Registrar General, "SRS-Based Abridged Life Tables 2003–07 to 2006–10," 2012, www.censusindia.gov.in/vital_statistics/SRS_Based/Cover_Page.pdf.

13 International Institute for Population Sciences, *District Level Household and Facility Survey* (DLHS 3).

14 Ibid.

15   Government of India, Ministry of Health and Family Welfare, "Coverage Evaluation Survey 2009," 2010, https://nrhm-mis.nic.in/frm_ces2009.aspx.

16   Mita Choudhury and H. K. Amar Nath, "An Estimate of Public Expenditure on Health in India," National Institute of Public Finance and Policy, May 2012, www.nipfp.org.in/media/medialibrary/2013/08/health_estimates_report.pdf.

17   World Health Organization, "Global Health Expenditure Database," http://apps.who.int/nha/database/StandardReport.aspx?ID=REP_WEB_MINI_TEMPLATE_WEB_VERSION.

18   World Bank, World DataBank, "Health Expenditure, Public (% of Total Health Expenditure)," http://data.worldbank.org/indicator/SH.XPD.PUBL.

19   David H. Peters, Abdo S. Yazbeck, Rashmi R. Sharma, G. N. V. Ramana, Lant H. Pritchett, and Adam Wagstaff, *Better Health Systems for India's Poor: Findings, Analysis, and Options*, Health, Nutrition, and Population Series (Washington D.C.: World Bank, 2002).

20   Ibid.

21   Government of India, Planning Commission, *Twelfth Five Year Plan*, vol. III: Social Sectors (2012), 1–46, http://planningcommission.gov.in/plans/planrel/12thplan/pdf/12fyp_vol3.pdf.

22   A discussion on these gaps can be found in the successive Five Year Plan documents prepared by the Planning Commission.

23   Government of India, Secretary (Health), "NAC Recommendations on Universal Health Coverage (UHC)—Progress to Date," presentation to the National Advisory Council, New Delhi, November 29, 2013.

24   Planning Commission, "High Level Expert Group Report on Universal Health Coverage for India."

CHAPTER 8

MODERNIZING TRANSPORT INFRASTRUCTURE

RAJIV LALL AND RITU ANAND

Infrastructure services—electricity, telecommunications, roads, rail, ports, and airports—are critical to the development of a strong, modern, and efficient economy. Transport services are key to productivity and competitiveness. Extending transport infrastructure to new areas creates jobs and catalyzes growth, opening up opportunities for industry, trade, and tourism. Transport is also an important determinant in the alleviation of poverty. By reducing transaction costs and facilitating access to markets, roads enable better prices for farmers and improved access to credit, thereby allowing greater productive investment by the rural population. They also provide better access to jobs, education, and health care facilities.

India has experienced a notable acceleration in the pace of transport infrastructure development since the 1990s. After four decades of sluggish growth, the national highway network expanded dramatically, from 34,000 kilometers of roads in 1991 to 71,000 kilometers of roads in 2011, absorbing the lion's share of the incremental growth in freight traffic over the period.[1] But it is the improvement in the road infrastructure of rural India that has been particularly noteworthy. Since 2001, about 400,000 kilometers of roads have been built or upgraded to provide all-weather access to more than 85,000 small rural villages, or habitations, across the country. The vast bulk of this expansion was achieved under the aegis of the remarkably successful Pradhan Mantri Gram Sadak Yojana (PMGSY) program, a central government–sponsored scheme launched in 2000 to connect the 57 percent of remaining unconnected eligible habitations to markets and cities. Elsewhere, the country's port and airport infrastructure have also undergone rapid growth. Over the past decade, India's maritime cargo handling capacity has grown by more than 2.5 times. Over the same period, its air cargo traffic has grown at over 8 percent per year, and domestic air passenger traffic has increased at over 14 percent per year. Expansion of rail infrastructure has been slower, though traffic carried by the railways has increased substantially. Rail passenger and freight traffic grew at a compound annual rate of close to 8 percent since 2001, making Indian Railways (IR) the world's largest rail passenger carrier in 2011 with 979 billion passenger kilometers and the fourth-largest rail freight carrier with 626 billion net ton kilometers.[2]

FUNDAMENTAL ISSUES FACING INDIA'S TRANSPORT INFRASTRUCTURE

The two most pressing issues that need to be addressed are the seriously inefficient and lopsided structure of the transport modal mix, and the acute overall transportation capacity constraints and absence of effective intermodal and multimodal transport connectivity.

Imbalance in Transport Modal Mix

Over the years, India's transport modal mix has become progressively skewed in favor of road traffic. The share of railways in freight transport has fallen steeply from 89 percent in 1951 to 36 percent in 2000–2008; over the same period, the share of freight traffic on roads has risen to more than 50 percent.[3] Passenger transport has undergone a similar trend. Poor quality of service, made worse by extreme capacity congestion and extremely high rail freight tariffs, has driven traffic away from railways. India's rail freight tariffs are among the highest in the world. This is because freight revenue is used to cross-subsidize deeply discounted—and politically driven—passenger rail fares. Passenger tariffs in India are one-fourth of those in China, one-ninth of those in Russia, and nearly one-twentieth of those in Japan. Even adjusted for purchasing power parity, they are far below at only 37 percent of tariffs in China, 15 percent of those in Russia, and 11 percent of those in Japan.[4] Freight tariffs, meanwhile, are the highest in India. Tariffs in China, for instance, are only 72 percent of the tariffs in India in nominal terms and 58 percent when adjusted for purchasing power parity.[5]

Given that a large part of India's freight traffic is transported over long distances and consists of bulk material, transporting it by rail would be both more economical and environmentally friendly than transporting it by road. The unit cost of rail transport is also lower, as are accident costs. It is estimated that the skewed intermodal mix of India's transport infrastructure costs the country up to the equivalent of 4.5 percent of GDP.[6] Raising the share of rail to at least 50 percent in freight transport, as is the case in China and the United States, should be a strategic priority of the new government and would entail a major expansion in railway capacity.

Overstretched Capacity and Low Efficiency

There is widespread consensus that inadequate infrastructure is becoming a drag on the economy. It is estimated that India's GDP growth could be higher by two percentage points if infrastructure bottlenecks were removed. Overall and across modes, the improvement and expansion of transportation infrastructure has clearly not kept pace with the increase in demand. On top of the infrastructure being insufficient, government investment in rail, roads, ports, and airports has been plagued by rampant delays at every stage. About half of all large (that is, costing more than Rs. 150 crore) central government infrastructure projects were behind schedule as of March 2013. Many of these projects were in the transport sector. In particular, 60 percent of road transport and highway projects were delayed, and 30 percent of rail projects were delayed. But the time and cost overruns for the rail projects were much higher than in the case of road projects.[7] There are several reasons for the delays, including difficulties in land acquisition, rehabilitating and resettling people affected by the project, shifting utilities, and obtaining clearances, especially environmental clearances. In addition, many rail projects are started without sufficient funding. Such widespread construction delays not only increase project completion costs, but also have aggravated the deteriorating situation of overburdened capacity, resulting in increased congestion, traffic delays, and associated additional costs, with serious implications for the economy's competitiveness.

India has an impressively vast network of roads, comprising national and state highways, and district and rural roads, but it suffers from highly variable quality and lack of maintenance. The roads are also grossly unsafe and their capacity is constrained. Over the years, the main aim has been to extend connectivity and build new roads, and only more recently with the National Highways Development Program has there been a concerted effort to augment capacity on trunk routes for wider roads, allowing faster speeds.

The national highways, which carry about 40 percent of total road traffic, constitute barely 2 percent of the road network.[8] Yet, only 25 percent of the country's national highways are four lanes or more and meet the required quality standards.[9] As a result of inadequate highways and access-controlled expressways, the average speed of trucks plying Indian roads is estimated at around an abysmal 20 kilometers per hour.[10] Delays at interstate and intrastate checkpoints and toll booths add as much as 25 percent to total journey times. Due to all these factors, trucks in India cover a maximum of 250–400 kilometers per day, compared with 700–800 kilometers in developed countries.[11] Congestion on national highways has also contributed to a rapid decline in road safety. Road accidents in India account for 10 percent of the world figure, though India's share of the global road fleet is only 1 percent.

Similarly, the trunk routes of railways connecting the four main metropolitan areas and the east-west diagonal across the country are oversaturated. These routes constitute 16 percent of the IR's track network but carry 50 to 60 percent of the rail passenger and freight traffic. The situation is exacerbated because India's rail system is mixed use, with freight train operations given lower priority than passenger trains over the shared network.[12] Consequently, the average speed of a freight train in India is 25 kilometers per hour, nearly half that of freight trains in the United States.[13]

While port capacity in India has reached 1.25 billion tons, most of the twelve "major" ports under central government control remain congested, with average berth utilization rates of about 90 percent compared with an international average of 70 percent, and average turnaround times of about

4.4 days compared with less than a day in Singapore.[14] Were it not for the rapid development of privately owned "non-major or minor ports" under the jurisdiction of state governments, the situation would be much worse.

Airfreight transport suffers from similar constraints. Airports, mostly all under the control of the central government, were not planned to deal with cargo traffic. As a result, the efficiency of Indian airports is low, with dwell times ranging from three to five days relative to four to twelve hours at leading global airports. This is in large part due to the long time taken for customs clearance.

The bottom line is that demand far outstrips the supply of infrastructure, with negative consequences for the Indian economy as a whole. Going forward, India's infrastructure capacity needs are expected to double every decade, according to the Planning Commission. The Twelfth Five Year Plan calls for a total investment in infrastructure of Rs. 50 lakh crore between 2012 and 2017, of which about 40 percent is slated for the transport sector. Transportation of bulk commodities is projected to place heavy demands on the transport system, requiring major capacity addition in rail and other modes. In particular, substantial investment will be required to ensure the transportation of coal from mines and ports to power generating plants. Without such investment, the country's energy security could be compromised.

PRIVATE PARTICIPATION: NECESSARY FOR CAPACITY EXPANSION

With some notable exceptions, such as PMGSY in the case of rural roads, the overall performance of the government as a builder and operator of infrastructure has been disappointing. Due to chronic fiscal constraints, the government has underinvested in infrastructure. And its declining managerial capacity has led to systematic failure to fully meet the targets set in one Five Year Plan after another since independence. Partly by default and partly as a matter of conscious policy, the private sector has emerged over the past fifteen years as an important player in the development of the country's infrastructure. Over the period of the Eleventh Five Year Plan (2007–2012), India invested close to Rs. 20 lakh crore in infrastructure, of which more than 35 percent was on account of privately developed projects. Indeed, were it not for private participation in infrastructure development, the Eleventh Plan would have fallen substantially short of its capacity creation targets.

While it is well known that mobile telecommunications in India, driven by the private sector, have been highly successful and widespread, the magnitude of the private footprint in other infrastructure sectors has also become significant. The transport sector, with the exception of railways, has had a large amount of private sector participation mainly through build-operate-transfer concessions. Under these schemes, the concessionaire is responsible for designing, building, operating, and financing the infrastructure to be developed, though the government can provide up to 40 percent of the project cost as viability gap funding. While the concessionaire collects and retains the agreed user charges, it also bears all risks, including construction, operational, and commercial. Minor ports, which are under the jurisdiction of state governments, handled 26 percent of India's maritime bulk in 2002 and 25 percent of its container cargo traffic. Today these ports, which are essentially privately managed through long-term concession agreements with state governments, handle 42 percent of bulk cargo and 85 percent of all container traffic, and they are as efficient as ports in Singapore and Antwerp. More than 60 percent of India's passenger air traffic and 70 percent of its cargo air traffic is now handled by the private sector because six major airports, including those serving the four main metropolitan areas, started operating under private concessions over the past decade. The Indian roads sector has arguably engaged in the largest ongoing public-private partnership (PPP) program anywhere in the world. Under the central government's flagship National Highways Development Program, about 40 percent of the 17,500 kilometers of new roads and lanes completed over the past decade have been in the form of build-operate-transfer concessions. And a staggering 83 percent of contracts awarded for road widening under the highways program since 2005 have been executed as PPPs.

Private participation in India's infrastructure is remarkable not only for its scale and the contribution it has made to asset creation in a compressed period of time, but also for the improvement it has brought to quality and service delivery.

However, of late the momentum has stalled. India is now experiencing a backlash against private participation that it can ill afford. Investment in infrastructure has fallen drastically. This drop can be attributed to, among other things, lengthy land acquisition and environmental clearance procedures. These procedures have resulted in construction delays and consequent cost escalations, regulatory uncertainties, high financing costs, and aggressive bidding and debt accumulation, which have also contributed to weakening contractor financial health. A large number of contractual disputes are also pending between private developers and various government agencies. Developers are not willing to bid for new projects as they are financially overextended. Lenders have become extremely cautious about disbursing funds to projects that are yet to receive clearances and have raised up-front equity requirements. All this has led to a logjam in the infrastructure sector. If the role of private players in infrastructure development is to remain sustainably on track, important lessons from the past decade need to be internalized.

PPPs: Too Much, Too Soon?

Public-private partnerships, the bedrock of capacity expansion in national highways, central and state government ports, and airports, have come to a virtual standstill. Why? In a nutshell, the institutional, administrative, and regulatory capacity of the government has not been able to keep pace with the private sector's exuberant and often aggressive ambition in the area of infrastructure development. Infrastructure development through PPPs entails more sophisticated management and oversight by the government than direct government implementation of projects. It requires skills in government agencies for structuring complex contracts and managing transparent bidding processes that ensure a level playing field for private participants. It also demands strong regulatory oversight to monitor the performance of—and prevent abuse by—private operators. The transparency of government decisionmaking assumes great importance, as do the predictability and stability of the regulatory framework, and the speed and fairness of sanctions and dispute resolution. Many of the current problems and challenges have emerged from infirmities in all these areas.

Lack of Government Preparedness. In the rush to have a pipeline of projects, the government diluted qualification norms and also often put projects out for bid that were not fully prepared. For example, the National Highways Authority of India bid out projects with only part of the necessary land available and unencumbered. Subsequent problems in land acquisition have delayed the commissioning dates for a large number of road projects, adversely affecting their viability. In fact, land acquisition has become progressively harder and has become a major sticking point and cause of disputes between the highways authority and road concessionaires.

Burdensome Multiagency Approval Process. Of the myriad permits required for infrastructure projects in India, environmental clearances have proven the most notoriously cumbersome for road and port projects. Not only is obtaining these clearances time-consuming because they involve sign-offs from different layers of government, but their issuance is also uncertain because of stakeholder involvement and community participation requirements, a process that can be abused by local political interests. Even simple matters, such as local clearances for shifting utilities, have tended to get mired in local bureaucracy.

Coordination Failures. The lack of integrated planning and coordinated execution across government agencies has had an impact on the commercial viability of many private sector transport projects, especially in the port sector. The efficiency of several private ports has been compromised because of poor connectivity to major road or rail transport arteries. The linkages simply were not planned. Similarly, insufficient attention to customs administration has contributed to congestion at ports as additional capacity has come onstream. Fragmentation and overlapping responsibilities have blurred accountability and exacerbated delays in getting permissions lined up.

Fragmented Regulation. Regulatory oversight in transport is uneven. Sometimes it is spread over many agencies with overlapping jurisdictions, and sometimes it is applicable only to certain entities. For instance, tariff regulation, by the Tariff Authority for Major Ports, is applicable only to major ports, so private concessionaires operating in major ports end up being at a competitive disadvantage vis-à-vis minor port operators that are free to set tariffs. This uneven playing field has contributed to major ports' rapidly losing market share to minor ports.

Regulatory Uncertainty. Ex post facto and retroactive changes in the policy and regulatory framework have sent confusing signals to private investors. For instance, in the airport sector, a regulatory body called the Airports Economic Regulatory Authority was set up in 2009 after all four major airport concessions were awarded. The agency is now revising the tariff basis for these airports, which obviously affects their financial performance.

Conflicts of Interest. The interface between the public and private sector has led to a complex situation, especially where the public sector body is an implementing agency. For instance, in the case of highway development, there is not sufficient distance between the Ministry of Road Transport and Highways responsible for policymaking and the National Highways Authority of India, leaving the latter vulnerable to political pressure. In addition, the NHAI is at once a signatory to as well responsible for overseeing PPP agreements. Because the highways authority is thus an interested party, which might not fulfill its contractual obligations such as ensuring that the right of way is clear of encumbrances, it may not perform its oversight duties in an impartial manner. In such a scenario, an aggrieved private operator has no fast-track dispute resolution route. This is reflected in the huge number of pending disputes.

Bid Manipulation and Other Abuses. The private sector has not been blameless. In the roads sector, private concessionaires with their own construction companies have had a tendency to overstate project costs and then use debt financing to recoup their actual equity contribution up front. Another technique that has been used in the case of airport and metro projects is to bid aggressively to win the concession, then to pressure the concessioning authority to renegotiate or reinterpret certain aspects of the original agreement.

Infirmities in Contract Design. In many cases, contracts have been loosely designed, leaving room for discretion on the part of the concessioning authority and reinterpretation on the part of the concessionaire. In the case of roads, the government's approach has been to rely on watertight model contractual agreements that include a formulaic tariff-setting mechanism. While these agreements have eliminated abuses that might arise from broadly written contracts, they are proving to be perhaps too rigid in the face of genuinely unforeseen circumstances.

All these issues have added significantly to the execution risk of greenfield infrastructure projects. They have also resulted in very costly delays that have compromised returns for private investors and asset quality for the debt financiers. Most important, they have undermined trust between government and private parties. Unless urgent and pragmatic measures are taken to address the situation, it will be hard to induce the private sector to participate on the scale needed to ensure that India meets its targets for expansion of transport infrastructure capacity.

REFORMING INDIAN RAILWAYS: A STRATEGIC IMPERATIVE

To address the serious imbalance in the country's intermodal transport mix, revitalizing Indian Railways is of utmost importance. Unlike the furious pace of activity in other transport sectors, the railway sector has barely started reforms. The IR faces three fundamental challenges: severe capacity and resource constraints, confusion between social and commercial objectives, and organizational dysfunction.

Capacity and Resource Constraints

An important cause of the capacity and resource constraints of Indian Railways is the way it prices its services. Passenger trains utilize nearly 65 percent of network capacity but contribute less than 30 percent of the revenue.[15] Deeply discounted passenger rail fares that remained unchanged from 2002 to 2012 and the resulting revenue losses have left the IR chronically under-resourced. The IR's inability to generate surpluses, coupled with the government's overall fiscal constraints, has resulted in systematic under-investment in rail. Expenditure on railways as a share of transport expenditure has steadily fallen from 56 percent in the Seventh Plan (1985–1990) to 30 percent in the Eleventh Plan (2007–2012).[16]

Confusion Between Social and Commercial Objectives

While the government expects Indian Railways to run as a commercial and financially self-sufficient organization, New Delhi cannot resist using it as a vehicle for important public goods such as connectivity to remote unremunerative locations, subsidized passenger services, and transportation of essential commodities below cost. The comingling of these activities causes serious problems. It has led to uneconomic capacity expansion (unremunerative lines constructed) without compensation from the central or state government budgets, loss of focus in project execution (as multiple disparate pet projects are initiated rather than concentrating on easing capacity constraints or improving operations), and poor cost management (as resources are spread thinly over too many projects, resulting in time and cost overruns).

Organizational Dysfunction

The IR remains a monolithic, departmentally organized giant with more than 1.3 million employees whose productivity levels, though improving, are still far below international benchmarks. Each department is staffed by separate cadres. This has undermined strategic coherence and led to internecine battles for resources. Many expert committees have recommended restructuring the Railway Board and zonal railways, separating policy from operations, reorganizing the departments into business lines with profit and cost centers, and focusing on core business areas.

While the IR has not corporatized as a whole, it has experimented with setting up some corporations to provide select services and develop special projects on a more transparently commercial basis. Among these, Concor, a cargo container company, was set up about twenty-five years ago to provide logistics services. Also, some of the new railway lines have been built and operated by separate corporations under the IR. More recently, the IR established a corporate entity for implementing the dedicated freight corridors, an ambitious project to augment the overstretched network capacity on the trunk routes and raise productivity by enabling heavier, longer, and faster freight trains to operate with lower unit costs. The corporation has successfully acquired most of the required land and started work on two dedicated freight corridors on the eastern and western corridors. Studies are under way for four more corridors.

The vast majority of assets and operations, however, remain with the IR and suffer from its poor track record of project execution and maintenance, diffusion of priorities, and its compulsion to pursue uneconomical projects without transparent subsidy compensation. More radical action is needed.

LOOKING AHEAD

Reboot Indian Railways

The importance of overhauling the IR and stepping up investments in the railways cannot be overemphasized. A first step in the direction of separating policy from operations would be to follow up on the recent cabinet decision to set up a Rail Tariff Regulatory Authority that would help depoliticize tariff setting. The regulatory authority should go beyond tariff setting to include setting of service standards as well.

The IR must reform its accounting systems to enable better business decisions and improve financial discipline. Identifying profit centers through transparent accounting will also increase its access to additional sources of financing and enable credit to be raised from the private sector. In parallel, the IR must actively pursue opportunities for mobilizing resources from the private sector through PPPs and through partnership to monetize (at least in part) its land bank. It should also explore freeing up resources by shedding its non-core activities such as its rolling stock manufacturing operations.

Learning from the experience of building the dedicated freight corridors, the IR should adopt a programmatic, rather than a project-specific, approach to investment planning. This would have many advantages. It would enable planning in an integrated way as part of a strategic program and result in a bigger impact than discrete unrelated projects. The announcement of the program would also draw many subsidiary industries. And importantly, it would help reduce politically motivated projects.

Revitalize Private Participation

Speedy resolution of the mounting disputes involving government agencies and private developers is key to restoring trust between the two parties.

In this regard draft legislation already exists to set up specialist courts to adjudicate disputes over public-private contracts and cut down the time it takes to resolve these matters. The judges in these courts will need to have deep sectoral expertise in public policy, law, business, and finance.

Going forward, the government needs to ensure that all preparatory activities are completed before projects are offered to private developers. In particular, the government must be able to deliver on land acquisition and clearances for concessions. Government departments and PPP cells should be strengthened to ensure that they are able to perform their roles well. An option is to set up a high-level PPP unit within the central government that includes qualified professionals with extensive experience and knowledge of the challenges and lessons learned from previous projects. Such an agency could monitor and manage the growth of PPP, help structure higher-quality PPPs, and identify and filter unrealistic bids or instances of collusion.

The private sector also must be induced to behave more responsibly. While it is not easy to design incentives to change their behavior, financiers have an important role to play in disciplining and discerning genuine promoters. The Reserve Bank of India is tightening up and facilitating recovery by banks more than in past cycles, causing serious pain to promoters and equity holders. Stricter provisioning norms and support for making resolution of bad assets more effective and timely are just two measures that could send strong signals to financiers and their clients.

Rationalize Regulatory Oversight and Ensure Independence

One alternative to the piecemeal approach that led to the proliferation of regulatory bodies and tribunals is to have a single regulator across all the transport sectors. While there are compelling reasons for adopting a single regulator, it is unlikely to happen given vested interests. Still, several other things can be done to streamline and strengthen regulation. Most important is to provide functional autonomy to the regulatory agency. In road transport, expert regulation is important to impartially monitor compliance of PPP agreements between NHAI and private concessionaires, resolve disputes after the concessions have been awarded, and regulate service quality. The priority for ports is to unify national and state regulatory oversight and distance the same from the Ministry of Ports and Shipping.

Replicate Success Stories of Government-Built Infrastructure

The private sector can never substitute for government in infrastructure development. It is imperative that government learn from its successes to improve the delivery of transport infrastructure. In this regard, the central government should in particular expand the footprint of the PMGSY program for rural roads and further strengthen collaborative models for road development with state governments.

Pursue Institutional Reform and Capacity Building

A first principle is that there should be a separation of the institutions that administer or monitor policy from those that provide service, to avoid conflicts of public interests with provider interests. In the case of the National Highways Authority of India and the Ports Authority, policymaking should be clearly separated by creating more distance between these agencies and their respective ministries.

The general level of skills in concerned government agencies needs to be upgraded. In the road sector, for example, the dominant mindset is that of road engineers, who are typically not equipped to deal with contractual terms, negotiations, and contract management. Capacity building among road engineers must be a priority.

Address Coordination Failures

There is a strong case for forcing collaboration between various ministries to focus on the issues of intermodal imbalances and connectivity. Australia, Brazil, Canada, Germany, Japan, Russia, and the United States, which collectively carry more than 90 percent of the world's rail freight outside India, all now have unitary transport ministries. Even China has recently expanded the ambit of its Ministry of Transport by bringing together all transport responsibilities except railways. India should seriously think about consolidating the separate transport sector ministries (roads, ports and shipping, railways, civil aviation) into a single Transport Ministry at the central government level so as to establish integrated national transport policies that transcend or augment individual modal interests.

The agenda for reform presented here is very ambitious. But then again, so is the country's goal for the modernization of its transport infrastructure. If India is to overcome the acute capacity constraints and infrastructure imbalances that impair its growth potential, it must act resolutely and expeditiously.

NOTES

1   Government of India, Planning Commission, *Twelfth Five Year Plan 2012–2017*, vol. 2, annexure 15.2, 254.

2   Government of India, *Report of the National Transport Development Policy Committee*, chaired by Rakesh Mohan, forthcoming.

3   Ibid.

4   Planning Commission, *Twelfth Five Year Plan 2012–2017*, vol. 2, 213.

5   Ibid.

6   Government of India, *Report of the National Transport Development Policy Committee*.

7   Government of India, Ministry of Statistics and Programme Implementation, "Monitoring of Infrastructure Projects," PIB Release, August 6, 2013, http://pib.nic.in/newsite/erelease.aspx?relid=91303.

8   Planning Commission, *Twelfth Five Year Plan 2012–2017*, vol. 2, 214–15.

9   Ibid., 215.

10 TCI and IIM-Calcutta, *Report on Operational Efficiency of Freight Transport by Road in India 2011–12* (Calcutta: Transport Corporation of India and Indian Institute of Management, 2012), 12.

11 Ibid.

12 Government of India, *Report of the National Transport Development Policy Committee*.

13 Planning Commission, *Twelfth Five Year Plan 2012–2017*, vol. 2, 194.

14 Ibid., 238.

15 Government of India, *Report of the National Transport Development Policy Committee*.

16 Ibid.

CHAPTER 9

MANAGING URBANIZATION*

SOMIK LALL AND TARA VISHWANATH

POLICY PRIORITIES

India's new government should pay immediate attention to three priority areas as they try to harness economic growth and manage social inclusion associated with urbanization.

First, to enhance productivity, policymakers should invest in the institutional and informational foundations to enable land and housing markets to function efficiently, while deregulating the intensity of land use in urban areas. This measure would require better coordination between planning for land use and planning for infrastructure, such that densification can be accompanied by infrastructure improvements. An incremental model of experimentation focusing on a few areas—say, around infrastructure corridors and neighborhoods—and then scaling up based on community-level consensus building can help in implementing densification reforms.

---

* This chapter's text is based on a longer World Bank report on Indian urbanization led by the two authors. See Tara Vishwanath, Somik Lall, et al., *Urbanization Beyond Municipal Boundaries: Nurturing Metropolitan Economies and Connecting Peri-Urban Areas in India* (Washington, D.C.: World Bank, 2009), https://openknowledge.worldbank.org/bitstream/handle/10986/13105/757340PUB0EPI0001300pubdate02021013.pdf?sequence=1.

Second, to improve livability and social inclusion, policymakers should rationalize the rules of the game for delivering and expanding infrastructure services, such that service providers can recover costs yet reach out to poorer neighborhoods and peripheral areas.

Third, for both growth and inclusion, investments in improving connectivity between metropolitan cores and their peripheries are needed, since these are the areas that will attract the bulk of people and businesses over the medium term. Connectivity improvements include investments in network infrastructure and logistics to facilitate the movement of goods, while also easing mobility for people.

Land policy, infrastructure services, and connectivity—coordinated improvements in this triad can help India reap dividends from improved economic growth and social inclusion that can come with well-managed urbanization.

INDIA'S URBANIZATION: AN OVERVIEW

Urbanization typically goes hand in hand with structural transformations within countries.[1] Changes in people's decisions on where to live, firms' decisions on where to locate production, and the economic composition of locations—alongside their spatial expansions—are all part of the urbanization process.

Today these changes are occurring rapidly in India. According to the 2011 census, 90 million people were added to India's urban areas over a ten-year period. Industrial jobs are concentrating in the suburbs of metropolitan areas, while on the outskirts of the largest metropolitan areas, high-technology and export-oriented manufacturing jobs are growing fastest. These suburbs are delivering economies of agglomeration and specialization, leading the production of goods and services that India trades with the global economy. But without a regional planning framework to integrate peri-urban areas with metropolitan areas, India faces challenges in managing its fast-expanding urban areas.

Urbanization has led India's impressive economic growth of the past twenty years. GDP grew by 7.2 percent a year in the first decade of this century, increasing the economic demand for India's urban areas in a manner seen in dynamic emerging economies that have rapidly urbanized and industrialized. For instance, India now has significant global market share in products such as vehicles, pharmaceuticals, industrial machinery, and electrical and electronic equipment that often benefit from agglomeration economies and whose global demand is growing at 5–15 percent a year. In fact, while India is known for its information and communication technology (ICT) services exports, what is less well known is that its $159 billion in manufactured goods exports in 2008 amounted to more than three times the ICT services exports. Much of India's economic growth has been unleashed by dismantling the entrenched, elaborate mesh of permits and regulations known as the "license raj." Rescinding licensing requirements, overhauling public enterprises, scrapping quantitative import restrictions, reducing trade tariffs, and liberalizing rules on foreign direct investment are among the liberating changes.

How urbanization is managed has implications for both economic efficiency and equity. For economic efficiency, the important question is to identify whether productivity gains through agglomeration economies are being adequately tapped. Put differently, are agglomeration benefits being stymied by policy distortions, and can specific reforms reduce these inefficiencies? For equity, are the benefits of these transformations spreading geographically? And can policies support the spread of economic activity?

Three notable stylized facts on India's urbanization have a bearing on public policy:

- Metropolitan dominance in economic activity

- Metropolitan stagnation

- Metropolitan suburbanization

India's urban geography has evolved since liberalization in the early 1990s—but policy distortions and infrastructure shortfalls undermine performance. India's largest metropolitan areas, with their good access to domestic and international markets, are still the choice of entrepreneurs looking for the most potentially profitable sites. But overregulated land markets are limiting urban densities and pushing up prices for land and property. As people and jobs move to the suburbs, their transport costs in maintaining contact with the core shoot up: short-distance freight costs are around Rs. 5 per ton-kilometer (km), twice the average in 2010 and twice China's average in 2002.[2] Suburbanization also poses challenges for urban mobility, which is increasingly constrained by public transport's limited role. Basic services in metropolitan peripheries are weak, with both access to services and the quality of services below what they should be.

Metropolitan Dominance

Analysis of data from the 2005 economic census shows that India's population and economic activity are highly concentrated around the seven largest metropolitan areas. Metropolitan areas are defined as the area within a 50-km radius of the city center. That's around the distance that can be traveled in two hours or less, approximating the extent of economic interactions within an urban area.

These seven largest metropolitan areas cover only 1.1 percent of the land area in India but in 2001 were home to 92 million people, or 9 percent of the total population and a quarter of the urban population. Their density is 2,451 people per square kilometer, almost eight times the

TABLE 1. POPULATION WITHIN MULTIPLE BUFFERS FOR THE SEVEN LARGEST METROPOLITAN AREAS, 2005

All figures in percentages unless otherwise indicated

| | Radius from the center in kilometers | | | | | | |
	Less than 50	50–100	100–200	200–300	300–450	More than 450	Total
Land area	1.1	3.3	11.9	16.7	24.7	42.2	100.0
Total population	8.9	4.5	13.7	16.3	20.6	36.0	100.0
Urban population	24.9	3.6	12.9	17.2	19.2	22.1	100.0
Rural population	2.8	4.9	14.0	15.9	21.1	41.3	100.0
Population density (per sq. km)	2,451	427	364	306	262	269	315
Urbanization rate[a]	77.7	22.4	26.2	29.4	25.9	17.1	27.8

a. Ratio of urban population to total population.

Source: Government of India, Ministry of Statistics and Program Implementation, "Provisional Results of Fifth Economic Census 2005: All India Report," 2006, http://mospi.nic.in/mospi_new/upload/economic_census_prov_results_2005.pdf; Government of India, Ministry of Home Affairs, Office of the Registrar General and Census Commissioner, "Census of India: Census Data 2001," 2001.

national average. As table 1 illustrates, the share of the urban population in this land area is 78 percent, well above the national average of 28 percent.

Some 18 percent of national employment is located in these seven metropolitan areas, and 29 percent of national employment in business services. These seven areas also account for 64 percent of employment in ICT services.

Metropolitan Stagnation

While India's metropolitan areas dominate the economic landscape, experience in other countries suggests a constant churn in location patterns between and within industries and cities: some types of firms agglomerate, others disperse. Industries that are just starting out or that recently underwent a major technological advance tend to locate in large cities to maximize learning spillovers. Over time, as they develop and factors such as cheap labor or land come into play, they are inclined to disperse. This dispersion is enabled by reliable transport networks ensuring connectivity and market access. In India, however, where transport networks are inadequate, industries that exhibit agglomeration economies more often remain in the vicinity of large cities.

While India largely conforms to international experience in its geographic specialization patterns, the slow pace of change is surprising. As leading areas of concentration grow beyond a certain size and density, the economies from agglomeration are outweighed by "diseconomies" of agglomeration—such as congestion—suggested by rising rents and wages. The slowdown and subsequent partial reversal of spatial concentration normally happens at a late stage of development. This turning point was at a per capita GDP of $7,000 for France and about $10,000 per capita for Canada and the Netherlands.

By comparison, with income levels of less than $1,500 per capita, India should expect economic concentration to increase for years to come. It is here that India puzzles. The top panel in figure 1 shows, as expected, that districts in all cities with more than 1 million people accounted for an outsized share of total formal manufacturing employment. But the conundrum is that concentration in those two categories was stagnant, even falling in the big seven metropolitan cores and their suburban districts, offsetting the gains made by districts in cities with 1–4 million people.[3]

FIGURE 1. SPATIAL TRENDS IN TOTAL FORMAL MANUFACTURING AND SERVICES EMPLOYMENT

District Share in Manufacturing Employment

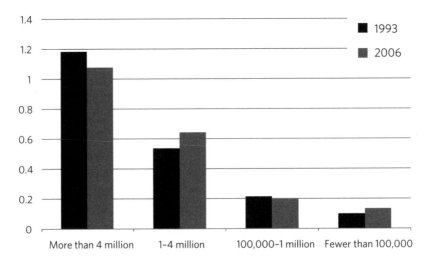

District Share in Services Employment

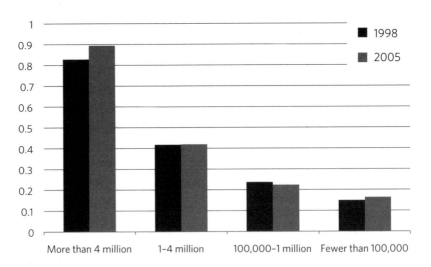

Source: Manufacturing trends are based on Ministry of Statistics and Program Implementation (1993 and 2006). Services trends are based on Ministry of Statistics and Program Implementation (1998 and 2005).

Similarly, the bottom panel shows no more than a hint of a rising concentration in services in the two largest categories combined.

How does one interpret this overall stability in spatial patterns of employment? This is a complicated question because development paths differ across countries. Still, international experience suggests that manufacturing concentration in India's leading metropolitan and suburban areas should not start leveling off for a while. The aggregate stability in spatial concentration indicates that the forces opposing concentration, such as congestion, are alarmingly strong in India's largest metropolitan areas.

Metropolitan Suburbanization

Behind the seemingly stable economic concentration in India's largest metropolitan areas lies a rapid spatial restructuring. According to spatially detailed data from the 1998 and 2005 economic censuses, industry is moving from metropolitan core areas to the suburbs and metro fringes.[4]

Manufacturing employment in India's largest seven metropolitan cores (defined as areas within 10 km of the city center) decreased by 16 percent from 1998 to 2005 (figure 2). Yet in the suburbs and immediate peripheries

FIGURE 2. EMPLOYMENT GROWTH IN METROPOLITAN CORES AND PERIPHERIES BY SECTOR, 1998–2005

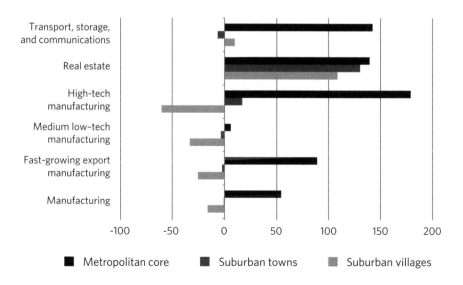

Source: Ministry of Statistics and Program Implementation, 1998 and 2005.

(a 50-km radius excluding the core), it increased by nearly 12 percent, a rate twice the national average. This readjustment between the cores and suburbs is most evident in high-tech and fast-growing export manufacturing industries: during the period that the cores had a 60 percent drop in high-tech industries, for example, the suburbs' gain in that segment was by the same amount.[5]

All suburban areas in India (between 10 and 50 km from the urban core) are experiencing the same manufacturing boom. This is the case regardless of whether these suburban areas are officially classified as rural or urban. In fact, the pace of manufacturing employment growth from 1998 to 2005 was fastest (41 percent) in rural areas closest to the largest metropolitan areas. While we observe overall stagnancy of the big seven metropolitan areas, there is clear evidence that high-tech and other emerging manufacturing industries are relocating to the immediate suburbs and peripheries of these very cities, as opposed to locations farther away. Moreover, though metropolitan suburbanization is a worldwide phenomenon, it usually happens at the middle to advanced stages of development.[6] Thus India's early suburbanization suggests that the overall stagnancy of metropolitan areas is partly due to firms' being pushed out of the cores. The next section offers an overview of why, and points to challenges in some detail.

POLICY DISTORTIONS HINDERING ECONOMIC AND SPATIAL TRANSFORMATION

The analysis above highlights considerable stability in the spatial distribution of people and jobs. After India's economic liberalization, one would have expected rapid economic concentration in large metropolitan areas with good market access. That's what happened after China's economic liberalization in the 1980s as well as in other dynamic emerging economies that rapidly urbanized and industrialized. But no discernible gains in economic activity are in evidence in India's metropolitan areas. This stagnancy points toward two overlapping scenarios. First, Indian cities have restrictive rules on converting land for new urban uses, and the intensity at which land can be used by industry, commerce, and housing. For example, even though the international best practice to accommodate growth in cities with limited land (as in Singapore and Hong Kong) is to raise the permitted floor space index (FSI)—the ratio of the gross floor area of a building on a lot divided by the area of that lot—the Municipal Corporation of Greater Mumbai did the opposite, lowering the permitted FSI to 1.33 in 1991.[7] In fact, the FSI was fixed at 4.5 in Nariman Point (the city's premier business district) in 1964. In India's otherwise liberalized policy environment, stringent regulations on development densities are pushing businesses and people out of urban cores. The land use constraints are also boosting housing costs to the point where poor and middle-class households can scarcely afford to live there.

Second, the growth of metropolitan suburbs may well be a reaction to draconian land policy. However, moving to the suburbs is costly for both firms and workers. Transport costs for freight are among the highest nationally between the metropolitan core and its periphery, and infrastructure access and quality of services—water, electricity, sanitation—is much worse in the urban periphery than in the core. These challenges have a negative impact on productivity, mobility, and livability.

THE CENTRALITY OF LAND POLICIES

In most cases, efforts to accommodate urban expansion will imply the need for land acquisition, which will bring with it a set of challenges. Indian policymakers have recognized this predicament, and land acquisition policies have been at the center of the policy debate. Today India lacks many of the institutions needed to facilitate the functioning of land markets, such as a transparent system to convert land use, a clear definition of property rights, a robust system of land and property valuation, and a strong judicial system to address public concerns.

The recent Land Acquisition and Rehabilitation and Resettlement Bill makes a concerted attempt to balance efficiency from urbanization and infrastructure development with equity in terms of the welfare of displaced residents. The bill is the first of its kind in almost one-hundred and ten years, amending the Land Acquisition Act of 1894, and is a commendable effort highlighting the need for poverty and social impact analysis and hinting at the need to use a sales comparison approach for valuation.

While the Land Acquisition and Rehabilitation and Resettlement Bill does not (and cannot) address the key issue of facilitating rural-urban land use conversion and cannot in itself solve the complex issue of unclear property rights, it does deal with the question of land valuation.

However, the bill leaves room for two issues to be addressed. First, India lacks a system that can independently verify and publicly access valuation of land; the bill relies on sales deeds or agreements for similar lands. However, high stamp duties, which the bill refers to, have historically created incentives to underreport land and property values, which are not frequently updated through surveys. Over time, institutions should be built that improve the information foundations of the valuation process, including training a cadre of appraisers in property valuation, ensuring transparency in the valuation process, and making information on land values widely accessible. Unless institutional capacity exists to help discover and disseminate the value of land, there is considerable scope for undervaluing land during the acquisition process. But this cannot be achieved unless stamp duties are reduced from the current exorbitant levels.

Second, to compensate for this inefficiency, the bill proposes arbitrary markups. Depending on the property's true value, this could lead to underinvestment or community resistance to allow land redevelopment. It will be very important to assess the impact of this compensation and, if necessary, make an adjustment.

Since stronger institutions governing land use conversion, property rights definition and adjudication, and land valuation are just emerging and land markets will take time to mature, India may want to look at alternative options for the short and medium term. One such alternative that is gaining acceptance is land readjustment, as it has many advantages for land assembly. The premise of land readjustment, is to provide public infrastructure at a shared cost to landowners and the municipality. It works by assembling a readjustment area, providing infrastructure and basic services, and then reallocating land back to participating private landowners. The reallocation is based either on pre-adjustment land holdings or land values, but the land amount decreases on the assumption that the land's value has risen because of the added infrastructure. The land readjustment process allows land to be developed without going through the complex transactions characteristic of eminent domain. Rather than buying all existing properties commercially or using eminent domain, the government agency can invite owners to participate in the project as capital investors. In return, after the area has been developed, owners are assured of receiving a property of at least equal value, near their original property. Adjustment processes appeal to landowners because they can stay where they are, avoiding the significant social and emotional ruptures that often accompany relocation.

Being in essence a participatory tool, land readjustment is able to a great extent to bypass the public discontent and protests that land acquisition may generate. Land readjustment may thus be more politically feasible than land acquisition invoking eminent domain in some situations, such as when there is distrust among the parties involved. As a gradual, essentially bottom-up approach, it also offers time to learn from the process itself. However, land readjustment requires efforts from public authorities such as the redrawing of boundaries and the associated adjustment of property rights. In some cases, it also requires local officials to initiate the project, as in Japan, and negotiate with affected landowners for a set of general agreements for the undertaking. Today, international practice is leaning toward land readjustment and away from land acquisition using eminent domain for two reasons: its participatory nature and the fact that it does not require substantial up-front capital.

Land readjustment is most commonly used to expand urban boundaries on the periphery of cities, though it may also be used in urban areas for redevelopment. A number of countries practice land readjustment, but its application is context-specific. Before implementing such a practice, countries must assess whether enabling institutions exist to facilitate the adoption of selected ideas of land readjustment. If not, a detailed plan to create such institutions is necessary before the practice can take off. Second, countries must ascertain what other institutions are required to implement a modified land readjustment system that fits the specific context of the country. One of the most interesting international examples is that of Germany. Germany is perhaps the oldest model for land readjustment, and it has been replicated in many countries. Its success and acceptability is grounded on three main issues: well-defined property rights; streamlined, independent, and transparent evaluation processes; and a strong judicial system to address public concerns.

If India's policymakers are to consider land readjustment methods for land assembly and as an initial instrument to defray the cost of infrastructure, they will first have to focus on evaluating whether institutions are ready to initiate the process, and then identify particularities of the local context that require changes to the international models of land readjustment.

Managing Urban Densities for Vertical Expansion

Just as land assembly and land valuation are challenges in terms of accommodating urban expansion, so is managing densities within cities and finding ways to finance urban expansion and city renewal. The ongoing debate on density regulation and floor space index should be placed in a broader urban planning framework. This framework should include FSIs, zoning and use controls, height and bulk controls, and requirements for public space and rights-of-way. International experience can shed light on important insights about which planning practices can promote sustainable economic growth.

FSIs provide the opportunity to manage densities by creating mechanisms where initial densities are regulated but developers are allowed to exceed the limits by paying for additional densities. Regulations on coverage areas and FSIs can be combined to create different density structures. In this context, it is important to stress that there is no optimal FSI. The level of the FSI depends on many things, among them existing spatial structure, street patterns, infrastructure capacity, and social and cultural factors. But the key lesson is that FSIs and these factors must be linked to formulate efficient and desirable spatial structures. For large metropolitan areas, this typically means moving from a traditional monocentric spatial structure with a single central business district to a polycentric structure with multiple, well-connected activity centers.

However, urban regulations such as restrictive FSIs limit densification in Indian cities, capping densities at levels much below international good practice. India's urban planners often justify the low urban densities by pointing out that cities' existing infrastructure systems would collapse if densities were increased. So they argue that development should be shifted to new towns and suburban industrial estates while preserving the size of existing urban areas. Granted, the infrastructure limits in Indian cities can be severe. But these arguments ignore the opportunities of monetizing increases in land values to finance higher capacity and higher quality infrastructure networks, and to increase the supply of office space as well as affordable housing for low- and middle-income groups.

Mumbai's FSI ratios, at around 1.0–1.5—low compared with international standards—have significant consequences. Because low FSIs push development to the outskirts of the urban area, sprawl ensues. Sprawl is caused by development limits in areas where the market would otherwise allow higher density to compensate for high land prices resulting from high accessibility. And FSI-induced sprawl affects households through such daily costs as more time and expense for commuting.[8]

Furthermore, Indian cities have blanket FSIs that cover large areas—thus missing opportunities to strategically increase densities around infrastructure networks. In fact, "granularity"—or extremely local variations—in FSI design and in coordination of land use to exploit infrastructure placement is the bedrock of good urban planning. Best international practice in cities such as New York, Seoul, and Singapore suggests that planners need to keep in mind that while density should not overwhelm infrastructure capacity, neither should it suboptimally use infrastructure networks.

In New York, for instance, FSIs in commercial districts in Midtown and downtown Manhattan allow much higher densities than residential areas on the Upper East and West Sides. Also, FSI adjustments should go hand in hand with infrastructure investments. A good practice example in this coordination is Singapore, where FSIs vary by location and type of use as well as infrastructure availability. In areas near metro stations FSIs are typically higher because the transit system can accommodate the increased density and activity.

Finally, it is important to stress that FSIs are part of an overall planning strategy and that they cannot be considered in isolation. FSIs and higher infrastructure investment should be viewed as the components of a virtuous cycle. Similarly, if strong infrastructure is in place, higher densities can be permitted, thus enabling higher FSIs.

Challenges for Commuting and Moving Freight

Because of land shortages and building regulations, populations and businesses are driven away from metropolitan cores to the outskirts of large metropolitan areas. Deficiencies in getting around compound the issue. A good, reliable urban transport system allows people to make efficient choices between where they live and where they work. Alternatively, a weak system only exacerbates the problems of stringent regulations in land markets. People may, for instance, be forced to live in slums if the formal housing market is unaffordable or they cannot access less expensive housing on the outskirts of cities because the transit system is unreliable or costly.

In Indian cities, congestion poses a major challenge. The combination of narrow roads and increased private car ownership means that motorized travel speed in all cities is barely faster than riding a bicycle. Public transport has not kept up with the expanding mass of urban commuters, and even though initiatives are under way to address this issue, its limited integration with other modes of transport and onerous land use planning are holding down how much it is used. One measure of public transport ridership (across modes) credits Mumbai with a high share of about 45 percent; in New Delhi, it's less than 20 percent. Those compare with more than 60 percent in Moscow and 50 percent in Singapore.[9] Urban transport experts suggest that limited integration with other modes of transport, partly because of land use planning, keeps down the amount of public transport use. Though a global role model in construction and operations quality, for example, the New Delhi metro is not well integrated with high-quality feeder services. It carries only 6,520 riders per system kilometer, well below Mexico City's 19,200, Moscow's 21,400, or Sao Paulo's 27,800.[10]

The cost of public transport also is a factor in low transit ridership. Public transport in Indian cities is the least affordable among cities in a cross-country sample using a public transport affordability index, adjusted for per capita income. The cost in Mumbai, for instance, is more than twice that in London and five times that in New York. While affordability scores are largely driven by relative prices of public transport, public transport also tends to be less attractive and people are inclined to walk or ride a bicycle. But with small increases in income, people prefer to ride a motorcycle rather than ride a bus, as the marginal cost of using a motorcycle is much lower. In New Delhi, petrol costs Rs. 50 per liter and, with mileage per liter on a typical motorcycle of 80 km, the marginal operating cost per kilometer is Rs. 0.60—versus a cost of Rs. 1.50 per kilometer for a bus and Rs. 1.80 on the metro. In addition, the convenience and social image of motorcycle ownership reduces the incentive to use public transport (despite the burden on congestion and pollution).

Just as urban transport services are key for connecting people to jobs in a city, city businesses require an adequate logistics system and road infrastructure network to reach local, regional, and national markets. Market access provides incentives for firms to increase production scale and to specialize.

As businesses relocate to the suburbs, however, they face increasing market-connection costs. Freight rates between metropolitan cores and their peripheries are as high as Rs. 5.2 per ton-km ($0.12)—twice the national average and more than five times the rates in the United States. One reason for India's high transport costs is the use of smaller, older trucks on metropolitan routes. There is also a higher share of empty backhauls (truckers returning without a load) on metropolitan routes. And trucks on metropolitan routes travel about 25,000 km annually—just a quarter of what is required to be economically viable. To improve coordination and reduce the cost of metropolitan freight movements, trucking firms could adopt logistics management systems or form trucking associations.

The Indian logistics system is also plagued by inefficiencies caused by poor infrastructure and equipment, high handling costs, theft, and damage. Together those make costs to users much larger than in other countries at a similar stage of development. It has been estimated that the deficiencies in its logistics cost India an extra $45 billion a year.[11]

Spatial Disparities in Access to Basic Services

Access to basic services and the quality of those services are the foundation of households' living standards and firms' performance, but India still has a long way to go in providing universal access to such services. No major city in India provides more than a small percentage of its population, if any, with continuous water supplies. Yet in Jakarta access is 90 percent and in Manila it is 88 percent. In New Delhi, 59 percent of industrial establishments experience low water pressure. And countrywide differences in access are large, with access to services such as sewerage and drainage worsening as city size decreases. Rural areas experience the lowest access levels.

Wide spatial variations exist within India's largest seven metropolitan areas. These areas overall have better access to services than do rural areas, but wide variations exist between their cores and peripheries. While 93 percent of households in the core have access to drainage, for example, the share falls to 70 percent a mere 5 km from the core. Survey data from large cities such as Bangalore also confirm that access to network services such as piped water is concentrated in the core and that it falls rapidly toward the periphery.

Inefficiencies in delivery and tariffs that do not cover costs jeopardize sustainability and hold back services expansion. In principle, user charges should generate revenue that is at least enough to cover operation and maintenance (O&M) costs and asset depreciation, and to yield an adequate return on assets. The operating ratios (O&M cost/revenue) from a small sample of 20 Indian cities, however, indicate that only a third of water utilities cover their O&M costs. Bhopal, Indore, Kolkata, and Mathura rank at the bottom, and financial sustainability is a serious concern for them. Beyond institutional improvements, water utilities must make an effort to achieve 100 percent metered connections. Of the 20 cities, Bangalore, Coimbatore, Mumbai, and Nashik are the only ones with at least 70 percent metered connections. Nagpur has 40 percent, and none of the others achieves even 10 percent.

A COORDINATED RESPONSE FOR MANAGING URBANIZATION IS IMPERATIVE

Working along these lines, policymakers will be able to knowledgeably come up with ways to manage economic efficiency and spatial equity trade-offs associated with India's urbanization. The constraints to agglomeration economies suggest inefficiencies in land markets and lack of coordination between land use and infrastructure improvements that together weaken the potential of urban areas. As policymakers work toward renewing existing cities and building new towns, they need to dismantle the country's urban planning "license raj." Economic prosperity is dependent upon getting urban planning right, and the country's policymakers have been grappling with the challenges. The Jawaharlal Nehru National Urban Renewal Mission (JNNURM), an ambitious government program launched in 2005, raised the profile of urban challenges by catalyzing about $24 billion of investments in infrastructure in Indian cities. According to March 2012 data from the Ministry of Urban Development, the mission has approved projects worth $11.2 billion from government-allocated resources. JNNURM envisaged that 23 reforms (11 mandatory and 12 optional) were to be implemented by 67 "mission cities" under JNNURM, including rationalizing stamp duty to no more than 5 percent by 2012, reforming rent control laws (balancing the interests of landlords and tenants), repealing the Urban Land Ceiling and Regulation Act, and recovering operation and maintenance costs from user charges (table 2).

TABLE 2. LAND AND PROPERTY REFORMS UNDER THE JAWAHARLAL NEHRU NATIONAL URBAN RENEWAL MISSION

Reform	States that have passed the reform (of 31 states)	Cities that have passed the reform (of 67 cities)
Rationalization of stamp duty	23	n.a.
Reform in rent control	15	n.a.
Repeal of the Urban Land Ceiling and Regulation Act	30	n.a.
Revision of building by-laws	n.a.	52
Simplification of land conversion laws	n.a.	52
Property title certification system	n.a.	0
Earmarking land for "economically weaker sections" and "low-income groups"	n.a.	54
Computerized process of registration	n.a.	51

Note: n.a. = not applicable.
Source: Jawaharlal Nehru National Urban Renewal Mission, http://jnnurm.nic.in.

Although the intended reforms are laudable and comprehensive, their implementation and impact are not yet clear. The evaluation design is largely based on self-reported information, and inputs and processes are assessed more than outcomes and impacts. To illustrate, consider three publicly available studies:

- *Appraisal by the Planning Commission (March 2010), carried out under the midterm appraisal of the Eleventh Five Year Plan.* A desk review done by an expert committee of the Planning Commission concluded that JNNURM, while effective in renewing focus on the urban sector and in making huge investments in urban infrastructure, had shown lackluster performance when it came to reforms critical to improving accountability and urban governance. It found that capacity building remained a key constraint for effectively implementing infrastructure projects and reform measures and that most cities had not embraced the notion of integrated urban planning when preparing their development plans, even though that is required by JNNURM.

- *Appraisal by the High Powered Expert Committee for Estimating Investment Requirements for Urban Infrastructure Services (March 2011).* After its own desk review, the committee concurred with the Planning Commission. It also highlighted JNNURM's failure to make cities financially sustainable and noted the limited progress in municipal bonds and public-private partnership arrangements.

- *Independent appraisal by Grant Thornton (May 2011).* The Ministry of Urban Development commissioned an independent midterm appraisal by the consulting firm Grant Thornton, whose findings were included in the ministry's annual update on JNNURM for 2010–2011. This appraisal was more rigorous than the previous two and included field visits to 41 cities. The lack of municipal capacity, allowing only a minimal role for local bodies in preparing city development plans or detailed project reports, was noted. In addition, the appraisal found that no environmental or social impact assessments were made during preparation of detailed project reports and that stakeholders were not consulted.

JNNURM has undoubtedly raised the profile of urban issues among policymakers. But there is yet to be an overall comprehensive impact evaluation study of JNNURM. The various assessments so far have highlighted challenges in capacity building and project selection. Since the Twelfth Five Year Plan is looking at options for shaping the second phase of JNNURM, an assessment of progress to date, including any impediments in implementation, should be a priority.

One of the important decisions facing policymakers is to determine who is responsible for implementing urban reforms in a federal system with overlapping national, state, and municipal jurisdictions. Some very local or neighborhood decisions on densification and infrastructure planning are often decided by the state government, while the guidelines on land valuation are handled by the national and state governments, with some input from districts (not necessarily municipalities). Likewise, urban basic services, such as water supply, are often provided by state public health and engineering departments. These approaches pass up potential economies of scale and scope from different service options across settlements with varying densities.

Policymakers should also identify incentives for coordination among jurisdictions and administrative units, which would allow service providers to exploit economies of scale. The experiences of other countries suggest several criteria for designing metropolitan governance structures. Among them are: including efficiency in exploiting economies of scale and the ability to reduce negative spillovers across municipal boundaries; equity in sharing costs and benefits of services fairly across the metropolitan area; accountability for decisionmaking; and local responsiveness. In India, agencies such as the Bangalore Metropolitan Region Development Authority and the Mumbai Metropolitan Regional Development Authority have been set up to encourage metropolitan-wide functional and investment coordination. How effective these institutions are in performing their intended roles, and their ability to manage efficiency, equity, and accountability across the metropolitan area, remains to be seen.

NOTES

1   See World Bank, *World Development Report 2009: Reshaping Economic Geography* (Washington, D.C.: World Bank, 2008), and Michael Spence et al., *Urbanization and Growth* (Washington, D.C.: World Bank/Commission on Growth and Development, 2009).

2   Tara Vishwanath, Somik Lall, et al., *Urbanization Beyond Municipal Boundaries: Nurturing Metropolitan Economies and Connecting Peri-Urban Areas in India* (Washington, D.C.: World Bank, 2009), https://openknowledge.worldbank.org/bitstream/handle/10986 /13105/757340PUB0EPI0001300pubdate02021013.pdf?sequence=1.

3   District data on all manufacturing employment (including establishments smaller than factories) from the economic censuses of 1998 and 2005 show the same trends (Ministry of Statistics and Programme Implementation 1998 and 2005).

4   Ministry of Statistics and Programme Implementation, Central Statistical Organisation, *Economic Census 1998: All India Report*, and Government of India, Ministry of Statistics and Program Implementation, *Provisional Results of Fifth Economic Census 2005: All India Report*, 2006.

5   Vishwanath, Lall, et al., *Urbanization Beyond Municipal Boundaries*.

6   For Brazil, see Peter Townroe, "Location Factors in the Decentralization of Industry: A Survey of Metropolitan São Paulo," Staff Working Paper 517, World Bank, 1981, and Eric R. Hansen, "Why Do Firms Locate Where They Do?" Discussion Paper UDD25, World Bank, 1983. For Korea, see Dong Hoon Chun and Kyu Sik Lee, "Changing Location Patterns of Population and Employment in the Seoul Region," Discussion Paper UDD65, World Bank, 1985, and J. Vernon Henderson, T. Lee, and J-Y Lee, "Externalities and Industrial Deconcentration Under Rapid Growth," mimeo, Brown University, 1999. One review paper highlighted that the general trend of urban development included dispersal from the center to the periphery of both population and employment, with the largest metropolitan areas converging to decentralized and multiple subcentered areas. See Gregory K. Ingram, "Patterns of Metropolitan Development: What Have We Learned?" *Urban Studies* 5, no. 7 (1998).

7   World Bank, *World Development Report 2009: Reshaping Economic Geography* (Washington, D.C.: World Bank, 2008).

8   Alain Bertaud, "Mumbai FSI/FAR Conundrum: The Perfect Storm—The Four Factors Restricting the Construction of New Floor Space in Mumbai," http://alain-bertaud.com/AB_Files/AB_Mumbai_FSI_conundrum.pdf, 2004.

9   Vishwanath, Lall, et al., *Urbanization Beyond Municipal Boundaries*.

10 "City Pages," Metrobits, http://mic-ro.com/metro/selection.html, accessed June 2011.

11 Rajat Gupta, Hemang Mehta, and Thomas Netzer, "Building India: Transforming India's Logistics Infrastructure," *McKinsey Quarterly*, 2010.

→

CHAPTER 10

RENOVATING LAND MANAGEMENT

BARUN S. MITRA AND MADHUMITA D. MITRA

THE CENTRALITY OF LAND

India's land management regime has for decades been mired in obsolete laws and misguided policies that distort markets, enable corruption, and deny fundamental property rights. Current land policies are a hodgepodge of outdated laws and even more obsolete ways of thinking, many of which are rooted in colonial India or even in classical Hindu law.

Land is the only asset that most Indians, even the poorest, possess to at least some degree, but technicalities often prevent them from claiming legal ownership. A functioning land market founded on strong property rights would expand the opportunities for economic advancement for those who possess land, empowering them as citizens in a democratic India. Such a market would also allow those with wealth to access and invest in property and engage with landowners in mutually beneficial transactions, rather than trying to use their waning political influence to access land.

Twin difficulties lie at the core of India's land management challenge today. First, the land market is broken, stymied by high transaction costs, including a range of taxes and duties, rampant corruption, and inappropriate regulatory and zoning burdens, which perpetuate the gap between supply and demand, and consequently corruption. Second, it is necessary to reform the land acquisition system, which has deprived millions of Indians of their property without just process or compensation. Several recent pieces of legislation—notably the Right to Fair Compensation and Transparency in Land Acquisition, Rehabilitation, and Resettlement Act—are well-intentioned. But they remain untested and create serious concerns among property developers, who worry that they will impede growth, raise the cost of land purchases and complicate the process of capitalization of land assets. Correcting these two fundamental flaws will not be a quick or easy process, but the next government ought to take several priority steps—including lowering land-related taxes and fees, delegating zoning regulations to local bodies, and creatively reforming the land record system—to do so over its five-year term.

DISTORTED MARKETS AND REGULATORY BURDENS

High Transaction Costs

The most fundamental problem associated with land in India today is the high cost of transactions. This has completely distorted the market for land. The distortion is best evidenced by the National Sample Survey Organization (NSSO) survey on land in 2003–2004, which found that about 40 percent of farmers would like to sell their land and move out of agriculture. At the same time, $100 billion worth of domestic and foreign investments—largely infrastructure and mining projects—have been stuck due to land-related disputes and environmental regulations.

The land market is thus characterized by this enormous gulf between supply and demand. Sellers cannot easily find a buyer at an appropriate price, while buyers can't easily access the willing sellers. This gap between supply and demand has allowed middlemen, who offer to meditate at a price, to thrive, further driving up transaction costs.

It is common knowledge that the cost of real estate in urban centers across India is referred to in terms of "forty-sixty," "fifty-fifty," "sixty-forty," and so on. This means that 60, 50, or 40 percent of the real price would be paid in cash or in kind and will not be reflected in the official price at which the transfer will be registered. It is not unusual for real estate brokers to refuse an offer if they learn that one intends to buy or sell a property by making the full payment and taking responsibility for the full legal duties and taxes.

In this environment, it is hardly a surprise that corruption thrives in and around the real estate market. Such corruption has become so institutionalized that even when a buyer and seller agree to pay the sale amount in full, legally, one would still have to pay about 1–2 percent of the transaction value as bribes at the government office where such transactions are registered. Without this "speed money," the bureaucracy could raise any number of objections to the sale, delaying the transaction and causing a greater loss.

Infrastructure and real estate are perceived to be the most vulnerable to corruption and fraud in India because they are so highly regulated. Corruption studies indicate that need-based services, like land records and registration, housing, access to forests (for fuel wood and other produce), the Mahatma Gandhi National Rural Employment Guarantee Act, and banking and police, provide the most opportunities for corruption. Politicians and bureaucrats exercise a great deal of discretion over land regulation. Bribes are paid to departmental officials as well as to deed writers and property agents. In fact, deed writers and property agents serve as such a seamless conduit for a hierarchy of public servants that the illegal cost of the transaction is hard to distinguish from the statutory fees. Anecdotally, it is common knowledge that the real estate sector is where politicians and public servants park their ill-gotten wealth.

In an article written in 2011, a back-of-the-envelope calculation by Barun Mitra and Mohit Satyanand of the Liberty Institute in New Delhi estimated that "black money" totaling about 1–2 percent of India's GDP was being generated on account of real estate and land transactions.[1] The buyers and sellers seek to declare a lower price for the property in an attempt to reduce the burden of taxes, fees, and duties. Rarely are fully "white" transactions found unless the seller and the buyer are required to disclose the full value of the transaction for settling loans or other forms of legal reporting. On paper, efforts such as fixing circle rates (government-set minimum rates for land prices) at assumed market rates to prevent revenue leakages have not worked because the rates are rarely based on on-the-ground realities.

More formal bribe estimation studies provide an understanding of the total amounts involved in corruption. Transparency International's *India Corruption Study* in 2005 estimated that bribes worth Rs. 31,260 million ($625 million) were paid for land administration services in a year. This includes services to get property registered and mutated and to settle property tax dues. The *India Corruption Study* of 2008, which focused on households below the poverty line, mostly in rural areas, found that an estimated Rs. 1,234 million ($24.7 million) was paid in bribes for land records and registration services by the 23,000 surveyed households in a year. Just two of the sectors, land records/registration and housing, together contributed nearly a third of the total bribes paid. In terms of perception of levels of corruption, the study ranked police services as the most corrupt, followed by land records/registration, and housing.[2]

Economists Bibek Debroy and Laveesh Bhandari, in their 2012 book *Corruption in India*, tried to estimate levels of corruption across a whole range of sectors. The authors estimated that 1.26 percent of India's total 2010–2011 GDP was the total "private earnings of public officials." Of the total bribes paid, about 13.6 percent was from real estate, ownership of dwellings, and business services.[3]

To break this cycle of inefficiencies and corruption, India's next government must facilitate an efficient land market by substantially reducing transaction costs, lowering regulatory barriers, and making the process as transparent as possible.

The first step toward achieving this goal demands that policymakers reconceptualize poverty with regard to land. Poverty has been traditionally characterized by the lack of capital—in this case, land. The time has come to expand this definition to include the inability to capitalize those assets already held. A functioning and efficient land market would help unlock the capitalization potential of land as a primary asset. For decades, governments have been looking at land and real estate sectors as sources of easy revenue under the misguided belief that this affects only the rich who can afford to pay. The error pertains to the belief that capital in the form of land should be taxed since the owners may not have directly contributed to the appreciation of its value.

But the impact of high transaction cost is affecting all, and taxing capital assets is contributing to the misallocation of resources, tax avoidance, and corruption. Rather than taxing capital, the focus needs to be on optimizing the use of capital assets by reducing transaction costs as much as possible. The focus of taxation should be the income from the capital deployed, or on consumption based on higher income.

This would require greatly reducing or eliminating various taxes, duties, and fees that impinge on land and real estate transactions, including stamp duties, registration fees, capital gains taxes, transfers, and mutation costs. A minimal registration fee to cover the cost of maintaining transfer and transaction records should be adequate.

Zoning and Regulations

Opaque and rigid zoning and land use regulations have invariably failed to keep pace with the rapidly changing situation on the ground. This has led to gross corruption both within government and among middlemen who specialize, for a price, in expediting changes in land use.

The price of land is determined by its use. Agricultural land typically fetches the lowest price. The price climbs as the land is designated for more intensive purposes, such as residential, industrial, or commercial use. A substantial part of the conflict and protest surrounding land has been on account of compensation, when land price is seen not to reflect the compensation being offered.

Conversion of land use—particularly the conversion of agricultural land for non-agricultural purposes—is the biggest barrier to a fair land market. With demand for land for industrial and infrastructural purposes increasing, it is only a few powerful interests in collusion with public officials who manage to subvert the restrictive land use conversion laws at the cost of the wider public. As a result, ordinary people may have to lose their land for such interests to set up their projects.

While the purpose of restricting land use change from agriculture to non-agriculture was primarily to improve food security, this is no longer a significant concern. Furthermore, unlike during British rule, retaining land for the purpose of agriculture to generate revenue is no longer a valid proposition, as land revenue earned by the government is negligible. Apart from the corruption that is bred in the process of approval seeking from various government departments—from revenue to the income tax—to change land use, the whole concept is regressive and counterproductive.

Yet the government's National Land Utilization Policy 2013 discussion paper continues to harp on the need to meet food security and livelihood concerns by placing reasonable restrictions on the acquisition and conversion of certain types of agricultural land such as prime agricultural lands, command areas of irrigation projects, double-cropped land, and agricultural lands essential for livelihood of rural and tribal populations.

Another retrograde position that the government continues to pursue is the land ceiling policy introduced as part of the land reforms initiative postindependence. It imposes limits on agricultural lands that individuals, institutions, and corporations can hold. Similar laws in urban areas were abolished over the years after the government realized that it had created an artificial scarcity of land and consequent high prices. Even while acknowledging the futility of land distribution, the National Land Reforms Policy 2013 has desired that States lower the agricultural land ceiling to 5–10 acres in the case of irrigated land and 10–15 acres for non-irrigated land. This has not gone down well with the states that have learned from their experience that fragmented land holdings provide neither sustainable agriculture nor adequate livelihood support for rural households. States like Andhra Pradesh, Punjab, Rajasthan, and even West Bengal—a state long ruled by the communists—have raised their land ceiling limits since the policy was introduced in the 1950s. Instead of retrograde positions like the land ceiling, the central government should be looking at consolidating such fragmented land into viable farm units.

Under the Indian constitution, land is a state subject, but it is the only factor of production that is always local. The two other factors of production—labor and capital—are increasingly mobile. Maintaining land records at the local level and allowing communities to decide on local land use issues for themselves could significantly empower the people and local government while bypassing the current corrupt and burdensome system. It would also make many local bodies more financially viable, more autonomous, and less dependent on higher tiers of government.

It is therefore logical to constitutionally allocate jurisdiction over land-related regulations to the hands of the local government, either the city councils or village *panchayats*, so that local communities would be able to hold their local representatives more directly responsible for policies that may enhance or depreciate the value of their land assets. The biggest advantage of such a devolution would be that the local government bodies would become much more financially viable, and by that same token would be held much more accountable by their own community.

EMINENT DOMAIN AND LAND ACQUISITION REFORM

After decades of chipping away at the fundamental right "to acquire, hold and dispose property" enshrined in Article 19(1)(f) of the constitution, this right was abolished by an amendment in 1978. The right to property now remains only a statutory right in Article 300-A: "No person shall be deprived of his property save by authority of law." Any property right violation can no longer be challenged as a violation of a fundamental right.

Eminent domain—the seizure of private land by government—has long been a key aspect of land governance around the world. In India, there is little doubt that eminent domain has been grossly abused, particularly by invoking the emergency clause of the Land Acquisition Act, 1894. In the absence of constitutional due process, land acquisitions frequently occur with little demonstrable public purpose or just compensation. An estimated 40–60 million people have lost their land to public and private acquisitions over the past fifty years, and many of these people go decades without finding permanent resettlement. Some have been moved more than once.

Similar conveyances of property, known technically as alienation, occur through colonial laws such as the Indian Forest Act, 1927, and other laws intended to protect forests and wildlife that over the years have negated the rights of traditional forest-dwelling communities.

Absent a fundamental right to property, the 1894 law formed the basis for expeditious expropriation of land from private landowners. Other colonial and post-colonial laws also exist to take away private land for railways, electricity, telecommunication, mining and setting up special economic zones. Increasingly, the public purpose clause for exercising eminent domain has been frequently abused to favor private interests. District collectors have enormous discretionary powers to decide the urgency and compensation amount. The arbitrary application of compensation norms and lack of resettlement programs displaced large numbers of people from project areas and took away their livelihoods. Two recent legislative initiatives aim to reform this broken and undemocratic system.

In its first recognition that land issues are at the top of the political agenda, India's Parliament passed the Scheduled Tribes and Other Traditional Forest Dwellers (Recognition of Forest Rights) Act (FRA) in 2006. The law addressed the historic alienation of tribal populations and other traditional forest dwellers by granting legal recognition to their individual right to title over forest land that they had been occupying for self-cultivation or habitation as of December 13, 2005. These communities were also given community rights over forest resources, including ownership of all non-timber forest produce, and the right to protect, conserve, and manage community forests of their village.

The FRA is significant because it reflects the changing popular perception on land and property. It is the first legislation that seeks to recognize and protect land rights since the deletion of the right to property from the Indian constitution in 1978.

In 2013, once again, in a rare act of political consensus, Parliament acted to reform the rampant and historical injustices of forcible land acquisitions by passing the Right to Fair Compensation and Transparency in Land Acquisition, Rehabilitation, and Resettlement Act (LARR). The LARR aims at providing fair compensation, resettlement, and rehabilitation of people whose land is taken, safeguards for the well-being of tribal and disadvantaged populations, and a transparent process of land acquisition. Since it is an enabling statute, it permits state governments to complement it with their own laws without diluting its provisions.

The LARR sets out a convoluted determination of compensation likely to further distort the land market. The law provides for compensation up to four times the market value in rural areas and doubles it. In fact, the law retrospectively applies to cases where no land acquisition award has been made and in cases in which the land was acquired five years ago but no compensation was paid or the acquirer has not taken possession. Where acquired land is sold to a third party for a higher price, 40 percent of the appreciated land value (or profit) is to be shared with the original owner(s).

The most significant and contentious development has been on the issue of consent. Where public-private partnership projects are involved, the 2013 law requires the consent of no less than 70 percent of those whose land is being acquired. For acquisition by private companies, 80 percent must give their consent for the deal to go through. Given the fragmented land holdings and unclear land titles, private acquirers of land have been apprehensive about their ability to obtain consent, an activity that previously was taken care of by the government. The contention stems from determining who the legitimate stakeholders are and how to acquire their consent. Issues such as whether a referendum should be held among stakeholders, whether a community should be allowed to negotiate directly with the project sponsors, or whether a community can decide on a larger project when it has no real ownership over local land and natural resources open up a Pandora's box and fears of holdouts. To safeguard food security, the law also directs states to impose caps on the acquisition of multi-crop areas and other areas under agricultural cultivation, raising the prospect of undercapitalization of farmers' assets and reducing their ability to invest and improve their agricultural productivity as well.

As a positive feature, the acquisition process under the new law involves multiple checks and balances with the participation of local *panchayati raj* institutions before the start of any acquisition proceedings. Independent social assessment of proposed projects and monitoring committees at the national and state level are expected to ensure that the government's obligations are met.

The government is at pains to emphasize the distinction between "acquisition" and "purchase," saying that the LARR applies only to acquisition by the central and state governments for any public purpose, while private actors remain free to purchase land directly from landowners. The underlying intent of the policy to shift from land acquisition to land purchase is laudable, but it does not allay the disquiet among commercial land purchasers that the new law would make projects economically not viable, make land transactions more difficult, widen the gap between supply and demand for land, and further fuel conflict. This ostensible tension between property rights and effective land use and development remains a core challenge in making good on land acquisition reforms.

The patchy implementation of the FRA in most states shows that it will not be easy to shake off the deeply entrenched interests of public servants in maintaining the status quo ante. Providing adequate evidence in support of their claims to land title to the satisfaction of the authorities is proving to be a difficult journey for most of the poor and marginalized communities that live in and around forest areas.

REFORMING LAND RECORDS

The poor quality of India's land records impedes both the development of a sustainable land market and meaningful reforms in land acquisition. Improving these records should therefore be a top agenda item for the next government.

A comprehensive land settlement survey has not been undertaken since the British left India. Land records are not easily accessible, nor are they transparent, opening the doors for manipulation and corruption. At the same time, their importance cannot be overstated: without accurate and accessible records, meaningful reforms to India's land management will be virtually impossible.

Governments have been trying to digitize land records and make them more easily accessible since the late 1990s. It is estimated that there are about 900 million plots of land that need to be recorded and updated. But digitizing the existing records carries the prospect of transferring the present errors as well and adds a further layer of complication while introducing prospects for conflict and corruption.

The National Land Records Modernization Program (NLRMP), launched in 2008, hopes to provide landowners with a conclusive title guarantee by replacing the existing system of presumptive titles. The program calls for updating survey and settlement records, computerizing land records and registration, and modernizing record-keeping practices. The process would, in its ideal form, build a transparent and integrated system of online real-time land records, ensure automatic mutation, and facilitate a conclusive titling system.

But despite its lofty goals, the program's track record is not promising. Of the 672 districts in 35 states and union territories, only 379 districts in 32 states and union territories are currently covered under the program. Of these, only four states—Tripura, Gujarat, Haryana, and Karnataka—have achieved the final stage in the program by simultaneously recording property transfers in the Record of Rights register. Most states have managed only to computerize the existing not-very-reliable register and make the data available on the Internet, but only seventeen states and union territories have actually stopped issuing manual Record of Rights registers. Much work remains to be done to modernize the ground truthing process. Due diligence ground surveys are still undertaken with measuring tapes and with metes and bounds descriptions of land based on very old and nearly illegible maps. Only seven states and union territories have digitized the maps of their boundaries. The current goal of the central government to complete the various stages of the NLRMP is 2016, but given the slow progress of the project, it is highly unlikely to meet the deadline.

The NLRMP experience should demonstrate that the scale of the problem and its associated complexity make it unlikely that any central-ized state agency will be able to undertake such a massive exercise. A diver-sified and multilayer system with stakeholders, such as surveyors, insurance and financial companies, and local government bodies, could instead be invited to update and maintain land records in a transparent manner.

Using geographic information systems (GIS) and satellite imagery, it would be possible to decentralize the whole process, while allowing all of it to integrate as required. This would also enable the emergence of inter-mediaries that could focus on effectively undertaking due diligence to ensure that the relevant record and status of the land are correct before transactions are completed. Such a process will have the dual advantage of land records getting updated not in a linear manner from one end of the state to another, but depending on the diverse needs in different localities, a GIS platform will allow integration of the information from different locations, eventually building a comprehensive land records system.

The procedure laid down for the granting of titles under the FRA already provides an example of the bottom-up approach that allows com-munities to document and file their claims with the appropriate commit-tees set up by the state government.

A complete implementation of the NLRMP will not necessarily ensure transparency in land transactions. Calculation of fair compensation based on the latest market rates can be facilitated only on the basis of legal titles validated by law. This calls for early enactment of the Land Titling Bill enabling the states to grant conclusive title guarantees to land owners. Property transfers must legally validate transfer of titles rather than merely enabling registration of the deed. The need of the hour is to amend the law to allow registration of title instead of registration of deed.

DEEPENING DEMOCRACY

The extent of land alienation in India has sustained a growing number of land-related protests spanning the country over the past few decades. Across party lines, members of the political establishment are beginning to realize that, while they may want to invoke eminent domain to acquire private land to favor their cronies for some consideration, the political cost of doing so has grown significantly.

The impact of legislation and political approaches to stem the tide of popular anger against arbitrary land acquisition and displacement is already showing. In an unprecedented hearing of stakeholders, twelve *gram sabhas* (village councils) rejected bauxite mining for a multinational company's alumina refinery in Odisha's Niyamgiri Hills, where the Dongri Kondh tribal group's habitation and traditional livelihood would have been affected. The Supreme Court upheld the rights of the communities under the Recognition of Forest Rights Act to make such decisions, and tribal and forest dwelling communities have begun claiming their rights under the law.

These new initiatives are significant because they recognize land rights. But such politicized attempts to champion the rights of the people to land and defuse the current popular resentment also do not address the key issue of regularizing the land market. Such a market is necessary for ownership rights to be really meaningful. Property owners must have the right to alienate those rights, either in full or in part. Mortgaging, renting, leasing, and selling are all ways of extracting the capitalizing potential of land assets, providing an incentive for putting the asset to more productive use.

The silver lining lies in the growing recognition among a section of people, particularly small land owners, that rights without the freedom to capitalize will become a poverty trap. In parts of rural India where land was distributed among the landless in the 1960s and 1970s, some are beginning to articulate their own experience of this trap. They had received titles, with the caveat that they could not alienate their ownership rights. Today, many of them recognize that they can neither expand their agriculture nor move out of it, tied as they are to their land that cannot be capitalized. They are thus unable to escape the vicious cycle of poverty.

By recognizing ownership rights over land but grossly restricting delineation, as in the case of the FRA, government distributed lands, and lands held by certain communities, existing policies have undermined the capitalizing potential of land. If allowed to persist, this will further aggravate the huge mismatch between supply and demand for land, contribute to gross misallocation of resources, and significantly add to economic inefficiencies and corruption.

Clearly, India faces a land policy dilemma. While the misuse of land acquisition over the past five decades had eroded popular trust in the political leadership, as it showered undue benefits on a few well-connected and powerful people at the cost of the masses, the new land policy will adversely affect those who own land, as well as those who may want to access land.

With all this in mind, the new national government taking office in 2014 has some difficult work ahead. Reforming land management remains a sizable task, but the following actions ought to take priority:

- Clearly articulate the need to create a functioning land market, which will significantly reduce the need to invoke eminent domain.

- Partner with stakeholders in both the private and public sectors to build a modern land record-keeping infrastructure based on geographic information systems and other imaging technologies.

- Abolish land ceiling laws, particularly in agriculture, to facilitate consolidation of such fragmented land into viable farm units.

- Eliminate the capital gains tax. In a poor country, taxing capital is self-defeating.

- Drastically reduce or eliminate fees and taxes that impede land transactions and increase the potential for corruption, replacing them with a nominal fee to cover only the administrative costs of keeping up-to-date land records.

- Transfer authority over land-related regulation such as zoning, land use, and environmental concerns to local governments and councils.

- Severely restrict the scope of eminent domain to truly public purposes—with the consent of those affected—not to facilitate private investment and business projects.

- Recognize landowners' rights over forest and other environmental resources, as well as minerals, above or below the land.

- Enact a mines and minerals law that recognizes the rights of landowners and communities, and allow them to negotiate access and royalties directly with investors.

- Adopt a land titling law to grant conclusive title guarantee to landowners. Property transfers must legally validate the transfer of titles rather than merely enabling registration of the deed.

The new government cannot hope to turn the clock back and return to the days when the power of eminent domain could be invoked to favor the few at the cost of the many. Historically, the spread of ownership of property among wider sections of society has led to demands for accountability and political participation, and given rise to democracy. In India today, it is the poor and the marginalized who are demanding greater recognition of their land and property rights, indicating the depth of democracy's roots in the country. The political leadership can ignore this popular sentiment at its own peril. The choice before the new government is clear. Either it may attempt to stem the changing tide of popular perception of property ownership or seize the political opportunity and leverage the groundswell of opinion to bring about the much needed changes in laws governing land and related natural resources, and in so doing secure a place in history.

NOTES

1   Barun Mitra and Mohit Satyanand, "Chasing Black Money: In Search of Red Herrings," Discussion Paper, Liberty Institute, August 16, 2011, http://indefenceofliberty.org/story/4190/4288/Chasing-Black-Money-In-search-of-red-herrings.

2   Transparency International India, *India Corruption Study 2005* (New Delhi: Transparency International India, 2005). See also Transparency International India, *India Corruption Study 2008* (New Delhi: Transparency International India, 2008).

3   Bibek Debroy and Laveesh Bhandari, *Corruption in India: The DNA and the RNA* (New Delhi: Konark Publishers, 2012).

———————➤

CHAPTER 11

ADDRESSING WATER MANAGEMENT

———————————————————————————————➤

TUSHAAR SHAH AND SHILP VERMA

INDIA'S WATER CHALLENGE

The post-independence era has witnessed a deep transformation in India's water economy. Around 1950, India had an abundance of water resources, with more than 5,000 cubic meters per person per year. The key priority of government policy was to develop water resources to achieve national and household food security through massive investments in canal irrigation projects. Since then, the complexion of the challenge has morphed. Today, India is food-secure but increasingly water-insecure. A 3.5-fold expansion in population since 1950 has made India one of the most water-scarce countries in the world. Water availability is down to 1,200 cubic meters per person per year, barely sufficient to sustain economic growth and support human well-being.[1] The entire western Indian corridor from Punjab to Tamil Nadu is experiencing severe groundwater depletion and water quality deterioration.

In 2013, the World Resources Institute declared India among the world's 50 most water-stressed countries (the baseline water stress rank was 41).[2] The study also included Australia (ranked 45) in this league. However, the water stress that Australia faces has much less impact on its economy and the quality of its citizens' lives and livelihoods. The difference is that while

India "administers" its water economy, Australia "manages" it. India has focused on investment in infrastructure; Australia has concentrated on managing infrastructure. India has allowed the public sector share in infrastructure and services to shrink and has left the booming private informal water economy to its own devices. Australia has integrated the large public sector and a regulated private sector to dominate water service provision. India has hardly used pricing and economic instruments for demand management, barring mostly perverse subsidies. Australia has installed powerful devices for water demand management. India has enacted water laws that have remained unenforced and water policies that have remained only on paper. Australia has evolved an intricate system of licenses, permits, and water rights that shape the behavior of water users. Australia has built a large, organized, technologically savvy water industry; India has a large, unorganized, chaotic, informal water economy that is technologically primitive and beyond meaningful regulation. True, Australia became well-off before it became water-scarce, while India has become water-scarce long before it becomes well-off. Yet, there is a great deal India needs to imbibe from the experience of countries like Australia.

GRAND CHALLENGE I: CLOSE THE MANAGEMENT DEFICIT

India administers its water economy in a "resource development" mode; its biggest challenge now is to make a transition to "management" mode. This requires a focus on managing three components of the water economy: water resources, water infrastructure, and water services. The difficulty is that, thanks to poor management, the relative share of public systems in all three components has been declining. High-level officials glibly assert that the water challenge is not a challenge of resource scarcity, but one of resource governance and management. Yet, despite the vast challenges India faces, it has invested little in creating water management capacities, structures, and systems.

When it comes to water infrastructure, India is in a perpetual "build-neglect-rebuild" cycle, a sure indicator of poor management. As India urbanizes at a breakneck pace in the coming decades, it will invest massively in water infrastructure, especially urban and non-agricultural. However, without management capacities, these investments will yield poor returns, private or social. A major folly is to assume that the skills required to build an infrastructure are the same as those required to manage it. India does little to reskill engineers for successful management of water systems. There are more than a dozen state-level Water and Land Management Institutes. There are similar institutes for training in water supply and sanitation. The National Water Academy at Pune is supposed to provide higher-level skills. Several Indian Institutes of Technology (IITs) have strong hydrology departments. However, none of them offer training and education in *managing* water resources, infrastructure, and services.

Given the size and complexity of its water economy and its growing water challenges, India needs a much larger—and better—knowledge infrastructure than it currently has for research, training, and education. A first step would be to create a world-class water university with a focus on managing irrigation, urban and rural water supply and sanitation, and hydropower. Equally, India should invest in performance monitoring and benchmarking of public systems in irrigation, water supply, and sanitation.

GRAND CHALLENGE 2: IMPROVE PERFORMANCE OF PUBLIC IRRIGATION SYSTEMS

The decades following independence have witnessed tectonic shifts in the structure of India's water economy and its organization. While central and state governments and multilateral funding agencies continued to invest in gigantic irrigation projects, the overall management and performance of public irrigation systems suffered rapid deterioration. The colonial state managed irrigation systems as commercial enterprises; colonial India's irrigation department earned a 12 percent return on capital investment in irrigation until 1945. Irrigation managers levied and ruthlessly collected irrigation service fees at non-trivial rates, amounting to 25–40 percent of the value of output. Farmers complained about extortionate Irrigation Service Fees (ISF), but were assured irrigation service of a certain level because managers regularly invested in the maintenance and upkeep of the system.

Soon after independence, the situation began changing. The new welfare state relaxed norms of cost recovery. Some states found the cost of collection too high and abolished irrigation service fees altogether. Others refused to revise and rationalize the fee for decades. Gradually, collection discipline also deteriorated, with most states collecting just 10–15 percent of irrigation service fee demand based on highly subsidized rates. Budgets given to irrigation departments were barely enough to cover salaries, with little or nothing for operation and maintenance (O&M). By the late 1980s, many state governments banned new recruitment in their respective irrigation departments. Several states with millions of hectares under command areas were left with irrigation departments that were aging and shrinking. Gradually, as deferred maintenance mounted, irrigation command areas began to shrink. After 1990, India was faced with the sad prospect that investment in new projects and rehabilitating old projects kept pace, but the area actually served by public canals declined. When an irrigation service fee was vigorously collected, the paper trail created an excellent management information system. Now that the fee remains uncollected, there is no reliable information on how much area a system irrigates and the quality of service offered. Recent irrigation scams in Maharashtra and the late Y. S. Rajasekhara Reddy's *Jala Yagnam* (derisively referred to as *Dhana Yagnam*)[3] suggest that mega irrigation projects are driven by rent-seeking politicians. The focus is on the construction of irrigation systems, which offers opportunities for giving away lucrative contracts, and not on their management.

This situation calls for a major effort to revitalize the public irrigation sector. India already has about 40 million hectares (mha) of irrigation potential created from public irrigation systems. Of this, only 12–15 mha is actually used. The infrastructure already created can serve 2.5 times the area currently served simply by concentrating resources on clearing the backlog of deferred maintenance, tightening the management of irrigation systems, restoring the accountability relationship between farmers and irrigation staff, rationalizing the irrigation service fee and vigorously collecting it, and improving all-around management capacities in irrigation departments.

GRAND CHALLENGE 3: PROACTIVELY MANAGE AQUIFER STORAGE

While public irrigation has declined during the past five decades, private irrigation has experienced a veritable boom, based on groundwater wells and tube wells. From just around 250,000 in 1960, the number of energized irrigation wells in the country has soared to more than 20 million. At 65 mha under irrigation, this groundwater boom financed by private capital has given Indian agriculture three times as much irrigated area in fifty years as public irrigation investments did in two hundred years. Groundwater proved a "democratic resource" taking the benefit of irrigation to every corner of the country, far outside the reach of public canals. Groundwater wells also became the mainstay of small and marginal farmers eking out a living from their shrinking holdings by working their land more intensively. Farmers prefer well irrigation over canal irrigation because it is more reliable, available on demand, and offers greater water control, allowing them to adopt high-value farming systems.

In sum, then, over the past sixty years, Indian agriculture has shifted its reliance on irrigation from surface storage—large dams, small tanks, farm ponds, and canals—to aquifer storage. The country has some 215 billion cubic meters of government-managed surface storage that serve 12–15 mha; in contrast, it draws on about 230 billion cubic meters of groundwater that wets 65 mha. While the booming tube well economy has promoted intensification and diversification of farming systems, the sustainability of the groundwater aquifers itself has been increasingly brought into question. As alluvial and hard-rock aquifers in western and southern India's semi-arid climes have been relentlessly pumped, many are getting exhausted. In 2006, the Supreme Court acted *suo moto* on the deepening groundwater crisis and mandated the Central Ground Water Authority to control the over-exploitation of groundwater. Predictably, nothing came of it because the country has never applied itself seriously to the challenge of sustainable aquifer management.

For the future of Indian agriculture, managing groundwater aquifers has become more critical today than ever. While surface storage has been managed by irrigation departments and communities, aquifer storage remains largely unmanaged on the demand as well as the supply side. There is arguably an inherent bias against the proactive management of aquifer storage partly because the water policy institutions such as the Central Water Commission, National Water Development Authority, and irrigation departments at the state and central levels are all dominated by a civil engineering mindset trained to focus on surface water resources. The Central Ground Water Board, the custodian of the nation's aquifers, seems unable to break out of its monitoring and research role to assume a larger resource management mandate.

On the supply side of aquifer management, an urgent need is to operationalize two practices: conjunctive management of surface and groundwater, and managed aquifer recharge. Both are happening to some extent, but primarily by default. If done by design, as part of a deliberate strategy, these practices can go a long way toward managing India's aquifers. As canal systems become increasingly marginalized as irrigation providers, the main purpose they serve is recharging the aquifers. If the area wetted by a canal is expanded by vigorous operation and maintenance, a much larger area will benefit from recharge than is the case now. In hard-rock aquifer areas outside canal commands, an intensive managed aquifer recharge program in a decentralized format can, over years, help restore aquifers to near pre-development levels, as has been shown in the Saurashtra region of Gujarat. Regular de-silting of reservoirs is another immensely beneficial tool for practicing managed aquifer recharge. Using droughts and the Mahatma Gandhi National Rural Employment Guarantee Act to operationalize this on a large scale, as is being done in Gujarat, would go a long way toward augmenting aquifer storage.

Another reason that managing aquifer storage becomes critical is the need to release surface storage for urban and industrial needs. China, which is thirty years ahead of India in economic growth, has shown that as cities and industries grow, surface storage originally built for irrigation gets prioritized for urban and industrial needs, while agriculture is relegated to groundwater irrigation. This has also begun happening in India. In both countries, it occurred over years by default and stealth without systematic planning. But India needs to expect this trend to unfold, and it needs to plan the transition intelligently. There is also an argument in favor of surface storage over groundwater for water supply because it is free from geogenic contaminants such as fluoride, nitrates, arsenic, and cadmium, which are now found in high concentration in groundwater in large parts of India.

At 75 billion cubic meters per year, domestic and industrial water demand in India is already a third of its public reservoir storage of 215 billion cubic meters.[4] Most Indian cities are looking to distant reservoirs to meet growing water demand. During droughts, it is common for district collectors to ban irrigation and reserve reservoir water for municipal supply. This unplanned, ad hoc transition is inefficient, ineffective, and wasteful. Water losses en route are frequently 70 percent or more. Carryover storage is often insufficient to meet drinking water needs during a drought. To increase inflows in a major dam that feeds Jaipur, for example, the government of Rajasthan recently dismantled 30,000 anicuts in the catchment. Arguably, there might be merit in reducing canal irrigation from such dams, and prioritizing them for urban and industrial water needs, but encouraging managed aquifer recharge in the catchment so that groundwater can sustain irrigated agriculture.

GRAND CHALLENGE 4: INTEGRATE SELF-PROVISION, THE INFORMAL ECONOMY, AND PUBLIC PROVISION IN WATER SUPPLY AND SANITATION

Three-quarters of rural Indians self-supply their water directly from nature with minimal treatment; this figure is smaller and shrinking for urban India, but vast numbers of urban Indians still use self-supply to supplement public supply.[5] Self-provision is the result of the inability of public systems to meet demand; the informal economy is a response to the opportunity to profitably serve demand. Tanker water markets in urban India are pervasive and booming. However, private service providers are beginning to play an active role even in the sanitation space. During recent years, for example, several hundred specialty tankers—"honey suckers"— have been pressed into service by private sanitation service providers in Karnataka and Tamil Nadu to remove sewage from apartment blocks for use as farmyard manure.

India is in the throes of massive urbanization. However, its municipal water infrastructure is unable to keep pace with the growing population. As towns grow into cities, they need huge investments in upgrading and expanding their water supply and sewerage network. An even more pressing problem, however, is the revenue and business model. The critical mistake India may make is of trying to replicate the rich, industrialized countries' levels of service. But this would amount to throwing good money after bad. Copenhagen, Glasgow, and Essen have among the best water supply and sanitation service regimes in the world, but the tariff they collect ranges from $6.30 to $7.60 per cubic meter. At the other end are Ashgabat, Damascus, Khulna, and Chandigarh, where water supply and sanitation services are poor by global standards. There may be several reasons for this, but an important one is that utilities raise less than $0.05 per cubic meter as water tariff. In central Mumbai, some of the most expensive real estate in the world, filling a swimming pool from public water supplies costs Rs. 7 per cubic meter, while tanker water supply used for drinking by slum dwellers costs Rs. 80 per cubic meter. It will take decades until Indian water supply and sanitation utilities are able to raise tariffs to European levels even in purchasing power parity terms. India needs to find ways to improve water supply and sanitation services while keeping average tariffs at affordable levels.

According to the Central Pollution Control Board, urban India generated more than 42 billion liters of wastewater every day in 2011–2012.[6] The current sewage treatment capacity can handle less than a third of this; worse, due to poor upkeep and maintenance, only 55 percent of the treatment capacity is operational.[7] Treatment plants in most urban centers act merely as accumulators, and large quantities of untreated wastewater is released. No wonder the Ganga, Yamuna, and most other Indian rivers look and smell like drains as they pass through cities.

Several municipalities have planned investments in primary, secondary, and even tertiary treatment plants for recycling wastewater. However, the cost of tertiary treated water is high, and only industries can afford it. A largely ignored potential customer of wastewater is the peri-urban farmer. Each city can be reimagined as a high-class irrigation system that releases near-constant volumes of water on a daily basis, year-round. Much "waste" in wastewater is valuable nutrients that farmers pay a great deal to buy in the market. The 15 billion cubic meters of wastewater that Indian cities release annually can potentially irrigate 3 mha, nearly twice the command area of the Sardar Sarovar Project.[8]

Thousands of farmers in peri-urban areas already use municipal wastewater to irrigate crops. One 2012 study estimated that nearly 18,000 hectares were being irrigated by wastewater in and around seven cities in Gujarat.[9] Limited availability of freshwater, the rapid pace of urbanization, and farmers' preference for nutrient-rich wastewater are the key drivers

contributing to rapid expansion of wastewater irrigation. Several municipalities have devised formal or informal arrangements with peri-urban
farmers. Rajkot Municipal Corporation, for instance, has been supplying
water to two registered wastewater cooperatives since 1962.

The Indian discourse on water supply and sanitation involves leapfrogging from the current highly rationed public urban water supply to 24/7
supply, from near-zero tariff to full metered tariff, from minimal wastewater treatment to 100 percent treated wastewater being released into rivers.
A more realistic scenario is that India will go through a long intermediate
phase before it reaches this ideal state. It seems very likely that self-provision,
informal markets, and wastewater irrigation will grow in this phase. The
challenge is to create water supply and sanitation governance regimes that
meaningfully integrate self-provision, the informal economy, and public
provisioning into a viable and sustainable system.

Much of wastewater irrigation today is happening by default, rather
than by design, because wastewater is seen mostly as a problem and not as
a resource. In the near future, a greater proportion of India's freshwater
resources will need to be diverted for municipal and industrial uses.
Wastewater recycling and irrigation present an opportunity in urban and
peri-urban planning. Done well, municipal and industrial wastewater
systems can act as reliable and efficient irrigation systems for millions of
hectares of cultivable land.

GRAND CHALLENGE 5: REDUCE THE ENERGY FOOTPRINT OF GROUNDWATER IRRIGATION

India's groundwater boom has come at a high collateral cost: nearly bankrupt power distribution companies. During the heyday of rapid rural electrification, governments provided all manner of subsidies and incentives to
electrify irrigation wells. To save on transaction costs of metering and con-
sumption-linked billing, some state electricity boards dismantled meters
and shifted to a flat electricity tariff. This gave a strong fillip to groundwater irrigation but also turned farm power subsidies into a weapon of vote-
bank politics. Tamil Nadu, Punjab, and Karnataka declared free power;
going one better, Y. S. R. Reddy, the late Andhra Pradesh chief minister,
guaranteed free power until 2017 as a pre-poll promise. Governments are

supposed to reimburse this subsidy to the power distribution companies, but most reimburse only a part. The distribution companies meet the balance by avoiding essential investments, by borrowing commercially, and by raising the tariff to non-farm consumers. Many distribution companies have accumulated so much debt that no bank wants to lend to them anymore. Free power has also led to feeder-level anarchy and deterioration in the power supply environment, affecting rural quality of life and economic activity. Politicians are averse to arresting and reversing this downward spin because they fear electoral backlash. However, the overall cost of free farm power for rural societies in Tamil Nadu, Andhra Pradesh, and Karnataka is so high that there is scope to create a vote-bank by cutting power subsidies and improving the rural power supply environment.

This is precisely what Chief Minister Narendra Modi did in Gujarat. In 2003–2006, he invested Rs. 1,250 crore in the *Jyotigram* scheme for separating electricity feeders serving tube wells from those serving villages, imposed a power ration on agriculture feeders of eight hours per day, assured 24/7 power supply on village feeders, initiated legal proceedings against more than 100,000 power thieves, drastically enhanced vigilance to curb theft, and made meters mandatory on all new farm connections. Popular backlash aside, the electricity reforms won Modi a decisive majority in the 2007 elections. Gujarat's electricity utilities, which lost money until 2000, have begun making profits.[10] They issued 450,000 new metered farm power connections, mostly to marginal, scheduled caste, and scheduled tribe farmers. Surveys show that reduced hours of power supply are more than made up for by a better quality, full voltage, uninterrupted power supply. Anarchy on the feeder is under control. Gujarat is the only state where the overall groundwater regime is improving. Above all, Gujarat's agriculture has grown steadily at an incredible 9.6 percent annually during these years.[11]

India's farm power subsidies have crossed Rs. 35,000 crore per year. Much of these are perverse, leading to waste of power and water. There are smarter ways of delivering power subsidies. In addition to the Gujarat model of intelligent rationing, there is the West Bengal model, where all tube wells are metered, remotely read, and subject to time-of-day tariffs under which off-peak night power is supplied to farmers at highly subsidized rates. Both of these methods can curb wasteful use of groundwater and reduce the deadweight burden of subsidies on power distribution companies. The challenge is implementation. States such as Karnataka are separating feeders like Gujarat did but are doing nothing to control the anarchy and theft on the feeder. Such piecemeal reforms are actually making things worse. In the absence of vigilance, many farmers hook onto the village feeder and steal power around the clock.

GRAND CHALLENGE 6: SOLARIZE INDIA'S GROUNDWATER ECONOMY

A big opportunity for cracking India's perverse groundwater-electricity nexus is offered by the precipitous and continuing fall during recent years in global prices of solar photovoltaic cells. Once considered prohibitively costly for irrigation pumping, solar power is destined to increase its presence in India's pump irrigation economy in the years to come. Capital costs are still beyond the reach of most farmers. As a result, state governments are aggressively promoting solar pumps by offering 70–90 percent capital cost subsidies.

The thinking underlying the current solar pump schemes, however, is patchy and piecemeal. The need is to promote solar pumps as an integrated energy-water-sustainable-farming solution. The electricity-groundwater nexus has bypassed eastern India, which has neither much electricity to offer to farmers nor proper transmission and distribution infrastructure. Eastern India is floating on one of the world's best aquifer systems, yet lack of energy renders its agriculture unable to benefit from intensive groundwater use. Eastern India's small farmers, ever dependent on expensive diesel to run pumps, are unable to benefit from irrigation even though they have no shortage of groundwater. Solar pumps offer the potential to quickly energize eastern India's groundwater economy. Solar pumps have a high fixed cost but almost no operating cost; thus, solar pump owners have strong incentives to sell irrigation services to neighboring farmers. The solar pump promotion strategy in eastern India should thus aim to stimulate vibrant, deep, and broad irrigation service markets at the village level. To do this, there is a need for a program that:

1. Offers a pro rata subsidy of, say, Rs. 50,000 per kilovolt (instead of a percent-of-capital-cost subsidy, which leads to gold-plating and corruption);

2. Allocates substantial funds (on the order of around Rs. 50,000 crore over a five-year period for Bihar, Odisha, Assam, West Bengal, Eastern Uttar Pradesh, Chhattisgarh, and Jharkhand) so that a large number of suppliers compete to get a share in the market;

3. Includes support for the establishment of a buried pipe network to neighboring farmers to stimulate water selling;

4. Does not put undue restrictions on the size of the pump and photovoltaic array that farmers can acquire;

5. Obliges suppliers to provide a five-year maintenance guarantee; and

6. Establishes rigorous third-party monitoring to ensure that suppliers keep their side of the deal. Such a program can install 10,000 megawatts of groundwater pumping capacity in eastern India, equivalent to 2.7 million five-horsepower electric pumps, and can create gross irrigation potential of 18–20 mha.

In India's western corridor, the solar pump promotion strategy must be totally different. The aim there should be to promote solar pumps to reduce the deadweight subsidy burden on power distribution companies, to decrease the huge carbon footprint of the groundwater economy, and to remedy the perverse incentive to overexploit groundwater implicit in the current electricity-groundwater nexus. The solar pump subsidy regimes currently in place fail to achieve any of these objectives. Take, for example, Rajasthan's scheme: restricting subsidies to 2-kilovolt pumps or less has meant that solar pumps are in addition to electric pumps rather than replacing them; an overall cap on annual allocation of funds has meant a high-margin, low-volume market for photovoltaic arrays; and a subsidy offered as a proportion of unit cost has produced strong incentives to inflate costs and gold-plate the product offering. Table 1 presents four alternatives to the existing schemes with their likely impacts vis-à-vis the four objectives.[12]

Option IV is by far the boldest option. It treats solar power like any other crop that a farmer uses his land and sunlight to grow in order to meet his own needs and to sell on the market. A 20 kilovolt-peak solar pump has a land footprint of 0.03 hectares (300 square meters). At 20 percent efficiency and with intensive management, this photovoltaic plant

TABLE 1. ALTERNATIVE POLICY OPTIONS FOR SOLARIZING PUMP IRRIGATION

	Objective	Likely Impact Relative to Current Situation			
		Size of the Solar Pump Market	Beneficial Impact on Power Distribution Companies' Finances	Groundwater Overdraft	Carbon Footprint of Groundwater Irrigation
I Remove existing restrictions linked to kilovolts, and micro-irrigation and farm pond on solar subsidy; enhance solar subsidy budget to Rs. 15,000 crore per year; provide a flat subsidy of Rs. 50,000 per kilovolt	Create a low-margin, high-volume business model for solar pump marketing companies	Negligible positive		Negligible positive	
II I plus offer subsidized solar connections only to new applicants for grid power connection for irrigation wells	Cap grid power connections to well irrigation to curtail subsidies and costs of fiberglass-reinforced panels	Low positive	Negligible Positive	Negligible positive	Negligible negative
III II plus offer existing holders of grid connection the option to surrender it in lieu of solar pump of the matching kilovolt	Solarize Rajasthan's pump irrigation	Moderate positive	Low positive	Very high positive	Low negative
IV III plus offer villages to take all their irrigation wells off grid by adopting solar pumps instead; offer solar farmer co-ops guaranteed buyback of surplus solar power to the grid at prices offered to megawatt-scale solar generators (as is done in Germany)	Transform irrigators from net buyers of subsidized grid power to net sellers of solar power to the grid	Very high positive	Moderate positive	Low negative	Very high negative

would generate up to 34,560 kilowatt hours (kWh) per year. At the current subsidized grid power prices, farmers in western India use, on average, 11,500 kWh of power per connection per year. Assuming the use of the same amount of power, a solar farmer would have a surplus of 23,000 kWh per year to sell to the grid which, at a feed-in tariff of Rs. 8 per kWh, can yield an annual income of Rs. 184,000 from a 300-square-meter plot. Solar power may well be the most lucrative crop a farmer can grow.

Option IV is also hard to implement, but it could transform the perverse electricity-groundwater nexus in India's western corridor from Punjab to Tamil Nadu: first, a solar pump of appropriate size would ensure farmers stable, uninterrupted six to eight hours of power for irrigation during daytime; second, farmers would have the incentive to maximize surplus solar power sales to the grid after pumping use because they get paid for it; third, to save power, farmers would have a strong incentive to adopt drip irrigation, mulching, and greenhouses; fourth, solar photovoltaic suppliers would have an incentive to maximize sales, to offer competitive prices in a large and growing market for photovoltaic for pumps; fifth, the governments would not need to find large swathes of land for greenfield megawatt-scale solar plants; and sixth, each solar pump that retires an electric pump would save the electricity utility around Rs. 50,000 per year of farm power subsidy. Moreover, taking tube wells off the rural grid makes power distribution companies' rural operations vastly simpler and financially viable.

GRAND CHALLENGE 7: SHIFT INDIA'S RICE/WHEAT SYSTEM EASTWARD

Much of India's investments in irrigation and subsidies on fertilizers, power supply, and food procurement have been justified in the name of national food security. Fifty years ago, when India was forced into a dependence on food aid and was raring to unleash the Green Revolution, it made a policy choice to invest heavily in states like Punjab and Haryana—its best bet for rapidly increasing foodgrain production. Today, the politically sensitive minimum support price has become a millstone around the government's neck. The new National Food Security Act will add weight to this millstone. As Punjab, Haryana, and Andhra Pradesh, among others, continue to deplete their scarce groundwater, the exchequer pays a high price for rotting food stocks.

In eastern and much of tribal central India, groundwater is relatively abundant, but villages often lack electricity supply. Farmers there are forced to depend on diesel, and this creates an economic paradox. In groundwater-scarce states, farmers face no economic water scarcity and pump like there is no tomorrow thanks to a free or nearly free power supply. In groundwater-abundant states, meanwhile, farmers are forced to economize on irrigation, resulting in low productivity. To add to their woes, farmers in groundwater-surplus eastern states are often unable to sell their produce to the government at the minimum support price due to limited procurement and storage infrastructure. The net result is that water-scarce northwestern and peninsular India exports "virtual water," water embedded in the foodgrains, to water-abundant eastern and tribal India. According to one estimate, Punjab, Haryana, and Andhra Pradesh export nearly 56 billion cubic meters of virtual water per year in the form of agricultural products. At the same time, Bihar, Jharkhand, and Odisha import 29 billion cubic meters of virtual water per year to meet their food requirements.[13]

Before India spends $120 billion to physically transport water to water-scarce regions under the ambitious National River Linking Project, India's food policies must be aligned with water (and land) endowments to correct the perverse direction of the domestic virtual water trade. Doing this would require encouraging farmers in eastern India to use their abundant groundwater resources to enhance their agricultural productivity. The first step to do this is to quickly expand the food procurement machinery. The second is to solarize eastern India's groundwater economy. This needs to be accompanied by improved availability of fertilizers, seeds, and other inputs. Western states need to be moved toward cultivation of high-value, water-saving crops for a growing domestic market and for export.

GRAND CHALLENGE 8: ADDRESS TRANS-BOUNDARY WATER SHARING

Few places in the world have as many water-related tensions as South Asia. The Indo-Pakistani water dispute is as old as the two countries. The historic Indus Water Treaty of 1960—under which Prime Minister

Jawaharlal Nehru ceded 80 percent of Indus waters to Pakistan (around 220 billion cubic meters), keeping only 20 percent for India's northwestern plains—has survived three wars, but tensions continue to simmer. India and Bangladesh have disputes over the sharing of the Ganga, Teesta, and other rivers. Viewed as a regional hegemon, India's actions are treated with suspicion by its neighbors. Huge opportunities for mutual gain through joint development of water resources between Nepal and India remain blocked because of Nepal's need to assert sovereignty and India's inability to make negotiations work. Despite these tensions, water forces the nations of South Asia to interact. Nearly all the water in Pakistan, Nepal, Bangladesh, and Bhutan comes from a river shared with at least one other South Asian state.

The elephant in the room, however, is China, with its territorial control over the vast Tibetan plateau, the world's largest freshwater repository, and its ability to construct mammoth water projects unhindered by dense human habitations found elsewhere within its own borders. China's aggressive dam building in the plateau region has already caused concern among its lower riparians in Southeast Asia, including Vietnam, Laos, Thailand, and Cambodia. While it continues building more dams upstream on the Mekong and Salawin Rivers, China now also plans very large hydroelectric and river diversion schemes on the Yarlung Tsangpo, which enters India as the Brahmaputra.

China reveals little about its dams and future plans. However, according to observers, China has already constructed ten dams on tributaries of the upper Brahmaputra, with three more under construction as part of a plan to build a total of 28. Of these the most worrisome to India is a gigantic 38-gigawatt hydropower project China is planning where the Brahmaputra enters India.[14] While all South Asian co-riparians have some mechanisms in place to negotiate water issues, China will not even enter into discussions. Despite India's repeated pleas, China has refused to constitute an intergovernmental dialogue or a joint water commission or a forum to discuss a potential treaty to deal with water issues between the two countries. As the upper riparian, China has in the past declined to provide flood alerts or forewarn India about water releases from dams. In mid-2000, a breach in an upstream dam in Tibet raised Brahmaputra waters in Arunachal Pradesh by a massive 30 meters, leaving 26 people dead and 35,000 homeless. This damage could have been contained if China had alerted India. Instead, the Chinese refused to even acknowledge the dam burst for months after the event. Similar unannounced releases of excess water by the Chinese caused flash floods in Himachal Pradesh in 2000, 2001, and 2005. During the October 2013 visit of the Indian prime minister to Beijing, a memorandum of understanding was signed to share hydrological information; however, the fine print says that all that China gave away was to share such data for fifteen more days during that month. Bangladesh, the lowest riparian on the Brahmaputra and the country that will bear the brunt of dam building by China in Tibet (as India will in Arunachal Pradesh), has even less say in this runaway appropriation and development of the Brahmaputra's vast potential.

The Indian leadership's toughest challenge is to bring China to the discussion table. So far, Indian water diplomacy has encountered two major obstacles: New Delhi's smaller neighbors find it obdurate and intransigent, and China has been able to get away with ignoring Indian interests. In both cases, India has been mortgaging its water future. With Nepal, India needs to replicate the win-win relationship it has built with Bhutan. With China, India needs to use growing bilateral trade as a tool for water diplomacy. China is already India's largest trading partner, and India is an important trading partner for China. As prime minister, Li Keqiang chose India for his first foreign visit with the stated purpose of seeking mutual trust and cooperation. India needs to build on this opportunity. Growing trade and economic interdependence may be the key to resolving regional water issues.

CONCLUSION

A resolute government in New Delhi can bring quick improvements by picking several low-hanging fruits. In the public irrigation sector, the Accelerated Irrigation Benefits Program should be thoroughly redesigned to prioritize investments in curtailing deferred maintenance and completing last-mile irrigation projects as per the original intent. The new government should restructure and mobilize the Central Water Commission for regularly benchmarking the managerial performance of 100 large public irrigation systems in a transparent manner. The National Irrigation

Management Fund, proposed in the Twelfth Five Year Plan to incentivize state governments to collect an irrigation service fee from farmers, should be implemented vigorously. All central irrigation support to states should be made conditional on regular management audit of irrigation systems. A new central water university should be established and assigned to build management capacities in irrigation and water supply bureaucracy at the central and state levels.

A nationwide managed aquifer recharge program should be implemented in a decentralized format, with special emphasis on the hard-rock aquifer areas of central and peninsular India, which constitute 65 percent of the Indian landmass. In basins with severe groundwater depletion, a portion of the available surplus water should be earmarked for redeeming accumulated groundwater deficits through managed aquifer recharge. To maximize the area under conjunctive management of surface and groundwater, canal system managers should be rewarded to spread surface water on as large an area as possible. At the same time, power distribution companies should be assisted either to collect agricultural power tariffs on metered consumption as in West Bengal or to effectively ration farm power supply as under the *Jyotigram* scheme in Gujarat. In western and peninsular India, the new government should also incentivize farmers—through guaranteed buyback at an attractive feed-in tariff for surplus solar power—to surrender tube well electricity connections against subsidized solar pumps and to grow solar power as a lucrative "crop." Together, these measures can ease the financial troubles of power distribution companies and bring groundwater depletion under control within five to seven years.

As a pilot, the new government should showcase fifty cities as highly reliable peri-urban irrigation systems with treated wastewater. It should fund municipal authorities or private utilities or both to invest in the treatment and orderly distribution of domestic and industrial wastewater to peri-urban farmers on full or partial cost recovery. When it comes to improving domestic water supply, urban and rural, India should be circumspect in leapfrogging to levels of service provision—such as 24/7 supply—that are way beyond the management capacities of local governance bodies. Instead, a redesigned Jawaharlal Nehru National Urban Renewal Mission should incrementally build on what exists. A 2011 Ernst and Young report estimates investment needs of $130 billion in India's water sector by 2030; however, this will materialize only when water utilities—public and private—figure out feasible approaches to pricing and cost recovery at levels that would make investments worthwhile.[15]

To kick-start eastern India's belated Green Revolution, the new government should quickly expand the grain procurement machinery in the eastern region; streamline input delivery and farm credit systems; empower chief ministers in eastern Indian states to offer bonuses on government-declared support prices of foodgrains; and create a Rs. 50,000 crore fund to stimulate vibrant, deep, and broad solar-pump–based irrigation service markets in eastern and northeastern India.

India's water crisis is often blamed on resource scarcity or insufficient investment in water infrastructure and services. In reality, the crisis can be blamed on a serious management deficit—management of the resource, of infrastructure, as well as services. In the normal course, the management will improve but only to the extent that water becomes an economic good and when consumers are able to bear the bulk of the cost of supplying quality water services. It is no surprise that Singapore, one of the most water-scarce places in the world, is able to offer one of the best water services to its citizens, who can afford to pay $10–12 per cubic meter of water. India's challenge is to provide better services at affordable tariffs. This is hard, but not impossible.

India has so far concentrated on only one option: public investment in infrastructure. It has placed very little emphasis on management improvements, governance reforms, and institutional innovations. This is why returns on public investments in water infrastructure in India have been poor and water projects have suffered from the build-neglect-rebuild syndrome. The country can make rapid strides in water security by emphasizing management improvements and institutional reforms rather than just public investment in water infrastructure. This shift of emphasis is the key water challenge facing the new government.

NOTES

1   The Falkenmark Water Stress Indicator defines water scarcity for a region or country in terms of renewable freshwater available per person per year. If the amount available is less than 1,700 cubic meters per capita per year, the region is said to be "water stressed." If it is between 500 and 1,000 cubic meters per capita per year, water scarcity is suggested to be a serious limitation to economic growth and human well-being; freshwater availability below 500 cubic meters per capita per year is defined as a key constraint to sustaining human life.

2   F. Gassert et al., "Aqueduct Country and River Basin Rankings: A Weighted Aggregation of Spatially Distinct Hydrological Indicators," Working Paper, World Resources Institute, November 2013, http://wri.org/publication/ aqueduct-country-river-basin-rankings.

3   *Jala Yagnam* (water worship) is a water management program implemented in Andhra Pradesh with the objective of bringing 3.3 million hectares under irrigation. The program has been mired in controversy with allegations of rampant corruption and poor quality construction work—hence the derisive nickname *Dhana Yagnam* (money worship).

4   Ernst and Young, "Water Sector in India: Emerging Investment Opportunities," September 2011, www.ey.com/Publication/vwLUAssets/Water_sector_in_ India/$FILE/Water_Sector_in_India.pdf.

5   Tushaar Shah and Barbara van Koppen, "Is India Ripe for Integrated Water Resources Management? Fitting Water Policy to National Development Context," *Economic and Political Weekly* 41, no. 31 (2006): 3413–21.

6   Government of India, Planning Commission, "Report of the Working Group on Urban and Industrial Water Supply and Sanitation for the Twelfth Five Year Plan (2012–2017)," Steering Group on Water Sector, November 2011.

7   Government of India, Central Pollution Control Board, "Evaluation of Operations and Maintenance of Sewage Treatment Plants in India—2007," January 1, 2008, www.cpcb.nic.in/upload/NewItems/NewItem_99_NewItem_99_5.pdf.

8   42,000 million liters/day = 0.042 billion cubic meters * 365 days = 15.33 billion cubic meters/year.

9   Alka Palrecha, Dheeraj Kapoor, and Teja Malladi, "Wastewater Irrigation in Gujarat: An Exploratory Study," IWMI-Tata Water Policy Program Highlight no. 30, 2012, www.iwmi.cgiar.org/iwmi-tata/PDFs/2012_Highlight-30.pdf.

10   See Tushaar Shah and Shilp Verma, "Co-Management of Electricity and Groundwater: An Assessment of Gujarat's Jyotigram Scheme," *Economic and Political Weekly* 43, no. 7 (2008): 59–66.

11   Ashok Gulati, Tushaar Shah, and Ganga Shreedhar, "Agriculture Performance in Gujarat Since 2000: Can Gujarat Be a *Divadandi* (Lighthouse) for Other States?" International Water Management Institute and International Food Policy Research Institute, May 2009, www.gujaratcmfellowship.org/document/Agriculture/ Agriculture%20Performance%20in%20Gujarat%20since%202000_IWMI%20 &%20IFPRI%20Report-_May%202009.pdf.

12 For a detailed discussion of opportunities and threats, see Tushaar Shah and Avinash Kishore, "Solar-Powered Pump Irrigation and India's Groundwater Economy: A Preliminary Discussion of Opportunities and Threats," IWMI-Tata Water Policy Program Highlight no. 26, 2012, www.iwmi.cgiar.org/iwmi-tata/PDFs/2012_ Highlight-26.pdf.

13 Shilp Verma et al., "Going Against the Flow: A Critical Analysis of Inter-State Virtual Water Trade in the Context of India's National River Linking Program," *Physics and Chemistry of the Earth* 34, nos. 4–5 (2009): 261–69.

14 See D. Jayaram, "China's Dams: A Security Challenge for South Asia," *International Policy Digest*, October 1, 2013, www.internationalpolicydigest.org/2013/10/01/ chinas-dams-security-challenge-south-asia, and Kenneth Pomeranz, "Asia's Unstable Water Tower: The Politics, Economics, and Ecology of Himalayan Water Projects," *Asia Policy* 16 (July 2013), http://mercury.ethz.ch/serviceengine/Files/ISN/167852/ ipublicationdocument_singledocument/ea67be3b-0eac-4629-a89f-8758417fb515/en/ Asia_Policy_16_WaterRoundtable_July2013.pdf.

15 Ernst and Young, "Water Sector in India: Emerging Investment Opportunities," 3.

CHAPTER 12

REFORMING ENERGY POLICY AND PRICING

SUNJOY JOSHI

INTRODUCTION

Despite more than two decades of sustained growth after its post-1991 integration into the global economy, India remains largely poor. According to the National Sample Survey (NSS) of the Indian government, the average all-India monthly per capita expenditure was less than $27 in nominal terms in fiscal year 2011–2012. India's energy challenge must therefore be viewed from the perspective of its development and growth needs, which have to be underpinned by the provision of modern energy to households.[1] According to the NSS, in 2011–2012, nearly 20 percent of households relied on kerosene as the primary source of energy for lighting and nearly 51 percent had to rely on firewood for cooking.

The *Integrated Energy Policy: Report of the Expert Committee* estimates that to deliver sustained growth of 8 percent up to 2031, a rate approximating the average rate of growth over the past decade, the country's primary energy supply would need to grow by three to four times.[2] Overall the annual average rate of growth in energy demand is projected to accelerate from 5.1 percent in the Eleventh Five Year Plan to between 5.4 and 5.7 percent in the Twelfth and Thirteenth Plans. By the end of the Twelfth Plan

(2011–2017), the country would be importing nearly 25–30 percent of its natural gas, 75 percent of its oil, and 23 percent of its coal requirements.

Indian policymakers are fond of defining the country's energy security in terms of the "three As" of availability, access, and affordability. However, all three appear at risk in the face of four formidable barriers we'll be discussing at length: the limited fiscal room to maneuver in the face of increasing deficits, exacerbated as they are by a burgeoning resources import bill; systemic inefficiencies in the management of resources; stiff competition from China in instituting cross-border energy linkages; and the rapidly changing global energy landscape in the face of challenges posed by climate change.

What has made these barriers difficult to overcome is the exaggerated emphasis in public discourse upon the "ownership" of natural resources, an overblown definitional bubble that stifles the country's ability to frame long-term policies that can help harness its own potential. The resulting convoluted and often perverse legal and regulatory structures that distort market forces and keep investors at bay are symptomatic of the state's inability to manage resources. Securing energy supplies in the face of these systemic barriers is a challenge of the first order.

INDIA'S FISCAL BURDEN: ENERGY IMPORTS AND SUBSIDIES

India currently imports nearly 76 percent of its net oil needs, 26 percent of its gas, and 20 percent of its coal.[3] According to the Indian government, India's oil import bill in terms of value has increased from $81.8 billion in 2009–2010 to $145 billion in 2011–2012 (all figures at current prices).[4] At the same time, India's current account deficit, of which energy imports constitute around a quarter of the total, touched a record high of around $88 billion, or 4.8 percent of the gross domestic product (GDP) in the financial year ending March 31, 2013.[5]

The expanding current account deficit reflects a systemic weakness in the Indian economy. Economic growth has faltered at under 5 percent. Investments have choked amid fading supplies and diminishing business confidence. To compound the current account deficit woes, looming fears of the withdrawal of quantitative easing by the U.S. Federal Reserve has increased pressure on Asian currencies with the U.S. dollar appreciating steadily. The Indian rupee, being one of the hardest-hit currencies owing to weak fundamentals that have stalled investment growth, has depreciated by more than 12 percent since March 2013.

Yet, a beleaguered United Progressive Alliance (UPA) government, buffeted by a series of corruption scandals, has chosen to head for the general election in 2014 armed with the National Food Security Act. As welfare measures go, the move may have been laudable, its only glitch being the country's inability to prune its spending to raise the required resources. The law will provide an additional $4 billion each year to the roughly $18 billion the country already spends on food subsidies. To this the addition of the $25 billion spent on subsidizing fuel,[6] $7 billion on electricity, and $10 billion on fertilizer leaves little fiscal room to maneuver.

Access and affordability are the arguments used to keep energy prices low even as the government finds itself ill-equipped to foot the bill for the subsidies it provides. Hence the temptation to administer them through price controls, whether on primary fuels, electricity, or fertilizer. However, price controls work only to restrict rather than expand access as a cash-constrained government juggles its subsidy bill from the country's balance sheet to the balance sheets of state-owned companies—a market intervention guaranteed to choke both production and supplies. The country finds itself unable to either increase production of primary fuels or acquire the economic capacity to finance their import.

Kerosene, diesel, and liquefied petroleum gas for household consumption—all petroleum products—are sold in India at prices that are lower than on the international market. The under-recovery burden to oil marketing companies is offset partially by fiscal subsidies from the government and in part by assistance from the upstream national oil companies. Yet, the full value of under-recoveries remains uncompensated, accounting for close to $18 billion in 2010–2011.[7] These under-recoveries undermine industrial competitiveness, compounding the structural inefficiencies of the subsidy regime.

Availability to the least empowered is the first casualty—modern fuels remain a privilege limited to few in India. NSS data for 2011–2012 reveal that despite claims of increased penetration of modern cooking fuels such as liquefied petroleum gas, 70 percent of rural households still use biomass. Although liquefied petroleum gas is an easily transportable fuel, the benefits of using it are disproportionately skewed in favor of urban house-holds. Less than 3 percent of the extremely poor in rural India, constitut-ing the lowest decile of the population, have access to it—a disadvantage that continues well into the next quartile. More important, among socially disadvantaged groups, the percentage of households using biomass has not only remained more or less constant, but may have even gone up in certain cases.[8]

Moreover, subsidies administered through price controls distort fuel choices. Diesel-fueled sport-utility vehicles of the super-rich romp city roads while farmers struggle to get their pump sets running. Supplies and services have failed to expand, diminishing both affordability and access as the least privileged end up paying most in terms of both time and money.

A similar effect is visible in the electricity sector. Agricultural tariffs are cross-subsidized by asymmetrically high industrial tariffs. Despite prom-ises of free power to poor agriculturalists, access to electricity remains directly proportionate to per capita spending. Worse, the effect of income on access is far more dramatic in rural areas, where 27 percent of house-holds use kerosene for lighting their homes, paying a very high price per lumen. For the poorest decile, this figure is 40 percent.[9]

Power theft and inefficiency are responsible for the loss of 30 percent of electricity in transmission and distribution. Cash-strapped state utilities, which lose money on every unit of power sold, resort to power cuts to trim losses. With accumulated losses estimated around $38 billion as of March 31, 2011,[10] state-owned power distribution companies can hardly be expected to be enthusiastic about extending power to more consumers.

In 2013, efforts to reform electricity distribution resulted in debt restructuring packages for state utilities overburdened by subsidies and dis-tribution losses. The new package provides for the restructuring of loans and tries to incentivize state governments to cut distribution losses. A Model State Electricity Distribution Responsibility Bill, 2013, tries to do through legislation what could happen more effectively through healthy, well-regulated markets. The government remains wedded to the idea that distribution losses can be prevented by more regulatory control and over-sight by yet more high-level committees. Under the circumstances, debt restructuring can give only a temporary reprieve, and losses will return to haunt balance sheets while politicians continue to distribute free power.

Staring up the fiscal wall, the government through 2013 tried to prune subsidies. It resorted to gradually raising the price of diesel, deregulating gasoline, and curtailing cooking gas subsidies. It doubled the price of gas in June 2013 in the hope that doing so would boost investments by oil and gas companies. However, a return to reforms originally announced in 1999, notified in 2002, but rolled back in 2004, and now reluctantly reintroduced in 2013, smacks of a desperation destined to inspire little confidence in investors.

A HALF-DISMANTLED PLANNED ECONOMY

Under the planned economy model adopted after independence, the Indian state gradually arrogated itself the responsibility for guardianship, extraction, and conversion of fossil resources into useful forms of energy. Thus the energy sector came to be dominated by gargantuan state energy companies such as Coal India Limited, Oil and Natural Gas Corporation, NTPC Limited (formerly National Thermal Power Corporation), and a whole host of smaller public sector undertakings. As a result, policy, legislation, rules, and regulations came to be devised exclusively for state-led operations, leading to an incestuous relationship with parent ministries or departments of the government.

To this day, government officials routinely sit on the boards of such undertakings, and executive positions in the undertakings often pass into the hands of officials. This overarching role of the state has been a natural corollary of a system of law and jurisprudence that maintains that ownership of all natural mineral resources vests not with individual landowners but with the state.

The structural adjustments forced by lending institutions in the 1990s initiated a process of piecemeal reforms in certain segments of this superstructure. Thus electricity reforms began in the hope that power shortages could be wished away by allowing private participation in generation. The retail segment of the value chain remained the holy cow, as distribution and marketing reforms lagged behind. Similarly, while policies for getting private sector participation in enhancing oil and gas production as well as refining occurred relatively quickly, when it came to allowing marketing and distribution to interface with the public through retail operations, the government developed cold feet.

To ease supply shortages of coal, half-hearted reform led to the random allocation of coal blocks—ironically enough called "captive blocks"—to select user industries having no experience with mining. The lack of fair and transparent allocation criteria then became the subject of adverse commentary by the Comptroller and Auditor General, leading to eventual cancellation of the licenses by the Supreme Court in 2011.

A spate of such allocations (including those of telecom spectrum) finally led a rather frustrated Supreme Court to hold up the "public trust doctrine" regarding the ownership of natural resources. In short, this doctrine ruled that while natural resources belonged to the nation, the government held them in trust, in a fiduciary capacity, for the public good. The doctrine of public trust has now come to be utilized repeatedly to question the powers and discretion of the executive to lay down rules for the exploitation and use of natural resources.

However, the doctrine has dealt a body blow to the so-called reforms, badly searing the few private sector entities that had inveigled themselves into these sectors.

While the public trust doctrine is sound in itself for the principles it advocates, the problem is not so much with the doctrine per se but with the *paramount* position it confers upon the notion of "ownership." If the government holds natural resources in trust, then it is also logical that the exploitation and use of natural resources be best and safely re-entrusted to its agents (that is, public sector undertakings) rather than "rapacious" private companies.[11] The consequence has been that government machinery, whose patronage networks were shrinking through creeping privatization, has begun using this doctrine to stall the process of reform itself. Even where extreme steps such as the cancellation of licenses awarded to private companies have not been taken, the public trust doctrine has led officialdom to adopt extreme and adverse interpretations of existing contracts and license conditions. Outcome has become subordinate to process.

The problem with the approach is that natural resources are by themselves valueless. Fossil fuel reserves buried kilometers under the ground, either undiscovered—or if discovered, unextractable—have zero value. Ownership per se confers no benefit upon the owner until resources are discovered, established, and efficiently extracted to derive maximum value from their use. None of this can happen without investment, technology, and human ingenuity. Only entities that best combine these three necessities confer maximum value upon otherwise valueless resources. Reforms are desirable only when their success encourages competition among all manner of entities (public or private) to bring in best practices, technologies, and efficiency across the value chain of resource extraction, allocation, and utilization.

As half-hearted attempts at privatization through captive coal blocks came to naught, supplies dwindled. The amended Mines and Minerals (Regulation and Development Act) notified in 2012 finally has allowed competitive auction of coal blocks—but still not to mining entities. It continues to restrict these auctions to end users such as iron and steel companies, power producers, and so on. Commercial coal mining operations still remain a pipe dream.

Alternatives like natural gas fare no better. Pricing reforms and marketing freedom were introduced with great fanfare in the oil and gas sector at the turn of the century. However, lack of commensurate reform in the power and fertilizer sectors has forced abandonment of market pricing in favor of a return to price controls and quotas. Several new development plans languish for want of approval. In more than a decade that saw nine rounds of auctions under the New Exploration Licensing Policy, only 110 of 254 blocks passed into the hands of private players[12]—which included a bare handful of foreign companies.[13] Despite more than 120 discoveries having been announced, a mere six were developed by 2012.[14] Today the number of blocks under exploration stands reduced to 178; all but 74 are in the hands of state-run entities.[15]

In a country that should have been desperate in trying to get investment into energy production at home, estimates are that nearly $53 billion of capital earned in India has left its shores in the past decade chasing energy deals abroad in oil, gas, and coal. Moreover, it is not just the private sector, but state-owned entities that also seem to be seeking safer investments overseas. Thus in the coal sector outbound investments totaled $16 billion;[16] in oil and gas, it was nearly $37 billion.[17] Investments abroad may be touted as essential for India's energy security, however, production overseas even by Indian companies invariably finds its way to the best available markets—and those are certainly not back home.

MANAGING ENERGY SOURCES: COAL, GAS, AND NUCLEAR

Contrary to popular perceptions of India as a resource-poor country, it is not singularly lacking in resources. India contains the world's fourth-largest coal reserves. Its brown coal resources lie yet un-estimated. Its thorium supplies are practically limitless. It is particularly abundant in solar, especially in the uninhabited deserts of Rajasthan. Amid stagnating or declining oil and gas production, barely 22 percent of India's 3.14 million square kilometers of sedimentary basins have been even moderately explored,[18] though most of these are deep offshore. International experts from IHS CERA recently presented their findings that these contained at least 91 TCF of gas—14 times the annual demand forecast by the International Energy Agency for 2035.[19] Estimates by a far more optimistic Directorate General of Hydrocarbons place the untapped conventional hydrocarbon resource at 20 billion metric tons—39 times the 2035 demand forecast. Therefore, if India remains such a huge importer, the problem is one of management and regulation, rather than scarcity.

The management challenge is best understood by the deficiencies in the coal sector. Coal is India's single largest fuel source, accounting for half the country's total energy use and producing two-thirds of its electricity.[20] India prides itself on the vastness of its coal reserves, and estimates are that it has enough to last for the next hundred years. However, environmental clearances, land availability, and evacuation constraints restrict access to huge swaths of coalfields, halving its extractable reserves.

Assuming India were to add 10 gigawatts (GW) of coal-fired capacity each year, by 2030 it could attain a peak capacity of 300 GW based on domestic coal.[21] Assuming conversion efficiencies on the higher side, this translates to an annual demand of 1.5 million tons of coal, three times the current levels. However, if these production levels are attained, the ratios of coal reserves to production would have fallen to well under forty years.[22] This in effect limits further capacity addition, unless improved mining as well as alternate technologies such as in situ gasification are successfully commercialized.[23]

The state-owned Coal India Limited is the largest coal producer in the world, meeting over 80 percent of India's coal needs,[24] extracting low-grade coal with an ash content as high as 45 percent from opencast mines.[25] It has struggled to raise output and meet supply commitments. In 2012–2013, coal shortages of 165 million tons affected the availability of power, weighing on the country's economic growth.[26]

Meanwhile, power plants dependent on imported coal suffered as international coal prices, with a standard deviation of about 15 percent from the mean across various coal indices, displayed a higher volatility than oil. The biggest sources of imports—Indonesia, South Africa, Australia, and the United States—today confront either increasing domestic demand or looming carbon curbs that restrict exportable supplies. With China and India accounting for a quarter of global trade, coal prices continue to be prey to demand fluctuations by India's giant neighbor. So, India's Twelfth Five Year Plan focuses on various means to curb the country's dependence on coal. At least half of the current plan's targets and all of the next are to be met using only super-critical units,[27] reducing emissions by 15 percent. Cleaner options would involve switching to gas, renewables, and eventually nuclear power.

Yet, as gas production falls prey to a regulatory crisis, 15 GW of gas-fired capacities lie stranded because domestic supplies are diverted for fertilizer production. Administered prices dismantled in 2002 have not only been reintroduced, but extended in 2007 to encompass even private producers. A complex system of quotas and allocations has returned to the sector, which, by depriving producers of the freedom to market gas, has made investors extremely wary of the regulatory regime.

Simultaneously, gas imports are limited by infrastructure. Depending on pricing policy, customers can burgeon or evaporate, making it impossible to predict demand and tie up long-term consumers. Investors are understandably shy of committing to pipeline or liquefied natural gas infrastructure in such highly fractured markets. Despite being surrounded by some of the most gas-prolific countries, India is yet to build its first transnational gas pipeline. Gas in 2012 accounted for a bare 9 percent of generating capacity—making India the only country whose share of gas in its fuel basket has declined in recent years.

One-third of the current installed power capacity of 225 GW comprises nuclear, hydro, and renewables. Increased availability of fuel after the U.S.-India Civil Nuclear Agreement did maximize capacity utilization in nuclear plants. However, low plant load factors in hydro and renewables reduce the share of non-fossil fuels to barely a fifth of the power fed into the grid.

Gupta et al. estimate that while India's ambitious target of setting up 63 GW of nuclear capacity by 2032 is unlikely to be met, even a modest 40 GW capacity by that time, if established, would "represent a 6 fold increase in 22 years accompanied by very significant development and maturation of breeder reactor technology ... [putting] India in an excellent position to transition to carbon-neutral systems after 2032, through rapid build-up of nuclear power."[28]

However, even this modest growth is held to ransom by a contentious Civil Liability for Nuclear Damage Act, 2010, more commonly known as the Nuclear Liability Act, which continues to frustrate suppliers. Foreign suppliers are worried that the liability law, inconsistent with international practice, places a disproportionate burden on them, with compensation payments forced upon equipment suppliers in case of any accident. Meanwhile, in the wake of the 2011 Fukushima Daiichi disaster in Japan, direct civil action against nuclear plants has become increasingly aggressive.

India's wind energy potential is at 103 GW for 80-meter hub height. Developed fully and integrated with a modern smart grid, it could substitute for about 30 GW of coal-fired plants. Similarly, the National Solar Mission seeks to set up solar capacities of 20 GW by 2020, substituting for about 5 GW of coal. The growth of wind and solar power generation, however, remains a prisoner to government subsidies. The importance of accelerated depreciation has been very visible in the expansion of wind power. In 2012–2013, when the government withdrew both accelerated depreciation and generation-based incentives, the sector added only around half of the targeted wind power capacity until October 31, 2012, leading to their reintroduction in the Union Budget in 2013. Poor and outdated infrastructure continues to constrain evacuation, limiting effective utilization of the power generated. Thus, while alternative sources of energy may reduce some dependence on fossil fuels, rapidly increasing demand for power until 2030 mandates maximum capacity addition in conventional fossil fuel–based thermal generation.

GEOPOLITICS AND THE GREAT WALL OF CHINA

Around the middle of the last century, India and China were at identical points along their separate development and demographic trajectories. In 1965, China's primary energy consumption was about two and a half times that of India. At the time of the Rio Summit in 1992, China was self-sufficient in oil, and in effect a net exporter. The subsequent year, it became a net importer, and by 2002 it overtook Japan as the world's second-largest oil consumer. The world woke up to the Chinese miracle.

A net importer of steel until 2003, China transformed into the world's largest steel exporter by 2006. As coal consumption doubled from 2002 to 2008, China also became the world's biggest carbon dioxide emitter, a full three years before it dethroned the United States as the largest energy consumer. This spurt in China's demand for energy came from a virtual explosion in the country's heavy manufacturing capacity fired by its export-led growth.

By comparison, with India's growth skewed toward services, its energy demand over the same period rose at a far more moderate pace. However, as both countries scoured the world for resources, comparison and even outright competition between the two have become more frequent.

Attempts by Indian state-owned companies to acquire equity oil in other geographies have repeatedly hit the Chinese wall. The far more aggressive Chinese have cornered assets from under the noses of their Indian counterparts in geographies as diverse as Angola and Kazakhstan. With a growing hunger for resources, China has become hyperactive, not just acquiring oil and gas assets abroad, but also diversifying its supplies to encompass Central Asia, Russia, Latin America, and extending into India's neighborhood.

As insurance against the risk of supply disruptions through the narrow Strait of Malacca, China has committed to developing Gwadar Port in Pakistan as a possible alternative transit point. It has recently started operating a gas pipeline in Myanmar, offering yet another strategic hedge for the maritime chokepoint. It has also put a substantial offer on the table—for the development of Iran's Chabahar Port, for which India has committed $100 million. The equivalent credit facility of $100 million offered to Iran by China may tempt the Iranians into a strategic rethink on which investment line they would prefer.

By comparison, in spite of more than twenty years of efforts, transnational gas supplies into India from Central Asia, Iran, Bangladesh, or Myanmar remain pipe dreams. Despite both countries' entering the global gas trade around the same time, India in 2012 imported 14 billion cubic meters (bcm) of gas—all as liquefied natural gas—and China imported 40 bcm, comprising liquefied natural gas and piped gas in equal measure. China is simply able to offer better deals and commands greater efficiency in putting up the requisite infrastructure.

Consequently, and sometimes to their frustration, Indian state-owned companies have found that successful acquisitions, whether in places as close as Myanmar or as far afield as Sakhalin, may merely mean investments to produce resources that head inexorably to feed the same market, namely China. Clearly, with an energy requirement 4.5 times the size of India's, China has managed to integrate itself far more successfully into global energy markets, outmaneuvering India across multiple geographies. While a dithering India meanders through repeated policy flip-flops, the Third Plenary Session of the 18th Communist Party of China Central Committee in November 2013 avowed its intention to commission a specialized leadership group to steer the country's market reforms. Significantly, "in a communique that mentioned the word 'market' 22 times, Chinese leaders attributed the 'decisive role' of the market economy in allocating resources."[29]

CLIMATE CHANGE: AN IMMINENT BARRIER

In 2009, Kojima and Bacon, examining the ten years preceding 2006, showed that India was one of the twenty countries in which emissions intensity (carbon dioxide emissions per unit of GDP) had declined both during the first half of this period and the second half.[30] So when China announced in Copenhagen that it would cut its emissions intensity by 40 percent by 2020, India had little hesitation in announcing a 20 to 25 percent drop.

Is that attainable?

According to the U.S. Energy Information Administration, India's emissions in 1995 equaled 0.64 tons of carbon dioxide per $1,000 of GDP (on a purchasing power parity basis).[31] Emissions levels declined to 0.55 tons by 2000 and had fallen to 0.48 tons by 2005, the benchmark year for the Copenhagen declarations of China and India. This was just a tad above that of the United States (at 0.47 tons).[32] Obviously, the reason for this drop during India's boom years was growth led by services rather than manufacturing.

Can the pattern be sustained? The much-maligned business process outsourcing industry, the poster boy of India's growth story that is accused of stealing jobs in the Organization for Economic Cooperation and Development countries, accounts for a mere 2 million jobs in a country where 12–15 million enter the workforce each year. Over the next few years, the only way to keep millions of unemployed youth from spilling onto the streets in protest is to create many more jobs in the far more labor- and energy-intensive manufacturing sector.[33] If it succeeds in achieving this necessary goal, India would find it hard to maintain—let alone reduce—the intensity of its emissions.

A shift to manufacturing, and expanding infrastructure, would also be accompanied by urbanization, increasing demand for commercial fuels. In the years since 2005 the rate of decline in emissions intensity has already decelerated, hinting that the declining trend may be petering out.

China, meanwhile, uninhibitedly exploited the post–Rio lack of multi-lateral consensus on emissions caps to fuel its growth with no carbon constraint. It continued building huge but inefficient and carbon-intensive manufacturing and production capacities. While India's intensity declined from 2000 to 2005, China's emissions intensity, which had fallen from 1.27 in 1995 to 0.83 in 2000, rose to 1.02 by 2005.[34] With big-ticket investments in infrastructure and heavy manufacturing already in place, China's stated reductions may easily be realized as its State Council announced a ban on the construction of new coal-fired power plants to cut air pollution in its megalopolises. Not to be outdone in new energy technologies, including renewables, China today also hosts more than 50 percent of the world's solar cell manufacturing capacity, along with 30 percent of global wind turbine manufacturing capacities.

So India's strategy of hanging onto China's coattails in climate negotiations may no longer yield dividends. Nor should one forget that the shale gas boom in the United States is simultaneously prompting emergence of a more aggressive votary for climate action across the Atlantic. Rising carbon costs and calls for climate action certainly mean bad news for increasing coal dependence. Even as India struggles to grow, therefore, it is likely to find itself increasingly isolated on the climate front.

THE WAY FORWARD

Over the next twenty years, dependence on coal will continue, hence the need to expand production capacities by opening up the sector rapidly to private participation to induce both capital and technology. Given the right mix of incentives, market forces must be encouraged to usher in new technologies in fuel extraction, carbon sequestration, and gasification when energy markets make these substitutions commercially viable.

Natural gas has been trading and is expected to continue being available at a significant discount to oil. As a consequence, the first policy thrust should be to allow market-led substitution for oil by gas rather than inefficient diversion of gas by allocation into feedstock for fertilizer or even as fuel in power plants. However, beyond a 300 GW coal-fired capacity, India must plan for carbon constraints by encouraging carbon-efficient fuel substitution by use of cleaner, available fuels. Natural gas emerges as an important bridge toward a future fueled more by renewables and nuclear power.

As for renewables, given low plant load factors, policy emphasis must shift to generation rather than capacity addition. Accelerated depreciation, viability gap funding, and other incentives must give way to generation-based incentives and interest subsidies.

Overall, while playing an increasing role, renewables will have limited utility for base-load generation, and so the nuclear option is not one that can be wished away for India. Ambiguities with regard to equipment supplier liability that have crept into the interpretation of the Nuclear Liability Act must be resolved. Nuclear suppliers are worried that the consequences of the law and its interpretation could open the doors to supplier liability and set a precedent for similar laws globally.[35] The latest opinion offered by the Indian attorney general—that in case of a nuclear accident, the Nuclear Power Corporation of India Limited will have the right to selectively enforce the recourse—has failed to assuage the U.S. supplier Westinghouse. While the executive may issue ingenious guidelines to "clarify" the law, it will likely need to be revisited in the Indian Parliament, the only constitutional body that can amend the legislation.

There are various inter-contractual safeguards between operators and equipment suppliers that cannot be substituted for by imposing statutory liabilities on suppliers. Operators of nuclear power plants must have the confidence and competence to negotiate and monitor their supply arrangements independently rather than hide behind an omnibus supplier liability act. It is therefore necessary for India to open the sector for more operators so that over time these competencies can develop.

Overall, while India's energy landscape may continue to be dominated by strong national energy companies, an efficient and technologically robust public sector is best created through competition with a strong private sector. That can happen only if the state adopts a hands-off approach and ensures a level playing field by not intervening to give selective advantage to one over the other through ambiguous regulatory ring fencing or through selective interpretations being offered to suppliers, as is the case in the Nuclear Liability Act.

Competition with private companies will help nurture competent state enterprises that do not need to be treated with kid gloves. Policy and regulation, whether for all statutory clearances, land acquisition, or administration of contracts and regulations, must be applied in a nondiscriminatory fashion. Energy resources acquire value only in their discovery and production. Grant of rights of exploration, production, and marketing in a transparent and fair manner is not transfer of ownership.

On the one hand, with the government creaming off all investible surpluses for fuel subsidies, state enterprises are left with little to invest in upgrading and depend on a politically volatile Middle East for 80 percent of their supplies. Simultaneously, on the other hand, more complex private petroleum refineries, which have greater technological flexibility in sourcing crude, are excluded from the domestic market by discriminatory marketing policies. The private refining capacity of 80 million metric tons per annum produces some of the best grade refined products for value-added exports that have made petroleum products India's single biggest export.

A public sector expected to pick up the tab for the government's redistributive largesse can never be competitive or have the ability to invest in technology, skill upgrading, and research and development for solutions to challenges that are unique to India. The treatment of state-owned companies as patronage distribution networks, which works to stall reforms, must cease. Therefore it is necessary to bring in greater professionalism through divestment. With the world's largest expansion in energy markets imminent in the country, India must become the nerve center for innovation in technologies such as clean coal, underground gasification, gas hydrates, carbon dioxide sequestration, nonconventional extraction, and renewables. It cannot afford to be relegated to a mere market for others.

Better-administered subsidies that do not interfere with markets and people's fuel choices are the only way to end the folly of policymakers' wasting their time on fuel allocations, only to find supplies run short. Rather than intervene in markets, the government must responsibly direct its support to end users. Technology has provided answers there, and the government has been experimenting with direct transfer schemes. However, the pace needs to be quickened and the process made more efficient.

A key failure of India's half-hearted process of reform has been the lack of strong and independent regulatory institutions that could have helped mediate the political economy of change in a fair and transparent manner. Organizations such as the Petroleum and Natural Gas Regulatory Board, the Central Electricity Authority, and the Tariff Commission have been unable to cut themselves loose from the apron strings of parent ministries. If reforms are to succeed, regulatory authorities must be given autonomy, which can unshackle them from political and bureaucratic control.

In the discussion above, we have seen how India's energy security—defined as the three As of availability, access, and affordability—confronts four formidable barriers. The barriers have been identified as the limited fiscal room to maneuver that constrains India's ability to import energy indefinitely; systemic inefficiencies that shackle the management of domestic resources; competition from a resource-hungry China; and the challenges posed to India's conventional energy economy by climate change.

What has made these barriers all the more formidable is the exaggerated emphasis in public discourse upon the notion of "ownership" of natural resources, an emphasis that amid all the scandals of corruption and rent-seeking has become an overblown bubble, constraining the country's ability to harness its own potential. Yet, if there is any lesson to be learned from the spate of half-baked, piecemeal reforms that have culminated in the Supreme Court's promulgating the doctrine of public trust, it is that governments by their very nature are poor and inefficient allocators of resources. Resources are best allocated by markets, rather than doled out through policy guidelines, which, straddling half a dozen ministries and a Planning Commission, can at best be suboptimal compromises negotiated among various inter-ministerial groups sparring with each other over pricing and fuel linkages.

NOTES

1 The linkages between development, growth, and access to modern energy are well documented. For more, see United Nations Development Programme, *Human Development Report 2007/2008: Fighting Climate Change: Human Solidarity in a Divided World* (New York: United Nations Development Programme, 2007).

2 Kirit S. Parikh et al., *Integrated Energy Policy: Report of the Expert Committee* (New Delhi: Government of India, 2006), http://planningcommission.gov.in/reports/genrep/rep_intengy.pdf.

3 "LNG in India: Contracts, Imports, Demand—Supply and Infrastructure," Indianpetro.com, May 28, 2013, www.indianpetro.com/articleView.do?articleID=114829&pgNo=0; Rakteem Katakey, "India to Exceed China as World's Coal Power, Buoying BHP," Bloomberg, June 28, 2013, www.bloomberg.com/news/2013-06-27/india-to-eclipse-china-as-world-s-coal-power-buoying-bhp.html.

4 India's oil import bill in terms of value has increased from Rs. 409,077 crore in 2009–2010 to Rs. 726,386 crore in 2011–2012. See Ministry of Oil and Natural Gas, "India's Oil Import Bill at Rs. 7,26,386 Crore in 2011–12," press release, August 23, 2013, http://pib.nic.in/newsite/erelease.aspx?relid=86628.

5 Asit Ranjan Mishra, "Chidambaram Lowers Current Account Deficit Target to $60 billion,"*Mint*, November 1, 2013, www.livemint.com/Politics/lTxeUOk4MwmkDs2hVkfufP/Chidambaram-sees-current-account-deficit-at-60-bn-or-less.html.

6 In 2013–2014 the Petroleum Planning and Analysis Cell of the Ministry of Petroleum saw its estimate of under-recoveries (due to price restrictions) of the state-owned Oil Marketing Companies shoot from Rs. 125,594 million to a record-high Rs. 161,000 million. The depreciating rupee now ensures that figures for the current year could scale new records.

7 "A Citizen's Guide to Energy Subsidies in India," Energy and Resources Institute and International Institute for Sustainable Development, 2012, www.teriin.org/events/INDIA_CITIZEN_GUIDE.pdf.

8 "Identity and Energy Access in India: Setting Contexts for Rio+20," *Energy Security Insights* 7, no. 1 (January–March 2012).

9 Ibid.

10 "Government Finalises Norms for Distribution Companies' Debt Recast," Press Trust of India, April 5, 2013, http://profit.ndtv.com/news/corporates/ article-government-finalises-norms-for-distribution-companies-debt-recast-320539.

11 See, for example, Shishir Asthana, "Is There a Case to Keep Shale Gas Out of the Reach of Private Players?" *Business Standard*, September 18, 2013, welcoming the move to exclude the private sector from shale gas development.

12 Rajya Sabha, "List of Questions for Oral Answers to Be Asked at a Sitting of the Rajya Sabha to Be Held on Tuesday, April 30, 2013/Vaisakha 10, 1935,"April 30, 2013, 147, http://164.100.47.5/EDAILYQUESTIONS/sessionno/228/301RS.pdf.

13 Ministry of Petroleum and Natural Gas, Government of India, "Comments Invited on Uniform Licensing Policy for Award of Hydrocarbon Acreages With New Contractual System and Fiscal Model," Memorandum O-19018/25/2013-ONG-1, September 20, 2013, http://petroleum.nic.in/comments.pdf.

14 "108 Hydrocarbon Discoveries Made in 36 NELP Blocks," Hindu Business Line, May 22, 2012, www.thehindubusinessline.com/industry–and–conomy/ article3446566.ece.

15 Ministry of Petroleum and Natural Gas, Government of India, "Comments Invited on Uniform Licensing Policy for Award of Hydrocarbon Acreages with New Contractual System and Fiscal Model."

16 International Energy Agency, *Medium Term Coal Market Report 2012* (Paris: OECD Publications, 2012).

17 "Gas Price at About $8, Chidambaram Hints Lowering Price for Fertilizer, Power Sectors," *Financial Express*, June 28, 2013, http://archive.indianexpress.com/news/ gas-price-at-about-8-chidambaram-hints-lowering-price-for-fertilizer-power-sectors/1135087.

18 Directorate General of Hydrocarbons, Under Ministry of Petroleum and Natural Gas, *Hydrocarbon Exploration and Production Activities, 2011–12* (New Delhi: Government of India, 2012), www.dghindia.org/pdf/1DGH%20Annual%20 Report%202011-12.pdf.

19 "Resource Assessment: Conventional and Unconventional Gas," Indianpetro.com, April 9, 2013, www.indianpetro.com/articleView.do?articleID=113307&pgNo=0.

20 Government of India, Ministry of Power, Central Electricity Authority, "All India Electricity Statistics, General Review: 2012," 2012.

21 Rajan Gupta, Harihar Shankar, and Sunjoy Joshi, "Development, Energy Security and Climate Security: India's Converging Goals," Los Alamos National Laboratory, http://cnls.lanl.gov/~rajan/Gupta_orf_writeup_v9.pdf.

22 The reserve portion (numerator) of the ratio is the amount of a resource known to exist in an area and to be economically recoverable (proved reserves). The production portion (denominator) of the ratio is the amount of the resource used in one year at the current rate.

23 Gupta et al., "Development, Energy Security, and Climate Security."

24 "About Us," Coal India Limited, accessed December 5, 2013, www.coalindia.in/ Company.aspx?tab=0.

25 Pukhraj Sethiya et al., "The Indian Coal Sector: Challenges and Future Outlook," PricewaterhouseCoopers, 2012, www.pwc.in/assets/pdfs/industries/power%E2%80 %93mining/icc%E2%80%93coal%E2%80%93report.pdf.

26 Saurabh Chaturvedi, "Coal India Share Sale Faces Hurdles," *Wall Street Journal*, May 20, 2013, http://online.wsj.com/news/articles/SB1000142412788732478700457849 4783635334730.

27 Supercritical power plants operate at temperatures resulting in higher efficiencies—up to 46 percent for supercritical plants—and lower emissions than traditional (subcritical) coal-fired plants. The "efficiency" of the thermodynamic process of a coal-fired plant power describes how much of the energy that is fed into the cycle is converted into electrical energy. The greater the output of electrical energy for a given amount of energy input, the higher the efficiency.

28 Rajan Gupta et al., "Development, Energy Security and Climate Security: India's Converging Goals."

29 Zhao Yinan and Fu Jing, "Leadership Charts Path," *China Daily*, November 13, 2013, www.chinadaily.com.cn/china/2013cpctps/2013%E2%80%9311/13/ content_17100151.htm.

30 Masami Kojima and Robert Bacon, "Changes in CO_2 Emissions From Energy Use," Working Paper, World Bank, October 2009, http://siteresources.worldbank.org/ EXTOGMC/Resources/co2_emissions1.pdf.

31 U.S. Energy Information Administration, "Carbon Intensity," accessed December 5, 2013, www.eia.gov/cfapps/ipdbproject/IEDIndex.cfm?tid=91&pid=46&aid=31.

32 Kojima and Bacon, "Changes in CO_2 Emissions From Energy Use."

33 The share of manufacturing in the Indian economy is a low 16 percent.

34 U.S. Energy Information Administration, "Carbon Intensity," www.eia.gov/cfapps/ ipdbproject/IEDIndex3.cfm?tid=91&pid=46&aid=31.

35 See, for example, M. V. Ramana and Suvrat Raju, "The Impasse Over Liability Clause in Indo-U.S. Nuclear Deal," *New York Times*, October 10, 2013, http://india.blogs. nytimes.com/2013/10/15/the-impasse-over-liability-clause-in-indo-u-s-nuclear-deal.

CHAPTER 13

MANAGING THE ENVIRONMENT

LIGIA NORONHA

THE CHALLENGES

Getting India back on track acquires even more significance in the environmental domain. Even the briefest glance at India's environmental record is both descriptive and sobering. The World Health Organization reports that thirteen of the G20's most polluted cities are in India.[1] A recent assessment of the global burden of disease estimates that outdoor air pollution causes 620,000 premature deaths per year in India.[2] A 2010 study by the Energy and Resources Institute (TERI) suggested that environmental degradation in India took a toll of about 4 percent of India's 2007 GDP; more recently the World Bank raised this economy-wide cost estimate to 5.7 percent of India's 2009 GDP.[3]

The two oft-heard arguments from supporters of economic growth regardless of its impact on the environment are that environmental concerns are an obstacle to growth and that, following the example of the developed world, India needs to grow first and then worry about the environment. However, this is a myopic view, as the developed world did not share India's high population density, nor was it developing at a time when local and planetary boundaries were already stressed. The mistaken perception that the environment is a hurdle to growth stems in part from the slow environmental clearance process that delays projects, as well as the failure to understand that economic activity is underpinned by the services that ecosystems provide and that a dynamic interdependency thus exists between economy and ecology. The environment matters because environmental degradation and pollution, while by-products of human activities, have a bearing on human well-being, affecting health and quality of life as much as livelihoods and economic activity. But this link is not recognized sufficiently.

"Management of the environment" refers not to actually managing the environment, which is not possible, but to influencing and shaping the interactions of humans and their activities with the environment. As a matter of policy, this involves engaging with the temporal, spatial, and agency dimension of ways in which ecosystems that contribute to human well-being are affected by human activities. The temporal dimension stems from the fact that the loss of ecosystem services has implications for human well-being not only today, but also intergenerationally. On a spatial level, the implications of such degradation vary in their extent and scale, from local to global. In terms of agency, a number of actors and actions are involved in the externalities created by growth, leading to both inter- and intra-generational inequalities in the distribution of pollution and access to resources.

But politicians have short time horizons, in which the impacts of degraded environments may not always be felt or seen or be of concern. This is a truism everywhere, and politicians in India are no exception. They focus more on projects and decisions that have clear beneficiaries, and the need to worry about the environmental impacts of such projects is of lesser interest because those affected may be invisible or voiceless or in the future. Politicians have even less interest if the costs or benefits of action or non-action are in the distant future and are uncertain, as is the case with climate change. However, surveys suggest that concern is growing among the Indian public about climate change and the state of the environment in Indian cities, creating a clear incentive for politicians to act.[4] The next big items on the electoral agenda after corruption will be environmental quality, action on climate change, and environmental justice. These issue areas are just waiting to spill onto the roads. The issue of corruption has merely bought politicians some time with regard to the environment.

The constitution of India has assigned functions, legislative competence, and fiscal powers to both the central and state government levels with respect to different subjects. Table 1 summarizes the distribution of subjects of relevance to sustainable development. The Seventh Schedule of the constitution, read with Article 246, in its three Lists—Union (the central government), State, and Concurrent—assigns subjects to different

TABLE 1. DISTRIBUTION OF SUBJECTS OF RELEVANCE TO SUSTAINABLE DEVELOPMENT

Governing unit	Subject	Schedule
Union	• Atomic energy, mineral resources necessary for its production • Regulation and development of oilfields, mineral oil resources; petroleum, petroleum products; other inflammable liquids • Regulation of mines and mineral development	VII
State	• Constitution and powers of local government units • Public health and sanitation; hospitals; dispensaries • Communication (roads, bridges, and so on, including inland waterways), subject to Lists I and III • Land • Water • Tax on sale and consumption of electricity	VII
Concurrent	• Vagrancy; nomadic and migratory tribes • Prevention of cruelty to animals • Forests • Electricity	VII
Local	• Urban planning, including town planning • Regulation of land use, construction of buildings • Economic and social development planning	XII
Rural	• Agriculture and agricultural extension • Land improvement, implementation of land reforms, land consolidation, soil conservation • Minor irrigation, water management, watershed development	XI

Source: Adapted from TERI, *Integrating Environment, Ecology and Climate Change Concerns in the Indian Fiscal Federalism Framework* (New Delhi: Energy and Resources Institute, 2009), 73.

Note: Schedule VII denotes legislative powers as recognized by the constitution; Schedules XI and XII enable states to devolve their powers and responsibilities to municipalities and *panchayats*.

levels of government. Environment, as a residual subject in the constitution, vests with the central government. Even where decentralization is provided for in the constitution, the corresponding institutional and fiscal support is inadequate. The states themselves are under no strict obligation to devolve functions relating to environmental and natural resource management, and the approach to funding it is top-down. Functional interaction between central and state authorities is limited, and the role of local bodies such as the *gram sabhas* and *panchayati raj* institutions is either limited or absent, more so in decisionmaking than in implementation.[5]

UNSATISFACTORY APPROACHES AND TRENDS
Centralism in Environmental Governance

At a time when the federating states and the polity in India are seeking greater say in national matters that concern them and want deeper political participation in the growth project, we observe that centralism in environmental governance has increased, with the constitutional role of the federating states diminishing, and that of local governments practically nonexistent. Our work suggests that the centrally sponsored schemes have become an increasingly important source of intergovernmental fiscal transfers, and since these often deal with matters of local significance, they are displacing local stakes and decisions. At the June 2012 Green Federalism conference organized by TERI in partnership with the Inter-State Council, the Ministry of Environment and Forests, and the Forum of Federations, it was noted that establishment of several central institutions has been instrumental in bypassing the state governments and that the federating states, too, have been lethargic in management of the environment, resulting in judicial intervention.[6]

There is evidence that existing environmental rules and policies, mostly command and control, while comprehensive, are often not enforced or are poorly enforced. Oversight institutions are weak, due to either inadequate capability and resources or lack of interest from those charged to provide this oversight. Institutional coordination is a key challenge, both vertically and horizontally. For example, provisioning of water supply and sanitation are, at the least, the concerns of ministries or departments dealing with water, rural development, urban development, local government, health, and agriculture. There is little interaction or communication among them on these issues. Inaccurate price signals lead to excessive and inefficient consumption, especially with regard to water supply across sectors, energy, and fertilizers. Environmental externalities are not reflected in pricing. Coal mining, for example, has many environmental and social externalities, from reduced air quality due to increased PM10 (particulate matter up to 10 micrometers in size) and sulfur oxides in the air, to impacts on water quality, loss of forests, and contributions to carbon emissions from coal combustion. Absence of wastewater charges and charges on mine waste result in the adoption of inefficient practices, making a strong case for the adoption of more market-based regulatory policies to supplement existing rules.

Command and control approaches alone do not work, in India or elsewhere, for several reasons: environmental risks are cumulative, and pollution sources have many pathways, are often multimedia, multiagency, and interactive. Second generation approaches on environmental governance in India focus on market-based instruments or even community-based initiatives and knowledge and institutions. But these, too, are not enough to address current problems.

Unsatisfactory Ecosystem Management

Three ecosystems are discussed below: rivers, forests, and coasts. These are of special concern because they are especially important ecosystems for India and are most under human stress.

Rivers

Rivers in India have become degraded and often serve as waste dumps and sewers in many parts of the country. For example, large segments of the Ganga are heavily polluted, and given the looming water security issue, this is indeed a serious concern, not just one of water availability but also of water quality.[7] In 2013, the Central Pollution Control Board identified 150 stretches of polluted rivers, the maximum stretches in Priority 1 being in Maharashtra, Uttar Pradesh, and Gujarat.[8] Rivers in India are also being dammed without sufficient attention to environmental flows required to keep the river system alive. This is especially so in the Western Ghats, but also in the Indus-Ganga-Brahmaputra river systems.[9]

As Ramaswamy R. Iyer, the former secretary of water resources, puts it, a river is not just a conduit for water, but "an integral part of the lives, history, politics, society, religion and culture of a people."[10] In the case of rivers and river basins, inadequate understanding of the role they play in human well-being leads to their being "chopped up," that is, not treated as an ecosystem but segmented for water-sharing purposes.[11] This affects the values that rivers represent for human well-being, as well as the functions they perform and ecosystem services they provide to support water availability, navigation, fish habitats, riverine livelihoods, and cultural practices; mangrove ecosystems, groundwater/surface water interface, and floods in support of estuaries. The direction and velocity of water flows and their distribution in time and location help define the extent to which the river system can support important ecological functions. Dams and diversions create loss of belonging if people are displaced; they can also affect seasonal rhythm and salinity patterns, cause changes in flow regimes, and make the estuaries in which the river systems open out more homogeneous over the year. As in case of other ecosystems, we notice that current approaches to management have migrated to reduced forms of ecosystem management. An "unconsciously holistic view of rivers gave way to a limited instrumental view brought about by two reductionisms: an engineering reductionism and an economic reductionism."[12]

Forests

Current policy seeks to balance forest preservation and development by using forest clearances; the mechanism of compensatory afforestation, which requires entities that need forest diversion to afforest land to compensate for the loss of forests; and payments based on the net present value (NPV) of different types of forest to compensate for forest ecosystem loss. NPV payments can range from Rs. 5.80 lakh to Rs. 9.20 lakh per hectare depending on density and quality of forests. As policy mechanisms, the purpose of compensatory afforestation is to rehabilitate forests. Payments based on NPV are meant as payment toward the protection of the environment and not in relation to a proprietary right. The payments so collected go to the Compensatory Afforestation Fund Management and Planning

Authority (CAMPA). The Comptroller and Auditor General's Report on CAMPA in 2013, however, suggested that Rs. 23,000 crore were lying unutilized in the fund in 2012 because of insufficient land for reforestation and delays in preparation of plans at the local level.

Compensatory afforestation was a result of a judicial intervention, which is often argued to be against the spirit of the federal structure because it results in too much encroachment by the central government on state matters that relate to forest lands. Through CAMPA, the central government is involved in micromanagement of forests beyond the forest clearance process, which the current regulatory framework requires of the central government. Moreover, the practice of obtaining non-forest land for compensatory afforestation for forest land that is diverted is seen to result in displacement of two different sets of people from their common lands without consultation, compensation, or the provision of alternatives. Quite apart from the administrative and federal issues that surround using allocations from the CAMPA fund, this policy instrument does not resolve the problems of habitat fragmentation and landscape restoration that are key to ecosystem and biodiversity protection.[13] However, given that this fund had around Rs. 30,000 crore as of 2013, it makes sense to use the funds to at least rehabilitate degraded forests, restore landscapes, and consolidate habitats.[14]

Coasts

Coastal ecosystems present a special case for environmental governance, not only because of their enormous developmental appeal historically and for being privileged with better infrastructure and other facilities, but also because coasts are land-ocean interfaces, which makes these zones very uncertain, complex, and vulnerable to natural and human processes. A mix of economic and environmental values and personal and community stakes is attached to subsystems, with implications for how choices are made to conserve or develop. Multiple users, for example, modern and traditional fishermen, small shack owners and large hoteliers, land use for power plants and for use by tourists and residents, imply greater competition for coastal space and increased potential for conflict over resources.[15] This also gives rise to the emergence of self-elected political actors who see opportunities for gain from this conflict. It is in this context that the

Coastal Regulation Zone (CRZ) Act was put in place in 1991 and revisited in 2011 to protect the coast and regulate its spatial use. The premise of the CRZ to protect the coast, and the environment and traditional livelihoods dependent on it, has not been met, however, and it is not clear how this would be achieved.[16]

AGENDA FOR THE NEXT FIVE YEARS

Environmental governance in India needs a fresh approach. It cannot be just a top-down enterprise led by the central government. The thinking needs to go beyond enacting rules and regulations to a greater focus on outcomes and results that emerge from a sense of shared understanding and common purpose for scientists, policymakers, experts and lay people, governments and business. The command and control approaches that India has deployed cannot sufficiently address current environmental and natural resource problems that are defined by the need to reduce emissions and pollution of unclear origin. Nor can these approaches regulate efficiently and equitably the use of space and resources that are contested by multiple groups with different interests. A new framework for environmental governance is required, one that is multilevel, multi-actor, based on ecosystems and outcomes rather than on mere compliance. This framework needs to reflect an understanding of the interrelationships of food, energy, and water, and the linkages between ecosystems and human well-being.

Five agenda items are proposed for the next government. They focus on framework issues and suggestions for improvements in the management of environmental pollution and in ecosystem-based management for forests, rivers, and coasts.

Agenda Item 1: Adopt the Principle of Subsidiarity in Environmental Management

The central government needs to apply the principle of subsidiarity to the case of environmental management in India to ensure that different levels of government take responsibility for those dimensions of environmental quality within their jurisdictional boundaries, leading to better environmental management across the board. This requires an understanding of the "span" of the public goods and services that are provided or need to be provided. Since many environmental issues are local and regional in nature, addressing them requires the involvement of local regional jurisdictions and the engagement of local people. This would also allow for greater public voice in the design of programs, enable feedback for the fine-tuning of policies, and reduce the number of layers of bureaucracy, thus making clear jurisdictional responsibilities for enforcement and service.

Table 2 summarizes some of the key aspects of a nuanced devolution of environmental responsibilities across levels of government. It is not comprehensive or final.

TABLE 2. WHO NEEDS TO DO WHAT

Environmental management policy outcomes	Spatial limits of benefit incidence	Responsible government tier
Research and knowledge creation on environmental matters	Global and National	C, S, L*
Research on sustainable consumption and production systems	Global and National	C
Knowledge sharing	Global and National	C, S, L
Feedback and experimentation on policy innovations	State and Local	S, L
Determination of emission standards, such as for vehicles and fuel efficiency	National	C
Addressing interjurisdictional externalities	Regional (spillover)	Higher-level governments/ regional bodies
Capacity building for environmental law enforcers and line agencies	National, State, Local	C, S with support from NGOs (non-governmental organizations)
Incentives for private effort in socially valuable technologies	National, State, Local	C
Incentives for forest conservation	Global, National, State, Local	S, L
Cleansing of groundwater	State, Local	S, L

* C - Central; S - State; L - Local.

There is a need, however, to provide for intergovernmental fiscal and knowledge transfers, which are necessary when pollution and environmental damage cross jurisdictions. Positive incentives and rewards for rule enforcement and good governance are required to promote accountability and competitive service delivery. Reforms in urban local bodies are needed to better manage waste, both institutional and technical. Given that management involves regulating economic activity that degrades or pollutes, and that the distribution of subjections in the Union, State, and Local Lists is given, adopting subsidiarity is a matter of issuing clear policy and administrative directives to sublevels of government and providing the fiscal and capacity supports required to deliver improved outcomes, perhaps through the intergovernmental transfers of the 14th Finance Commission.

Empowering the Inter-State Council would help advance this agenda. Currently under the Ministry of Home Affairs, this is a constitutional body whose mandate is to examine and seek to resolve key issues and friction between states. Its mandate can also be expanded to address center-state issues since many contentious ones are mushrooming. Activating and empowering the Inter-State Council, while liberating it from the controls of the Home Ministry, which is part of the central government, is the best way to create a platform that can enable the discussions and the formation of a national consensus on environmental and resource management issues that are emerging as states and people become more federalist in their reasoning.

Agenda Item 2: Prioritize Mitigation of Air and Water Pollution

Managing air and water pollution in India needs to be a top priority of local governments working in synergy with state pollution control boards. The air quality situation in Indian cities is grave, as is the case in several water bodies. While a well-developed regulatory framework is in place for air and water, monitoring and enforcement are weak. States should strengthen the pollution control boards to take action against violators and impose penalties and charges, but they should also invest in the boards' resources and capacity. States should also support more participatory monitoring (as was done in the Western Ghats Expert Ecology Panel's report) and independent third-party auditors to improve outcomes.[17] Cleanup action plans should be taken up urgently by the states and the central government for those areas, regions, and river stretches identified by the Central Pollution Control Board as critically polluted, and no further development projects should be allowed there until pollution is significantly reduced.

In the transport domain, the central government should provide incentives through fiscal policy for fleet modernization and a road map for introducing improved fuel quality and vehicle technology tied to increased public health concerns around emissions. Public investments at the state level are required to increase the availability of bus fleets, metros, and informal public transport such as improved electric auto rickshaws, since any disincentives for plying private vehicles can work only if alternatives are available. States should incentivize the use of public transport through student and senior citizen discounts, and last-mile connections. Public transport will not have the desired response from women, however, unless cities' safety records are improved. For affluent areas in cities and metropolitan areas, congestion tax or vehicle quotas—both of which are incentives for carpooling—can be introduced, as they have been in Singapore, to penalize the overuse of personalized transport. Subsidies and tax exemptions for "eco cars" that produce fewer emissions should also be introduced by the central government.

The central government should urgently introduce reforms to manage waste and wastewater. This has to be at three levels: reduction of waste and wastewater at the source; onsite treatment where possible; and recycling of wastewater as water for nonconsumptive use, with waste converted into energy for decentralized distribution. To achieve these reforms, a three-pronged strategy should be enacted: training and capacity building of state and local bodies, resident welfare associations, and local market associations in partnerships with national and international research and training institutions; clear policy guidelines issued by the central government for waste minimization and recycling; and rehabilitation of waste dumps and landfills in public-private partnership mode.

Agenda Item 3: Adopt Green Accounting in National and State Income Accounting by 2015

Central to initiatives on greening the economy is attaching an economic value to ecosystem services and finite natural resources used in development activity, a practice often termed "green accounting" or "resource accounting." This is based on the premise that when the social and economic value that ecosystem services provide goes unrecognized, there are fewer obstacles to their destruction. Green income accounting seeks to modify income accounts to incorporate the use or depletion of environmental and natural resources. This adjustment can be done to conventional income accounts at the national or macroeconomic level or at the microeconomic level to assess the costs and benefits of an activity or project. The key objective of such accounting is to make visible the use of environmental resources in economic production; until now, their use has been invisible. The conventional treatment of these environmental resources, being free, has resulted in their overuse and exploitation. To be useful, valuation needs to involve appropriate stakeholders, especially local communities, and also be clear about what parameters are to be included in such exercises. In project decisionmaking, assuming that a free prior informed consent exists, such valuation can help arrive at decisions that are more ethical, efficient, and acceptable.

The next government should make a priority of preparing national and state income accounts adjusted for environmental impacts. This will be an important indicator of the quality of growth at the national and state levels. As an example, the Energy and Resources Institute did a green accounting for the minerals sector in Goa. Our study used four clusters of mining over an area of 520 square kilometers. The clusters differed in terms of the age of mining and were based on a 1997 study on social and environmental impacts of mining. Some impacts from mining were valued, and the information was used to adjust the income reported from the minerals sector in state income accounts. Our accounts, limited as they were in scope and methods, suggested that for 1996–1997, the contribution of mining to Goa's state domestic product was 15 percent of what was reported by the state as being the contribution of the minerals sector to state GDP. This adjustment to reported value added from mining serves to enable people and decisionmakers to realize that the inflated contribution attributed to minerals development ignores the conjunctive use of land, water, and forests and the impacts these resources have on other users. Despite the reductionism involved in green accounting, some values of impacts that help provide more realistic and "true" contribution of development activities to state income are better than no valuation at all. At the national level, initiatives are already afoot to introduce green accounting into net state domestic product estimates by the Central Statistical Organization.[18] In April 2013, the prime minister expressed the hope that the Ministry of Statistics and Program Implementation, in consultation with the Planning Commission and any concerned ministries, would seek to introduce the framework developed by Partha Dasgupta and others. An integrated environmental and accounting framework urgently needs to be implemented by the central government; this integration, several methodologies, and pilots have been much discussed for more than fifteen years. Valuation methodologies and frameworks thus exist, and are known, but training needs to be provided to the planning departments in all state governments if green accounting is to be enabled by 2015.

Agenda Item 4: Adopt More Progressive Frameworks for Mineral Resource Development and Resource Efficiency

There is no denying that India will need material resources in very large quantities to meet the development needs of its population. India currently has a low material consumption per capita relative to other countries. The projections done by a recent study suggest a 2.5- to threefold increase from 2008 to 2030 and a four- to fivefold increase by 2050 in terms of material requirements, assuming an 8 percent growth rate until 2030 and a 6 percent rate after that.[19] This demand will have a large and growing social and environmental footprint. India is rich in minerals, but many are found in ecologically sensitive areas and in regions inhabited by tribal populations. Mineral extraction operations' social license is already diminishing, given that resource and environmental governance measures have not been able to address the trust deficit observed among government, companies, and local people in mineral-rich regions. Nor has the government implemented the right compensation, consent, and benefit-sharing frameworks. It is clear, however, that we will need minerals to meet our mobility, housing, food, and energy requirements. India's mining sector has one of the lowest exploration spends globally. And over the past year, mining for iron ore has almost come to a halt in parts of India because of illegalities and other governance issues. Coal production has continuously been a cause for concern given the rising demand for this resource to meet energy needs. Yet there seems to be little urgency to pass the Mines and Minerals (Development and Regulation) Bill and to have in place frameworks that are more progressive in terms of taking on board environmental and social concerns, to ensure that mining happens in a well-regulated manner that produces more benefits for local populations. The current lack of action on this front only compounds the already difficult problem posed by rising import prices. Such global dependency will only rise, adding to new challenges to energy and mineral resource security. In this context, India needs to focus on putting in place the right frameworks and also adopt efficient resource use wherever possible to enable increased output with fewer inputs. It is clear that technology alone will not address India's need for materials in the long term. More specifically, the central government should do the following on a priority basis:

1. Establish stable and predictable tax and allocative policy regimes to attract long-term investments. The government needs to adopt business models (and fiscal systems) that are mineral-specific, depending on the policy objectives with regard to different mineral groups, for example: where mineralization is known and reserves are in abundance; strategic but abundant minerals, but with reserve uncertainty; and minerals critical to the Indian economy, but with different levels of information and technology needs.

2. Make resource efficiency an organizing principle of the economy and the sector in the interest of long-term supply security, competitiveness, equity, and sustainability. The government needs to put in place aggressive information, education, and communication campaigns for the "4 Rs"—Reduce, Reuse, Recycle, and Recover—to

ensure that resource efficiency is mainstreamed into the Indian economy. Further, the government should make investments in efficient food production, water- and energy-efficient technology, building material science, and appropriate policy instruments to incentivize efficiency along the product life cycle.

3. Make clear decisions on areas that are out of bounds for mining based on science and social consensus and have them spatially mapped as discussed below. Once these areas are clearly established, regulatory clearances in other areas need to be time-bound and fast-tracked.

4. Conduct environmental and social impact assessments responsibly. Anything else backfires. Shoddy environmental impact assessments also hinder the environmental clearance processes. The independence and integrity of the environmental impact assessment consultancy pool must be established and recognized.

5. Opt for partnerships in tribal regions that acknowledge their special status. Companies can consider use of model development agreements, when and if the free prior and informed consent of the *gram sabha* for mining has been obtained.[20]

6. Establish mechanisms or platforms to address grievances, resolve conflicts, and provide opportunities for stakeholder engagement and dialogue. Establish accountability mechanisms, as it is critical that decisionmakers are accountable to stakeholders and in particular citizens, who are the ultimate owners of mineral assets. Information must be provided across the whole chain of decisions.

7. Require mining companies to establish management information systems and web-based tools to track the sustainability performance of minerals projects. These would enable the general public to know how the mining industry is contributing to the public good and to track environmental and social impacts.

Agenda Item 5: Adopt a Reasoned Approach to Balancing Valuable Ecosystems and Development

Science and participatory decisionmaking need to be brought together to balance valuable ecosystems and development. To help achieve this, the next government should map ecologically sensitive areas across the country on a geographic information system platform using different parameters of ecological value, as was done by the Western Ghats Expert Ecology Panel. This mapping then needs to be used by states, in conjunction with *gram sabhas* and other popular institutions, to decide in a participatory manner which activities to ban, allow, and regulate, and which to promote. This approach, followed by the Western Ghats panel, suggested the use of ecologically sensitive zoning as a tool to balance the environment and development in the Western Ghats.[21] Ecologically sensitive zones should be based on scientific data that enable an understanding of ecological sensitivity and fragility that could pose long-term risks if people are exposed to degrading development activity. Human activities should continue in all these zones, but with prudent regulation. The zones should not stop development in ways that would hurt local people but should promote development that is responsible, environmentally friendly, and people-oriented.

In the case of rivers and river basins, the empowered Inter-State Council should work toward a national consensus on the complex and multidimensional nature of water. With regard to improved coastal management, the Coastal Zone Management Authority should identify ways in which multiple perspectives can be brought into the working of the Coastal Zone Management Act and levels at which information exchange is easiest, working within the framework of the subsidiarity principle. The *gram sabha* in Coastal Regulation Zone areas should be given the same standing as in scheduled areas and include the *gram sabha* resolution in CRZ clearances.[22]

In conclusion, future governments should ensure the mainstreaming of environmental considerations in development decisionmaking. This is of great urgency, given that environmental degradation is affecting the health and the quality of life of citizens and of India's economic productivity; unaddressed early on, this situation will only get worse as India develops. The central government has to focus on what needs to be done to improve Indians' quality of life as well as the country's environmental and resource security. Five agenda items have been identified around subsidiarity, green accounting, management of air and water pollution, progressive resource development and efficiency frameworks, and reasoned approaches to the balancing of development and ecologically valuable ecosystems. Decisionmaking on development needs to be stepped up through having prior vetted information, and CAMPA as a policy instrument needs to be revisited or fine-tuned.

A balance between growth and the environment should be the goal, made possible by recognition and pricing of externalities of development, adoption of technological innovations to reduce them to the extent possible, more deliberated choices on ecological valuable areas where degrading industrial activity should not be allowed, and a greater focus on improved environmental health outcomes. Development, if unsustainable, destroys the very basis of future economic growth, not least by destabilizing the climate. Ecological tipping points will profoundly affect human wellbeing and economic activity if these irreversible shifts in the behavior of natural systems are not factored into decisionmaking. The next government should factor this interdependency into policymaking and prioritize environmental management to improve the quality of India's growth. This will require more collaborative economic models that reflect equity, participation, and multilevel governance.

NOTES

1   Muthukumara Mani, *Greening India's Growth: Costs, Valuation and Trade-Offs* (New York: Routledge, 2014), 2.

2   Centre for Science and Environment, "Burden of Disease: Outdoor Air Pollution Among Top Killers," February 13, 2013, http://cseindia.org/userfiles/briefing_note-13feb.pdf.

3   Divya Datt and Shilpa Nischal, *Looking Back to Change Track* (New Delhi: TERI Press, 2010).

4   Centre for Science and Environment, "Burden of Disease: Outdoor Air Pollution Among Top Killers," and Energy and Resources Institute, *TERI Environmental Survey 2013* (New Delhi: Energy and Resources Institute, 2013), www.teriin.org/pdf/Environmental-Survey.pdf.

5   Ligia Noronha, Amrita Goldar, et al., *Integrating Environment, Ecology and Climate Change Concerns in the Indian Fiscal Federalism Framework* (New Delhi: The Energy and Resources Institute, 2009).

6   Energy and Resources Institute, "Greening the Indian Federal System: Views From the Centre and States," summary of conference proceedings, July 6, 2012, www.teriin.org/events/greening-gfi_summary.pdf.

7   See Government of India, Ministry of Environment and Forests, National Rivers Conservation Directorate, "Status Paper on River Ganga: State of Environment and Water Quality," August 2009, http://moef.nic.in/downloads/public-information/Status%20Paper%20-Ganga.pdf.

8   Government of India, Ministry of Environment and Forests, Central Pollution Control Board, "Polluted River Stretches in India: Criteria and Status," November 2013, www.cpcb.nic.in/upload/Latest/Latest_66_FinalPollutedStretches.pdf.

9   Latha Anantha and Parineeta Dandekar, "Towards Restoring Flows Into the Earth's Arteries: A Primer on Environmental Flows," *International Rivers*, May 2009, www.internationalrivers.org/files/attached-files/eflows_primer_062012.pdf, and Parineeta Dandekar, "'Damning' the Western Ghats." presentation at Save the Western Ghats Conclave, Mahabaleshwar, India, December 2009, http://sandrp.in/rivers/Damming_the_Western_Ghats_Presentation_SWGM_December2012.pdf.

10 Ramaswamy R. Iyer, "Chopping Up Rivers: From Segmentation to Holism and Harmony," paper presented at Strengthening Green Federalism: Sharing International Practices Conference, New Delhi, October 29, 2012.

11 Ibid., 6.

12 Ibid.

13 Praveen Bhargav, "'Greening India' But Losing Forests," *Hindu*, November 2, 2007.

14 Energy and Resources Institute, *TERI Environmental Survey 2013*.

15 Ligia Noronha et al., *Coastal Tourism, Environment, and Sustainable Local Development*, chapter 1 (New Delhi: Energy and Resources Institute, 2002), www.teriin.org/teri-wr/coastin/coastaltourism.pdf.

16 KAS India and Environment and Resources Institute, "Environmental Governance in the Context of Sustainable Development in India: The Case of Coastal and Marine Ecosystems," Policy Paper, April 2013, www.teriin.org/pdf/policy-paper_3rd-TERI-KAS.pdf, 6.

17 Esther Duflo et al., "Truth Telling by Third-Party Auditors and the Response of Polluting Firms: Experimental Evidence From India," *Quarterly Journal of Economics* (2013), http://qje.oxfordjournals.org/content/128/4/1499.full.pdf.

18 See Government of India, Ministry of Statistics and Programme Implementation, National Statistical Organization, *Green National Accounts in India: A Framework,* Expert Group Report, March 2013, http://mospi.nic.in/mospi_new/upload/Green_National_Accouts_in_India_1may13.pdf.

19 Indo-German Environmental Partnership, "India's Future Need for Resources: Dimensions, Challenges and Possible Solutions," November 2013, www.ifeu.de/abfallwirtschaft/pdf/ResourceEfficiency_Final%20Report_lowres.pdf.

20 Energy and Resources Institute, "Governance of Mining in India: Responding to Policy Deficits," TERI Policy Brief, July 2013, www.teriin.org/policybrief/docs/TERI_Policy%20Brief_June%202012.pdf.

21 See Government of India, Ministry of Environments and Forests, *Report of the Western Ghats Ecology Expert Panel,* August 31, 2011, http://moef.nic.in/downloads/public-information/wg-23052012.pdf.

22 Indo-German Environmental Partnership, "India's Future Need for Resources: Dimensions, Challenges and Possible Solutions."

CHAPTER 14

STRENGTHENING RULE OF LAW

DEVESH KAPUR AND MILAN VAISHNAV*

INTRODUCTION

Guaranteeing the rule of law is perhaps the most critical task facing any democracy. While the importance of the rule of law for underpinning contracts and promoting basic law and order is often emphasized, designing and enforcing just laws are even more fundamentally the basis of a fair society, providing the only checks and balances to protect the weak against the strong.

On paper, India has a long tradition of upholding the rule of law, distinguishing it from many of its autocratic peers and neighbors. This tradition is enshrined in India's constitution and subsequent statutes, protected fiercely by the courts, and held together by democracy and free elections. According to 2012 World Justice Project data, India fares well on indicators related to the openness of government and democratic controls. In the

---

* The authors would like to thank Madhav Khosla and Ananth Padmanabhan for valuable inputs on the Indian legal system, Danielle Smogard for her excellent research assistance, and Govind Mohan and T. V. Somanathan for helpful conversations. We also acknowledge incisive comments from Bibek Debroy, Ashley J. Tellis, and Reece Trevor. However, only the authors are responsible for the statements (and any errors) made herein. This article draws, in part, on Devesh Kapur, "The Law Laid Down," *Outlook India*, January 7, 2013. Available at http://bit.ly/16eOmCa.

category "limited government powers," which evaluates the checks on government, India ranks 37 of 97 globally, 1 of 5 regionally, and 2 of 23 among lower-middle-income countries.[1]

Yet the rule of law that exists on paper does not always exist in practice. According to the same dataset, when it comes to procedural effectiveness, India fares poorly. In the categories of "absence of corruption" and "order and security," India ranks 83 and 96, respectively.[2] The net result is that India has laws, but also a great deal of uncertainty about how those laws are actually implemented.

The literature on the rule of law distinguishes between its formal and substantive conceptions.[3] In the majority of this chapter, we use the term "rule of law" in a way that encapsulates the former idea that focuses on the procedural legitimacy of laws and institutions—which demands that laws are prospective, clearly drafted, properly enforced, independently reviewed—and emphasizes state capacity in the context of law making and enforcement. In this manner, the rule of law is not a single entity, but rather a spectrum of activities. The upstream end of this chain is the structure of the laws and statutes that govern any society, not to mention the lawmakers who write them. Next come the investigative arms of the state, followed by the prosecutorial agencies. The judiciary and penal system constitute the downstream end. Each component of this chain influences the strength and quality of the preceding step(s). Referring to the substantive aspects of the rule of law—in which the actual content of the laws is evaluated—we will also assess the ability of certain laws to adequately protect equality and justice.

In India, the entire rule of law supply chain, never very strong to begin with, has become deeply dysfunctional. India's legal undergirding is badly outmoded and constrained by a tendency to pass new laws rather than fix or eliminate old ones. Weak laws yoked to an even weaker enforcement system virtually guarantee that the powerful will transgress with abandon. Furthermore, the very lawmakers who write the laws are hardly exemplars of the rule of law themselves; nearly a third of state and national legislators faced pending criminal charges at the time of their election. This disturbing fact has a negative impact on the credibility of the entire rule of law supply chain, from lawmaking to enforcement.

Moving farther down the chain, the police and prosecutors need an overhaul. India's investigative agencies have become politicized and starved of resources, infrastructure, and leadership. The judiciary in India has many bright spots: the Supreme Court of India, for instance, is one of the country's most widely respected public institutions. Yet the courts, on the whole, face challenges from vacancies to backlogs and weak internal processes of self-regulation.

At the time of writing, India's once-robust economy has been badly hobbled. While external factors played a role in the current economic slowdown, the country has also fallen victim to corruption, weak institutions, and legal and regulatory uncertainty. A large part of its population is apprehensive of physical insecurity, and a spate of large-scale corruption scandals has shaken the faith of its citizens. Whatever government comes to power in 2014 must acknowledge India's mixed performance when it comes to enforcing the rule of law and take immediate steps to reverse this state of affairs.

LAWS

The Problems

The first element in the supply chain is India's archaic laws, many of which date to a colonial era that was very different from circumstances prevailing in contemporary India. Unfortunately, India does not require the expiration of certain laws after a fixed period of time.[4] At the central level, poorly drafted laws with ambiguities, amendments, clarifications, and exemption notifications (or their withdrawal) have led to contrary interpretations (and judgments) by various high courts and increased litigation. In part this reflects an enfeebled capacity in the Law Ministry at the central and state levels.

Furthermore, India's legal obsession is typically about enacting new laws and rarely about repealing or modifying existing laws. In 1998, the Jain Commission, a committee established by the Department of Administrative Reforms and Public Grievances, reviewed existing administrative legislation and identified laws to be amended or repealed. In its report, the commission sought the repeal of more than 1,300 central laws out of the 2,500 it reviewed.[5] The Law Commission has also periodically given recommendations for the revision of laws. Yet, apart from a onetime repeal of 315 amendment acts in 2002, progress has been decidedly modest. When it comes to similar state laws, which number into the many thousands and directly affect the day-to-day workings of business, India still lacks a reliable inventory. The multiplicity and complexity of laws make compliance, deterrence, and effective enforcement difficult and, in many cases, impossible. The result is circumvention by business while state functionaries harass and extract rents.

Potential Solutions

While line ministries often have little incentive to reform outmoded legislation, the union and state law ministries simply lack the capacity to do so. The revising, repealing, and updating of old laws are sorely needed, and the Law Commission should be given additional resources to undertake this task. Dedicating additional human resources at the upstream end to ensure greater precision in the drafting of laws could also attenuate future litigation.

One example of legislative consolidation and simplification is the model established by the Financial Sector Legislative Reforms Commission (FSLRC).[6] Like many other activities of the government of India, the financial sector's legislative framework contains regulations that date back decades when the objectives and demands of the financial system were quite different. The FSLRC was given a two-year mandate to evaluate and modernize the regulatory framework of the financial sector, identify any overlaps and inconsistencies, and develop a lasting unified financial code.

The FSLRC team was split into multidisciplinary working groups, composed of experts from finance and academia as well as regulators, to ensure a comprehensive evaluation. With each issue, the commission developed objectives for that area of the market, identified the sources of market failures, critically assessed the role of government in that area, and evaluated the costs and benefits of redrafting the legislation. This model could be adopted for other sectors in order to rid the legal system of outdated laws.

LAWMAKERS

The Problems

At the end of the day, lawmakers write the laws. The fact that many of India's leading lawmakers are also its foremost lawbreakers has a subtle but pervasive negative impact on the credibility of the rule of law in India. According to data compiled by the Association for Democratic Reforms, as of September 2013, roughly one-third of India's elected lawmakers at the state (31 percent) and national (30 percent) levels faced pending criminal charges at the time of their election. About half of these cases involve charges of a serious nature, which include murder, attempted murder, kidnapping, and crimes against women.[7]

To address the supply of "tainted" candidates in the electoral domain, the Supreme Court recently issued two landmark judgments. The first found that any member of the Legislative Assembly or member of Parliament currently holding office, upon being convicted by a court of law, would be immediately disqualified from the date of conviction. Under prior statute, convicted lawmakers could hold on to their seat as long as a court has stayed their conviction and appeals are pending before the courts. A bill introduced in Parliament by the government to supersede the court's judgment justifiably came under heavy fire. After Parliament balked, the government flirted with introducing an executive ordinance but wisely and swiftly reversed course.[8]

The second judgment found that any individual who was in jail or in police custody would no longer be allowed to run for office, even if that person was not formally charged.[9] The court, in its decision, reasoned that, "if a jailed person can't vote, a jailed person can't contest elections." Parliament swiftly moved to pass a bill, later signed by the president, that negated the court's ruling.[10] The court's ruling was problematic, given the temptation of politicians to misuse the police to punish political rivals.[11]

Potential Solutions

Beyond the issue of convicted politicians or those in jail, there is a larger issue at work: that lawmakers rarely face conviction due to shortcomings of the justice system. Despite the plague of politicians who have cases pending against them, since 2008, only 0.5 percent of elected members of Parliament and the Legislative Assembly have declared ever being convicted by a court of law, according to the Association for Democratic Reforms.

At the time of writing, the law minister had sought the opinion of the Law Commission on a bill to bar persons charged with heinous crimes (those such as rape, murder, and kidnapping that carry a minimum sentence of seven years in prison) from running for office. While the doctrine of presumption of innocence is rightly invoked in criminal jurisprudence given that the life and liberty of an individual is at stake, in public law, a larger public interest might necessitate invoking the Latin dictum *ei incumbit probatio qui dicit, non qui negat* (the burden of proof lies with who declares, not who denies).[12]

Restricting this penalty to heinous crimes helps guard against the predictable response from politicians that they are victims of politically motivated cases. The government could consider establishing special electoral tribunals charged with adjudicating serious criminal cases against political aspirants. This would be tantamount to a fast-track court—a policy of last resort—but there is hardly a better case for speedy justice than when it comes to those actually making the laws.

Because of the well-known complementarities of "money" and "muscle," the Election Commission of India has recommended additional reforms, which the next government should champion in an effort to forge an all-party consensus on reforming election finance.[13] For instance, the Election Commission could be given additional authority to regulate the functioning and potential de-registration of political parties. In addition, the commission should have the mandate to legally require that all parties get their accounts independently audited on an annual basis and that the results be made publicly available.

Furthermore, there are no clear guidelines for the Election Commission to act against a candidate who files affidavits containing false or misleading information. This loophole also applies to campaign expenditure statements.[14] The next government must ensure that candidates file accurate information about themselves and their campaigns and should authorize the Election Commission to take strong measures against those who do not make proper disclosures.

POLICE AND PROSECUTORS

The Problems

A citizen's first encounter with the justice system is typically with the police, a demoralized arm of the state, still governed under colonial-era statutes such as the Police Act of 1861. The primary objective of the police remains the maintenance of law and order rather than the prevention of crime. The former stems from the pre-Independence period in which the function of the police was essentially to act as crowd control by maintaining public order. This militaristic function is starkly different from the modern-day mandate of police forces to provide a public good that prevents crime and protects victims. Outdated colonial-era laws, rivalries between the Indian Police Service and rank-and-file officers, deep politicization of police institutions, and an overcentralized police hierarchy have also burdened the police.[15]

Over the years, several attempts have been made to reform India's police. Yet there are several reasons that the recommendations of numerous police commission reports gather dust. If there is one principle that unites Indian politicians, it is that a competent, autonomous police force is a threat to their common interests. Societal pressure to reform the police has also been limited. The middle class and the rich have exited public services across a broad spectrum, including relying on the police (as evidenced by the huge growth in private security services). And the centrality of identity politics for India's political and social movements has further weakened a common societal interest by making social representation in the police, rather than police effectiveness, their prime focus.

As a result, the police in India are somewhat in shambles, caught in a vicious cycle of demoralization and low popular support, continued politicization, and consistent starvation of resources. India has the lowest rate of police officers per capita—122.5 per 100,000 people—of any member state of the Group of 20. Furthermore, across India, the police vacancy rate stands at 25 percent.[16] Understaffed and undertrained, the police also lack many of the technological capabilities necessary to perform quality investigations. All of these factors, in turn, contribute to the low conviction rate that discredits both the police and the courts, highlighting one example of how inextricable the inefficiencies are in every branch of the criminal justice system.[17]

Indeed, the higher up the food chain one travels, the problems plaguing the police do not disappear. Take, for instance, the Central Bureau of Investigation (CBI)—the premier investigative police agency in India. The CBI investigates major cases in which the central government is a protagonist or where there are interstate disputes. Unfortunately, the CBI is widely perceived today to be a partisan arm of a capricious executive, used to reward or punish individuals on the basis of political imperatives.[18] Corruption investigations of several leading politicians, for instance, wax and wane according to the political alignment between these officials and the government of the day.[19]

The CBI's lack of independence can be traced to the rules governing how its director is chosen and the limitations on its jurisdiction.[20] For instance, the CBI can open investigations at the state level only if the respective state government explicitly approves. The Supreme Court, referring to a recent dispute with the executive branch, remarked that the CBI was little more than a "caged parrot speaking in a master's voice."[21] Similar issues plague the Central Vigilance Commission, which has no independent investigative powers and thus must rely on other government agencies to take up any corruption allegations it forwards.[22]

India's prosecutors, too, suffer from a variety of maladies. In almost every case where the defendant has deep pockets, there is a major mismatch between the quality of legal counsel. Government lawyers are poorly briefed, while corporate and political defendants have a battery of highly paid lawyers who have had much more time and often competence to undercut the public prosecutor's case.[23]

Potential Solutions

Police reform commissions set up by successive governments have articulated steps that both the central government and the states could take. Any future reform must be guided by five principles:

- *Subsidiarity:* The police are highly centralized at the state level yet need both greater centralization (empowering federal investigative agencies for such issues as terrorism) as well as decentralization (at the local government level such as traffic police).

- *Autonomy:* The police require greater autonomy from pernicious political control.

- *Accountability:* Greater autonomy needs to be complemented by investments in accountability, such as the creation of independent supervisory boards.

- *Personnel:* The gap between a tiny, very selective Indian Police Service and a large, ill-trained constabulary reflects the deep social stratifications of India. This requires changes in organizational structures and promotion pathways and much greater efforts at training lower-level recruits.

- *Resources:* Ultimately, change will be hard to come by without sharply increasing the resources available for the police, especially at the station house, or *thana*, level.

Even modest steps to address these issues can have positive effects on police functioning. A recent study undertaken on the Rajasthan state police found that simple reforms such as freezing the transfers of police officers and training officers in professional skills had positive effects both on public satisfaction with police forces and the quality of actual police work.[24] Such low-cost, administratively simple reforms have the potential to contribute to lasting change.[25]

After the Anna Hazare–led anticorruption demonstrations of 2011, there was a brief period of sustained focus on legislating a *Lokpal,* or anti-corruption ombudsman, to bring greater accountability to elected officials and senior-level government functionaries. The Lok Sabha passed the Lokpal and Lokayuktas Bill in December 2011, and, after much dithering, the Rajya Sabha eventually passed the bill two years later and the president signed it into law.

While it is too soon to tell whether the Lokpal will be an effective corruption-fighting agency, its very creation speaks to the degree to which politicians in India have been forced to come to grips with popular disquiet over malfeasance in government at all levels. There are a few provisions in the Lokpal law that will require special attention as the agency gets off the ground if it is to add value over the long term. For starters, the Lokpal law mandates that states establish *Lokayuktas* to address corruption charges against state and local government officials within one year, but it does not provide any further direction. At least eighteen states have already established *Lokayuktas*, but they vary considerably in terms of their authorities. As with the passage of the 73rd and 74th amendments on decentralized governance, there is scope for states to sabotage these institutions from the outset. Furthermore, regarding the functioning of the Lokpal itself, the agency requires approval by state authorities in order to investigate central government officials seconded to state governments. This defeats the purpose of creating a unified body that will decide all cases of sanction for prosecution. Second, rather than experimenting with an open selection process for the nine members of the Lokpal, the bill establishes a selection committee as well as an advisory search committee. The creation of multiple substructures overseeing what is essentially a closed process will limit the pool of candidates considered for the agency and reduce transparency—an ironic outcome for an agency in charge of transparency and accountability in government. Finally, it remains unclear how the Lokpal will receive complaints from those who are affected by or witness corrupt acts. The bill provides no assurance that either the local authorities will cooperate with the initial gathering of evidence or that, once a complaint is made to local authorities, they will act swiftly to refer the case to the Lokpal and begin a process of preliminary inquiry.

COURTS

The Problems

While India's judiciary forms the bedrock of the legal system, the courts in India suffer from an apparent paradox. On the one hand, in the face of a weakened executive and gridlocked legislature, the courts (particularly the Supreme Court) have attempted to fill a vacuum of authority and policymaking. Yet, on the other hand, the institutional underpinnings of the judiciary are growing weaker over time.[26]

The single biggest affliction of the Indian justice system is the snail's pace at which it proceeds. Each year, the courts take on more cases than they are able to process. As of June 2012, the Indian judiciary faced a backlog of roughly 32 million cases. As of 2011, approximately 24 percent of court cases had been pending for at least five years, while 9 percent had been pending for more than ten years.[27]

But there is also the issue of judicial capacity, which raises questions of manpower as well as quality. As of June 2012, the Supreme Court had a vacancy rate of 13 percent. This rate is relatively low compared to the High Courts and District Courts, which have vacancy rates of 29 and 21 percent, respectively. To provide a sense of manpower shortage, in the United States there are 108 judges per million citizens, while there are a mere twelve judges in India for the equivalent population. Underlying these weaknesses is a lack of financing. With the caveat that these figures do not account for state-level judicial spending, the Planning Commission allocated Rs. 1,470 crore for modernizing and upgrading the court system during the Eleventh Plan period (2007 to 2012).[28] This allocation amounts to only 0.07 percent of total plan outlays, on par with the meager resources budgeted for the Ninth (1997 to 2002) and Tenth (2002 to 2007) Plans.[29]

Judicial appointments with respect to the upper judiciary are decided by a collegium consisting of the chief justice of India and the four most senior judges of the Supreme Court. While the collegium evolved in part as a method of protection against political interference, it lacks transparency, does not deliberate according to a fixed set of criteria, and does not stipulate any recourse for addressing issues of malpractice.[30]

In many ways, the judicial process itself has become the punishment.[31] The extraordinary alacrity with which the courts grant adjournments has ensured that the powerful will always outlast the weak, making a mockery of what constitutes justice. The ease with which the judiciary takes on and intrudes on the space of the executive is in sharp contrast to timid efforts to improve the effectiveness of the courts for more basic tasks. Modest efforts in reforming the administrative organization of the courts have been outstripped by the sheer growth in caseloads.

To address the massive backlog, the government set up a National Mission for Justice Delivery and Legal Reforms in August 2011 with a five-year mandate. It has coupled this with Rs. 5,000 crore to state governments to improve the delivery of justice, from increasing the number of court working hours to creating "court managers" in every judicial district to assist the judiciary in its administrative functions.

As an additional method of reducing the burden on the judiciary, successive governments have moved to establish quasi-judicial tribunals and other alternative dispute resolution mechanisms (arbitration, mediation, conciliation, and *Lok Adalats*). Unfortunately, to date, tribunals have a rather checkered record overall. For starters, tribunals offer a mechanism for speedy justice but they leave unaddressed the core institutional problems that led to their creation.[32] Second, tribunals have been established in areas where specialized knowledge is required, yet they have been largely staffed by retired judges and bureaucrats who are generalists.[33] Third, they routinely lack even the most basic requirements of any office, such as office space and equipment, personnel, and an adequate administrative apparatus.

Potential Solutions

The next government must move toward streamlining the judicial process. For starters, the next government should simplify the process of case management. Most problems of delay in cases actually arise due to the excessive emphasis on procedural fairness during the first hearing. All the tasks covered in this stage can be outsourced to private case managers, the way many governmental functions are now handled.

When it comes to the trial phase, courts should enforce a strict timetable with monitoring by judicial officers and imposition of costs to ensure strict compliance with prescribed time lines and the creation of predetermined events that can be easily tracked, such as the filing of motions.[34] The filing of a case often has negative externalities, but the moment a part of these externalities is shifted to the litigant and errant lawyers, the number of frivolous cases filed is likely to be considerably reduced. One method is to impose costs when civil cases do not disclose a cause of action or are hopelessly barred by the law of limitation or any other law.[35]

In May 2012 the Supreme Court established a National Court Management System to address issues of case management, court management, and setting measurable standards for performance of the courts. Under the court management system, a National Framework of Court Excellence is being prepared, which will set measurable standards of performance for courts, addressing the issues of quality, responsiveness, and timeliness. These are positive steps, and the next government must support them with sufficient human and financial capital. A better organized case management system also needs to be supplemented by addressing a major obstacle to the speedy delivery of justice: adjournments. The only way litigants can be forced to take adjournments seriously is by tying case outcomes to the prompt and timely manner in which they comply with case management deadlines. Ironically, even though both the Supreme Court and the executive have been interested in this issue, courts continue to lavishly grant adjournments, which substantially delays trial proceedings.

The clogged, dilapidated plumbing of Indian courts has led to multiple efforts to create alternative systems. For instance, the Gram Nyayalayas Act in 2008 ensures inexpensive and speedier justice in rural India. This scheme suffers from inadequate physical and human infrastructure. But perhaps the most difficult challenge is staffing the courts with a sufficient number of judges who are both competent and have integrity. One solution, recommended by the Law Commission of India and endorsed by several advisory bodies, is to create an all-India judicial service. This has obvious benefits, such as standardizing court functioning, the powers of lower court judges and their conditions of service; facilitating greater ease in bringing about judicial reform on a national scale; and expanding the applicant pool to the entire country rather than a particular state.

An all-India judicial service would complement the newly introduced Judicial Appointments Commission Bill, 2013, which seeks to scrap the opaque collegium system and replace it with a Judicial Appointments Commission. The Judicial Appointments Commission Bill should also be considered alongside another bill that seeks to reform the judiciary, the Judicial Standards and Accountability Bill.[36] This bill proposes several sensible steps to improve the quality and integrity of the judiciary, such as mandating that judges publicly declare their assets; establishing a judicial code of conduct; and creating formal processes for removing judges who violate this code of conduct.[37]

Finally, successive governments have established tribunals in order to circumvent the pathologies of the formal justice system. The next government must rationalize and rethink these alternative dispute resolution mechanisms. With the government having created 62 tribunals at last count, it has become even more important for Parliament to create a permanent mechanism that is well staffed and charged with settling intra-government disputes.

CONCLUSION

As India undergoes massive economic and political changes, its society is also gradually moving from a status to a contract society. If this change is to continue, further attenuating status hierarchies, improving India's rule of law institutions—and enforcing contracts—must be a top priority for the new government.

For far too long, reform of India's administrative and legal institutions was seen as a "second order" issue that could be addressed after critical economic reform measures were dealt with first. This sequencing, while understandable from a policymaker's point of view, was shortsighted given that the rule of law is the sine qua non not just for sustaining economic activity in a market economy, but also for upholding democracy itself, especially for the weak and marginalized. Even modest changes can have substantial impacts.

Many of the reforms recommended here do not entail huge budgetary outlays. This is not to deny that India's rule of law apparatus is badly starved of resources. But despite budgetary pressures, higher court fees, especially in the case of appeals filed by the government or corporations, can address these resource shortfalls. However, one should not minimize the large impact that even modest legal or administrative changes can have on the functioning of India's rule of law institutions writ large.

NOTES

1   World Justice Project, "Rule of Law Index: India Profile," 2012, http://
    worldjusticeproject.org/country/india.

2   In these same categories India ranks 3 and 4 regionally, and 14 and 22 in the lower-
    middle-income group.

3   Paul Craig, "Formal and Substantive Conceptions of the Rule of Law: An Analytical
    Framework," *Public Law* 467 (1997).

4   Bibek Debroy, "Reforming the Legal System," *Academic Foundation* 88, (2005): 4–5.

5   P. C. Jain et al., "Report of the Commission on Review of Administrative Laws,"
    Department of Administrative Reforms and Public Grievances, Government of India, 1998, 1–6,
    http://darpg.gov.in/darpgwebsite_cms/Document/file/Review_Administrative_
    laws_Vol_1.pdf.

6   Ila Patnaik and Ajay Shah, "Reforming India's Financial System," Carnegie Paper,
    Carnegie Endowment for International Peace, 2014.

7   Association for Democratic Reforms, "Criminalisation of Politics: Almost
    One-Third of Lok Sabha MPs Have Criminal Cases Against Them," September 29,
    2013, http://adrindia.org/media/adr-in-news/criminalisation-politics-almost-one-
    third-lok-sabha-mps-have-criminal-cases-agains.

8   "Rahul Gandhi Has the Final Word, Cabinet Withdraws 'Nonsense' Ordinance,"
    Indian Express, October 3, 2013.

9   However, the court ruled that disqualification would not apply to a person subjected
    to preventive detention.

10 Although Parliament passed a bill to negate the court's judgment, it neverthe-
    less asked the court to review its judgment. The court has agreed to do so. For an
    overview of this legislation, see PRS Legislative Research, "Bill Summary: The
    Representation of the People (Amendment and Validation) Bill, 2013," August 26,
    2013, www.prsindia.org/uploads/media/Representation/Bill%20Summary%20
    --%20The%20ROPA%20Amendment%20Bill%202013.pdf.

11 While the government could consider denying those in jail the right to run for office,
    these restrictions should be circumscribed—for instance, limiting it to those who
    were jailed six months before elections were called—so as to not incentivize politi-
    cians' merely placing people in temporary custody for political gain.

12 The Election Commission of India has made a similar proposal: it recommends that
    candidates be disqualified from seeking office if charges have been framed against
    them by a court for an offense punishable by imprisonment of five years or more and
    if such charges were framed at least six months prior to an election.

13 Milan Vaishnav, "The Demand for Criminal Politicians," Oxford India Policy Series,
    May 1, 2013, http://policyblog.oxfordindiasociety.org.uk/2013/05/01/the-demand-
    for-criminal-politicians.

14 For instance, the Election Commission of India has been pursuing a case against
    the former chief minister of Maharashtra, Ashok Chavan, for allegedly paying off
    journalists during his 2009 campaign. The government has openly challenged the
    commission's power to disqualify a candidate for falsifying election finance filings.

15   Arvind Verma, "The Police in India: Design, Performance, and Adaptability," in
Public Institutions in India: Performance and Design, ed. Devesh Kapur and Pratap Bhanu
Mehta (New York: Oxford University Press, 2005), 194–251.

16   National Crime Records Bureau, "Prison Statistics India 2012," 2013, http://ncrb.
gov.in/PSI-2012/Full/PSI-2012.pdf. India's corrections system also suffers from
human resource constraints. According to the 2012 Prison Statistics India report,
roughly one-third of sanctioned positions are vacant. Yet the jails are operating above
capacity; the occupancy rate for all of India is 112 percent. On both dimensions, of
course, significant variations exist across states.

17   Law Commission of India, "Expeditious Investigation and Trial of Criminal Cases
Against Influential Public Personalities," 2012, http://lawcommissionofindia.nic.in/
reports/report239.pdf.

18   S. K. Das, "Institutions of Internal Accountability," in Kapur and Mehta, eds., *Public
Institutions in India,* 149.

19   The most recent instances of such behavior involve the winding down of corruption cases against former Uttar Pradesh chief ministers Mayawati and Mulayam
Singh Yadav, both of whose fortunes have improved with their support of the
ruling government. See Mihir Srivastava, "The Congress Bureau of Investigation,"
Open Magazine, April 6, 2013, www.openthemagazine.com/article/nation/
the-congress-bureau-of-investigation.

20   Srivastava, "The Congress Bureau of Investigation," 152–53.

21   DNA India, "Coalgate Probe: SC Calls CBI 'A Caged Parrot,' Slams PMO and Coal
Ministry," May 8, 2013, http://bit.ly/15yBpTE.

22   Verma, "The Police in India."

23   Bishwajit Bhattacharyya, *My Experience With the Office of Additional Solicitor General of
India* (New Delhi: Universal Law Publishers, 2012).

24   Abhijit Banerjee et al., "Can Institutions Be Reformed From Within? Evidence
From a Randomized Experiment With the Rajasthan Police," National Bureau of
Economic Research Paper 17912, March 2012.

25   According to a senior Indian Police Service officer interviewed by the authors, only
1–2 percent of the police budget is dedicated toward human resource development
activities, community policing, and crime prevention programs. Research and training accounts for even less (roughly 0.8 percent).

26   Pratap Bhanu Mehta, "India's Judiciary: The Promise of Uncertainty," in Kapur and
Mehta, eds., *Public Institutions in India,* 159–60.

27   A. I. S. Cheema and Bibhuti Bhushan Bose, "Court News," 2012, 4–8, http://
supremecourtofindia.nic.in/courtnews/2012_issue_2.pdf. Between 2000 and 2010,
the number of cases admitted to the Supreme Court doubled (24,747 to 48,677). And
in 2004, 7 percent of regular hearing matters had been pending for more than five
years, while it was 17 percent in 2011.

28   Department of Justice, Ministry of Law and Justice, Government of India, "Report of
the Working Group for the Twelfth Five Year Plan (2012–2017)," September (2011),
http://planningcommission.gov.in/aboutus/committee/wrkgrp12/wg_law.pdf.

29   Government of India, "Report of the Task Force on Judicial Impact Assessment," June
15, 2008, http://lawmin.nic.in/doj/justice/judicialimpactassessmentreportvol1.pdf.

30 Devesh Kapur, "The Law Laid Down," *Outlook India*, January 7, 2013.

31 Centre on Public Law and Jurisprudence, "Justice Without Delay: Recommendations for Legal and Institutional Reform," Jindal Global University, 2011.

32 As Khosla argues, "The haphazard growth of tribunals has diverted attention from any serious reform of the high courts." Madhav Khosla, "The Problem," *India Seminar* 642 (2013), www.india-seminar.com/2013/642/642_the_problem.htm.

33 Unfortunately, the quality of justice tribunals have been able to deliver has varied considerably, in part because they are perceived as "excellent source of post-retirement opportunities" for those facing mandatory retirement from public service. Arvind P. Datar, "Tribunals: A Tragic Obsession," *India Seminar* 642 (2013), www.india-seminar.com/2013/642/642_arvind_p_datar.htm.

34 We thank Ananth Padmanabhan for bringing this idea to our attention.

35 The Civil Procedure Code allows the defendant in a civil action to file an application for rejection of the complaint in such cases. Where such applications are allowed— and the threshold for a plaint to survive such early frontal attacks is pretty low— some reasonable costs would act as a deterrent, forcing the plaintiff to factor in this cost at the earliest stage of the litigation, that is, when deciding whether to file a case or attempt to settle the matter.

36 Anirudh Burman and Vivake Prasad, "Legislative Brief: The Judicial Standards and Accountability Bill, 2010," PRS Legislative Research, March 18, 2011, www.prsindia. org/uploads/media/Judicial%20Standard/Final%20Brief%20for%20printing%20 -%20Judicial%20Standards%20and%20Accountability%20Bill%202010.pdf.

37 In addition to increasing both the quality and quantity of judges, thought should be given to extending the courts' working hours. On average a workday in an Indian court lasts between 5 and 5.5 hours, compared with 6.5 or 7 in other countries. Also in terms of working days, the Supreme Court is operational for only 180 days a year, while the High Courts and District Courts work 200–210 and 240–270 days a year, respectively. Some estimates claim that cutting down judges' leave is equivalent to increasing the number of actual strength by up to 25 percent. Debroy, "Reforming the Legal System," 28–29.

CHAPTER 15

CORRECTING THE ADMINISTRATIVE DEFICIT

BIBEK DEBROY

INTRODUCTION

The Indian economy is in bad shape. Real GDP growth was 5 percent in 2012–2013. In 2013–2014, it will be a shade above 5 percent if one believes the government and below 5 percent if one believes everyone else. This is a far cry from the 9-plus percent levels between 2005–2006 and 2010–2011, barring the 6.7 percent of 2008–2009. Compared to those high-growth years, both savings and investment have declined as shares of GDP. Employment growth has stagnated. Wholesale inflation is around 6 percent and retail inflation (measured by the consumer price index) is around 9.5 percent. Current account deficit to GDP ratios are high, and the exchange rate is not only volatile, but the rupee has depreciated sharply against the U.S. dollar. More signs of the malaise need not be enumerated.

Why has this happened? The external world is no longer as benign as it was between 2003–2004 and 2007–2008, and the contours of a global recovery are yet uncertain. Still, the ills aren't only exogenous. For instance, other economies have registered high growth rates, despite the relatively malign external environment. Between 2003–2004 and 2007–2008, India was among the fastest-growing economies in the world. But then its growth sputtered; by 2012, around 60 countries grew faster than 5 percent.

The differential in rates of growth between India and other developing economies has increased. Therefore, while exogenous factors are important, they do not represent the entire story. In the realm of the endogenous, with legitimate reason, high fiscal deficits (a revenue deficit problem, to be precise) and profligate public expenditure have been flagged, leading to high interest rates and crowding out private investments and even private consumption expenditure. Coalition politics and the legislative logjam have also been suggested as reasons, compounded by uncertainty over legislation concerning land acquisition, mining, and forests, with judicial intervention thrown in. Add to that excessive state intervention and control, as distinct from regulation, across sectors.

All these are valid arguments and are probed in other chapters in this volume. Here we focus on what we choose to call the "administrative deficit," as opposed to the fiscal deficit, the current account deficit, or the governance deficit. "Governance deficit" is an imprecise term. By administrative deficit, we mean an executive failure, sometimes also called an implementation deficit. This is the spirit in which Lant Pritchett described India as "a flailing state," focusing not on legislation and policy, but on their implementation.[1] However, it is the administrative deficit in the central government in New Delhi, not the delivery of services in state governments, that will be examined here. The core of the argument is that the administrative deficit has become worse under the second iteration of the United Progressive Alliance (UPA-II) than it was under UPA-I.

One needs to pin down what is meant by "the executive" and "administration," though this is often taken to be understood. The Indian constitution has three organs of state: the executive, the legislature, and the judiciary. Problems with the legislature and the judiciary are not our concern. While the constitution does not quite define the "executive," Articles 73 through 78 identify the prime minister, the cabinet, and the civil services in New Delhi as the apparatus of such executive decisionmaking. Interpreted thus, we would argue that there has been a collapse of both bureaucratic and ministerial decisionmaking, that this problem has worsened under UPA-II, and that one of the most important agenda items for the new government is to rehabilitate both. We argue that bureaucrats do not make decisions and that the trigger of the Seventh Central Pay

Commission can be used to incentivize civil service reforms. We argue that unwarranted decisionmaking has concentrated in New Delhi and that this can be reduced through decentralization. Finally, we argue that the ministerial system, through the cabinet, also needs energizing.

THE RISK-AVERSE BUREAUCRAT

India's anticorruption efforts, however necessary and well-intentioned they may be, have produced a chilling effect on public administration. Most notable among these is the Prevention of Corruption Act, which was enacted in 1988 and applies to public servants. It defines criminal misconduct by a public servant and covers instances of personal gratification, fraudulent misappropriation, and abuse of position as a public servant to obtain pecuniary advantage. In addition, Section 13(1)(d)(iii) defines the following as criminal misconduct: "while holding office as a public servant, obtains for any person any valuable thing or pecuniary advantage without any public interest."

These definitions are problematic. Bureaucrats are public servants. Any decision made by a bureaucrat tends to benefit a third party, and it therefore is impossible to predict ex ante the consequences of a decision. "Public interest" is a vague expression, difficult to pin down, so that clause of Section 13 is enough to make any public servant risk-averse. The Central Vigilance Commission is the primary channel for inquiries under the Prevention of Corruption Act, at least so far as the central government is concerned. It was set up in 1964 and given statutory status in 2003. Table 1 shows the number of complaints received by the commission.[2] These are complaints received and nothing more than that; the table does not show how the complaints were resolved. The increase in complaints over the years is reflective of countervailing pressure being exerted against corruption. This has been reinforced by instances of whistle-blowing, though legislation on whistle-blowing—formally the Public Interest Disclosure and Protection to Persons Making the Disclosures Bill—does not yet exist. It was approved by the Cabinet in 2010 and passed by the Lok Sabha in 2011, though it is still pending in the Rajya Sabha. Individual sections of the bill have been criticized, but that's not terribly pertinent for present purposes.

TABLE 1. COMPLAINTS RECEIVED BY THE CENTRAL VIGILANCE COMMISSION

2008	10,142
2009	14,206
2010	16,260
2011	16,929
2012	37,039

Source: Central Vigilance Commission, *Annual Report* (various years).

Anticorruption presents a double kind of problem: ensuring the culpability of dishonest civil servants while protecting honest ones. Both challenges have been flagged since the 1964 Committee on Prevention of Corruption, popularly known as the Santhanam Committee for its chairman. A Citizen's Charter and Grievance Redressal Bill, also known as the Right of Citizens for Time Bound Delivery of Goods and Services and Redressal of Their Grievances Bill, has been pending in Lok Sabha since 2011.

Both the whistle-blower legislation and the delivery of goods and services legislation are of limited utility in isolation. For instance, the two major Conduct Rules in India, the Central Civil Services (Conduct) Rules of 1964 and the All India Services (Conduct) Rules of 1968, are completely out of sync with these changes. To take one example, should serving bureaucrats be nominated to the boards of public sector enterprises? More important, before a court can take cognizance of an offense under the Prevention of Corruption Act, Section 19 requires the previous sanction of the competent authority. Then there are delays in granting sanctions. Technical problems with the way sanctions are granted are used to argue for acquittal. Trials take a long time. Article 311 of the Indian constitution makes it very difficult to take action against a civil servant. Conviction rates are low. These kinds of issues were probed by the fourth report of the Second Administrative Reforms Commission, which offered specific recommendations.[3] Here is an example:

The Delhi Special Police Establishment shall not conduct any inquiry or investigation into any offence alleged to have been committed under the Prevention of Corruption Act, 1988[,] except with the previous approval of the Central Government where such allegation relates to the employees of the Central Government of the level of Joint Secretary and above.... The Commission on balance is of the view that it would be necessary to protect honest civil servants from undue harassment, but at the same time in order to ensure that this protection is not used as a shield by the corrupt, it would be appropriate if this permission is given by the Central Vigilance Commissioner in consultation with the Secretary to Government concerned and if the Secretary is involved, a committee comprising the Central Vigilance Commissioner and the Cabinet Secretary may consider the case for granting of permission. In case of Cabinet Secretary such permission may be given by the Prime Minister.

Then there is the question of protecting the honest civil servant. Notice that some sections of the Prevention of Corruption Act shift the burden of proof to the accused. Notice also that there are several dimensions to corruption. In many cases of relatively petty corruption, the answer lies in eliminating monopoly and discretion and increasing transparency and accountability. However, almost tautologically, discretion cannot be eliminated at higher levels (joint secretary and above) of the central government. This is against the background of the aforementioned countervailing pressure and the central Right to Information Act of 2005. There is also a lack of clarity on the protection granted to civil servants who have already retired. Ideally, the necessary reforms, as documented in more than one report of the Second Administrative Reforms Commission, should have been implemented by the executive. Since they were not, a writ petition was admitted in the Supreme Court, which delivered a judgment on October 31, 2013.[4] Focusing only on the parts that pertain to the central government, this judgment directs the government to set up a central civil services authority, pass a Civil Services Act and have a fixed minimum tenure. In addition, the judgment requires civil servants not to act on the basis of verbal directions and instructions. Consider also the following:

No official should have any dealings with a person claiming to act on behalf of a business or industrial house or an individual, unless he is properly accredited, and is approved by the Department, etc.[,] concerned. There should be some system of keeping some sort of record of all interviews granted to accredited representatives. It is also desirable that officers belonging to prescribed categories who have to deal with these representatives should maintain a regular diary of all interviews and discussions with the registered representatives whether it takes place in the office or at home.[5]

It is possible to complain of judicial overreach and that some of these recommendations can't be implemented because they constrain efficient decisionmaking. However, the problem has arisen under UPA-II because the recommendations of the Second Administrative Reforms Commission, and those of other commissions that came before it, were not implemented. While some of those recommendations pertain to states, others could have been implemented by the central government, had it so desired. Failure to implement them contributed to greater risk-aversion on the part of the bureaucracy. An amendment to the Prevention of Corruption Act was introduced in Rajya Sabha in August 2013 and has been referred to the Parliamentary Committee, with a report expected at the time of writing. This takes care of some of the problems we have highlighted. However, one need not have waited until 2013 for the bill to be presented before Parliament. Using the trigger of the Supreme Court judgment, the agenda for the new government is straightforward: set up a central civil services authority, pass a new Civil Services Act; revamp the laws on corruption, and change the Conduct Rules. The new government should also swiftly pass the amendment to the Prevention of Corruption Act, which would take care of some of the problems.

"Bureaucrat Plus"

Reforms that enhance quality and productivity in the civil service are equally necessary. Pay Commissions represent a major vehicle for such possible reforms, but their actions have often led to bloating in government salaries. In September 2013, UPA-II announced the setting up of the

Seventh Central Pay Commission. As the expression implies, a Central Pay Commission is meant for "employees" of the central government, though its spillover impact on state governments and quasi-government employees (such as teachers) is impossible to avoid. The Fifth Pay Central Commission devastated state government finances in the late 1990s, and the Sixth Central Pay Commission did the same in the late 2000s. Estimates are that, at the central government level, the Seventh Central Pay Commission will cover 5 million employees, including those employed in defense and the railways, and 3 million pensioners. The Ministry of Labour and Employment in 2012 actually came up with a lower figure of 3.1 million because it excludes public sector undertakings.[6] A point often missed is about the distribution of these central government employees, spread across grades: 3 percent belong to the top Group A (known as gazetted officers), 8 percent to Group B, 63 percent to Group C, and 26 percent to Group D. Table 2 is for public sector undertaking employees, but it is indicative of government employees in general.[7]

TABLE 2. INCREASE IN GOVERNMENT SALARIES (PERCENT OVER 1971–1972 BASE)

	Per Capita Emoluments of PSU Employees	Average All-India Consumer Price Index
1980–1981	140.52	108.85
1990–1991	730.73	395.31
2000–2001	3,610.67	1,440.62
2005–2006	4,698.26	1,292.71
2011–2012	12,264.78	2,216.15

Source: Government of India, Ministry of Finance, *Economic Survey*, various years.

Therefore, there has been a substantial increase in real salaries in the government sector. Logically, this ought to happen if there has been a commensurate increase in productivity. Arguments are sometimes advanced about low salaries within the government and the need to raise these wages to attract and retain talent. But if one accounts for perks and allows for a job security premium, that is no longer a valid proposition. In addition, that argument about relatively low salaries is made about Group A posts, which account for a small percentage of employees. Especially for Groups C and D, salaries within the government, which have far lower variance than outside the government, are higher than for comparable jobs outside the government. It is too early to gauge the quantitative impact of the Seventh Central Pay Commission. But if the Fifth and the Sixth Central Pay Commissions are any indication, once this has percolated through to state governments, the fiscal costs—the incremental costs of implementing a new Pay Commission's recommendations—are between 1 and 1.5 percent of GDP. In the absence of productivity increases, which are difficult to measure within the government, this is a redistribution of resources from relatively poorer sections of society to those who are better protected.

Even if one looks only at recent years, there is a long list of committees that have examined the question of civil service reform. One of them, the Second Administrative Reforms Commission, advised that "many of the recommendations involving basic changes have not been acted upon and therefore, the framework, systems and methods of functioning of the civil services based on the Whitehall model of the mid-nineteenth century remain largely unchanged."[8] While civil service reform is a broad area, given the context of this chapter, the focus is on performance appraisal prior to vertical mobility, lateral entry, contractual appointments, and exit—all issues linked to productivity. Unlike the Fifth Central Pay Commission, the Sixth Central Pay Commission (2006) was conspicuously silent on these issues. Using the trigger of the Seventh Central Pay Commission, whose terms of reference have not yet been announced, these reform ideas need to be brought back onto the agenda and implemented.

DECENTRALIZATION AND THE FEDERAL ENTITY

India is a federal country and, in the foreseeable future, any government in New Delhi will be a coalition government with support from so-called regional parties. As such, that government will have to perform some careful introspection about how it conceives of the states' role in the policymaking process. Failure to achieve such clarity has exacerbated the administrative deficit by confusing the jurisdictions and priorities of the central and state governments.

The point has often been made that India is excessively centralized, especially compared with China. In part, the reason was historical and colonial, and this was reinforced by developments after independence. As the Commission on Center-State Relations observed in its report submitted in March 2010, "Looking back and as is well known, in the first three decades after the independence centralization of powers had been accentuated due to various factors such as the predominance of a single political party at the Center as well as in the States; adoption of planning as a strategy of National development in which investment decisions determined by the Union [central government], albeit through a consultative process, generally set the priorities for State budgets; the system of industrial licensing and control; and nationalization of major banks. The trend of judicial pronouncements during this period also tended to follow a similar spirit."[9] This contrasted with a considerable amount of cross-country literature on the benefits of decentralization. One has to be careful in using the word "decentralization," however. Within the decentralized governance ambit are aspects of political decentralization, administrative decentralization, fiscal decentralization, and economic decentralization. Some arguments in favor of decentralization are connected to the efficient provision of public goods and services and optimal levels of governance, in the sense of economies and diseconomies of scale in providing these public goods and services. Others are linked to rendering decisionmaking a participative process. While decentralization also implies the devolution of authority within individual states and the empowerment of the third, more local tier of governance, we will focus on central-state relations.

The management of central-state relations is one of the most important agenda items for the new government. Whether decisions involve a central counterterrorist center, a goods and services tax, or agreements with Bangladesh, they have been held up because of an inability on the part of the central government to talk to the states. There is a case for completely reexamining the Seventh Schedule, the section of the constitution that delegates governmental authority for a range of issues to the states (the State List), the central government (the Union List), or to both (the Concurrent List). Four major concerns ought to guide any such reforms.

First, it has often been the case that when subjects are in the Concurrent List of the Seventh Schedule, the central government has not effectively consulted states at certain key junctures, such as before introducing legislation in Parliament. Second, the Inter-State Council has not functioned efficiently. Third, there is a strong case for moving non–tax-related residuary powers from the Union List to the Concurrent List. Fourth, extending the argument beyond the Inter-State Council, the National Integration Council, the National Development Council, the Planning Commission, and the Finance Commission function as appendages of the central government and have no representation from states. Ideally, there should be no Concurrent List. Since most government intervention and public expenditure are in the social sectors, which are responsibilities of state governments and local bodies, the State List should be expanded and a local body list should be added.

However, passing the constitutional amendments that would make such changes possible is a long-term goal, beyond the ambit of the next government. Over the next five years, it makes the most sense to focus on fiscal transfers as a means of reforming central-state relations. The constitutional mechanism for transferring tax revenue from the central government to the states is through the Finance Commission. Article 280 does not provide for any other channel to distribute the net proceeds of taxes to states. Nor is there provision in the constitution for what are called Plan transfers, those executed by the Planning Commission according to development plans rooted in the Five Year Plan and discretionary transfers. However, with these becoming broad-based and with the Planning Commission increasing in importance, the Finance Commission's transfers are restricted to tax devolution and grants to cover non-Plan current expenditure, with grants-in-aid covered by Article 275 of the constitution. In any event, the Plan versus non-Plan distinction is artificial and prevents one from taking an integrated view, even for the limited purpose of transfers to states. (For that matter, the role of planning itself has been questionable since 1991.)

As for Five Year Plan expenditure and grants for capital expenditure, from the Fourth Finance Commission in the mid-1960s onward, right up to the Ninth Finance Commission in the late 1980s, these matters have been excluded from the purview of the Finance Commission, and its terms of reference have been progressively diluted.[10]

One therefore needs to abolish the Plan versus non-Plan distinction, drastically reduce transfers through the Planning Commission, and restore the constitutional mandate of the Finance Commission. For the Finance Commission, there has been conceptual confusion between transfers based on formulas and grants-in-aid, also linked to the definition of "special category" states that get preferential treatment. The setting up of the Fourteenth Finance Commission offers an opportunity to finally settle these issues.

Transfers routed through the Planning Commission have both discretionary and non-discretionary elements. For non-discretionary transfers, the Planning Commission uses the Gadgil formula, first used in 1969 and since 1991 known in its modified form as the Gadgil-Mukherjee formula. We have argued that the Plan versus non-Plan distinction should be abolished and all non-discretionary transfers should be through the Finance Commission. This brings one to discretionary transfers by the Planning Commission through central sector schemes and Centrally Sponsored Schemes (CSSs). Central sector schemes are few. Most transfers are through Centrally Sponsored Schemes—basically schemes that are largely funded by the central government but carried out by state governments and requiring matching contributions from non-special category states. The Planning Commission's own view on CSSs, at least in the course of the Tenth Five Year Plan, was the following:

> It would be better to do … fewer things well rather than messing up with a larger number of activities. … One of the ways to reduce the mismatch between the lofty intentions of the [government of India] and its poor implementation capability is by re-examining the whole concept of Centrally Sponsored Schemes, and by radically limiting its number and improving its flexibility. The share of the CSSs in the Plan budget of the Central Ministries has now increased to 70 percent against 30 percent in the early 1980s. This massive increase has however not been matched by improved monitoring, and effective control over diversion of plan funds for

salaries and other non-plan expenditure. Therefore the number needs to be curtailed drastically from more than 200 today to just about 20 to 40 so that systems for their monitoring can be developed. No Ministry should be allowed to run more than 3 or 4 CSSs, and the outlay for each scheme should not be less than 100 crore a year. At present less than 20 percent of the CSSs have an outlay of more than 100 crore a year. Weeding out smaller schemes will therefore reduce the total number of CSSs from 210 to about 40.[11]

The Commission on Center-State relations also recommended, "The number of Centrally Sponsored Schemes (CSSs) should be kept to the minimum.… Once a programme has passed the pilot stage and has been accepted as desirable for implementation on a larger scale, it should appropriately form part of the State Plan. The Central assistance towards CSSs should be kept to a minimum in relation to the Central assistance for the State Plans."[12] No such dramatic pruning has been done, and informal reports suggest that the number of CSSs has been reduced only modestly, from 225 to 195, despite a 2011 Planning Commission Report on restricting CSSs.[13]

Even beyond efficiency, delivery, and focus, there are other problems with CSSs. They encroach on items that are on the State List. In 1996, at a conference of chief ministers, it was agreed that all CSSs that impinge on the State List will be transferred to the states. But that decision has not been implemented. Because of the matching requirement, the financial burden on states increases. Conditions are imposed on states, often in areas that are the legislative domain of states. CSSs transfers are often made to autonomous bodies, bypassing the states. Some CSSs require the creation of a fresh and new bureaucratic system of delivery. In any event, CSSs amount to a unilateral decision by the central government to divert resources that would otherwise have been available to states. Therefore, CSSs should be pruned, and more "untied" funds should be available to states. These need not be completely untied, in the sense that there can be overall guidelines and some indication of the sector for which the funds can be used. Subject to that, states need to have far greater flexibility. If infant mortality reduction is the objective, the way to accomplish it will not be same in Jharkhand as in Kerala.

It would make sense to retain only those CSSs that are in some sense demand-driven. Examples are Swajaldhara (for drinking water), the Mahatma Gandhi National Rural Employment Guarantee Act, the Total Sanitation Campaign, National Horticulture Mission, National Rural Health Mission, National Urban Health Mission, Sampoorna Grameen Rozgar Yojana (for food and employment), Swarnjayanti Gram Swarozgar Yojana (for self-employment), Integrated Child Development Services, Sarva Shiksha Abhiyan (for elementary education), Pradhan Mantri Gram Sadak Yojana (for rural roads), Rajiv Gandhi Grameen Vidyutikaran Yojana (for electrification), EWS/LIG housing in urban areas, Indira Awaas Yojana (for rural housing), the Mid Day Meal Scheme, and Rashtriya Krishi Vikas Yojana (for agriculture growth). But even in such cases, the centralized template should be tweaked and weakened, so that states have greater flexibility.

MINISTERS WHO ADMINISTER

The administrative deficit can be traced in part to the existence of so many ministries and the disproportionate influence of ministers. The Constitution Amendment Act of 2003 specifies that the number of ministers in the Central Council should not exceed 15 percent of the total number of members in the Lok Sabha. UPA-II has 51 ministries and 79 ministers—in other words, nearly the maximum figure allowed by law. It is difficult to compute the annual costs of maintaining a minister and the minister's support staff, but it is considerable. The 15 percent is meant to be a maximum, not a minimum. Using that trigger of decentralization discussed above, there is a case for reexamining the need for so many ministries and ministers at the central level. For instance, if there is decentralization to the states, a single Ministry for Social Sectors could suffice. Nor does India require so many ministries for energy or for transport.

These ministries have also worked at cross-purposes. The Ministry of Environment and Forests vis-à-vis the others provides a case in point. Constitutionally, such issues are meant to be resolved through collective decisionmaking by the cabinet. Under UPA, however—and more so under UPA-II—this system has been short-circuited by a large number of Groups of Ministers and Empowered Groups of Ministers. There are no reliable figures on how many of these groups still exist. But according to journalistic reports, 183 such groups have been set up since 2004. The role of the cabinet has also been undercut by the dual power structure that the Congress party was forced to live with, compounded by the existence of the National Advisory Council. That is clearly a model of misgovernance, not governance. Therefore, the constitutional sanctity and collective responsibility of the cabinet needs to be reestablished, including that of the prime minister's office.

More specifically, on issues connected to land, forest, environment, and technology clearances, a few principles should be implemented. First, once a clearance has been granted, it should not be opened up afresh, retroactively. Second, there cannot be an open-ended system for clearances. If a clearance has not been granted within a certain number of days, it should be deemed to have been given. Third, such clearances can be parallel; they need not be sequential. Fourth, following the decentralization agenda, if a clearance has been granted by a state, or local bodies further down, why should the issue be reconsidered by New Delhi? These are the kinds of reasons that the Cabinet Committee on Infrastructure, renamed the Cabinet Committee on Investment, has failed to make the dent it should have had. At a rough count, an average infrastructure project requires 56 authorizations and clearances from 19 ministries.

In conclusion, the administrative deficit may not be talked about as much as fiscal and other deficits. But without its being corrected, growth and investments will not pick up. One doesn't need fresh commissions or committees to determine what needs to be done. Recommendations already exist; they merely need to be implemented. This is important because one often tends to focus on "policy." But any policy is only as good or as bad as the instruments used to deliver it. The British Prime Minister David Lloyd George once described the colonial civil service in India as "the steel frame of the whole structure," and this idea applies to administration in general. While we can legitimately debate and discuss the frame, let us first ensure that the steel is not rusted.

NOTES

1   Lant Pritchett, "Is India a Flailing State? Detours on the Four Lane Highway to Modernization," Working Paper Series RWP09-013, John F. Kennedy School of Government, Harvard University, May 13, 2009, http://dash.harvard.edu/bitstream/handle/1/4449106/Pritchett%20India%20Flailing%20State.pdf?sequence=1.

2   Government of India, Central Vigilance Commission, "Annual Report 2012," June 2013, http://cvc.nic.in/ar2012.pdf.

3   Government of India, Second Administrative Reforms Commission, "Fourth Report: Ethics in Governance," January 2007, http://arc.gov.in/4threport.pdf.

4   *T.S.R. Subramanian v. Union of India & Ors.* (Supreme Court of India, 2011), http://judis.nic.in/supremecourt/imgs1.aspx?filename=40943.

5   Ibid.

6   Government of India, Ministry of Labour & Employment, Directorate General of Employment & Training, "Census of Central Government Employees," May 2012, http://dget.gov.in/publications/ccge/ccge–2009.pdf. These data are for 2009.

7   Government of India, Union Budget and Economic Survey, *Economic Survey 2012–13*, Appendix Table 3.2, http://indiabudget.nic.in/es2012-13/estat1.pdf.

8   Government of India, Second Administrative Reforms Commission, "Tenth Report: Refurbishing of Personnel Administration—Scaling New Heights," November 2008, http://darpg.gov.in/darpgwebsite_cms/document/file/personnel_administration10.pdf.

9   For the full text of this report, see Government of India, Commission on Centre-State Relations, *Report of the Commission on Centre State Relations,* March 2010, http://interstatecouncil.nic.in/ccsr_report_2010.htm.

10 That pressure from the Planning Commission was responsible for this dilution is evident from the account given about non-acceptance of the recommendations of the Third Finance Commission. See Asok Chanda, *Federalism in India* (New York: Hilary House, 1965).

11 Government of India, Planning Commission, "Poverty Alleviation During the 10th Plan—Policy Issues," http://planningcommission.nic.in/reports/articles/ncsxna/ncsax2a.htm. More accurately, this was the view articulated by N. C. Saxena, but it was also a general view.

12 Commission on Centre-State Relations, *Report of the Commission on Centre State Relations.*

13 Government of India, Planning Commission, Committee on Restructuring Social Sector Schemes, "Report of the Committee on Restructuring Social Sector Schemes," September 2011, http://planningcommission.nic.in/reports/genrep/css/rep_css1710.pdf.

CHAPTER 16

BUILDING ADVANCED DEFENSE TECHNOLOGY CAPACITY

RAVINDER PAL SINGH

BACKGROUND

Due to rapid technological advances, new generations of weapons systems that are being developed enter the market at a rate which is shorter than their service life. This phenomenon has increased the obsolescence rate of new weapons, compelling military organizations to seek replacements of weapons without fully utilizing their life-cycle investments. Consequently, to maintain military competitiveness, much better capacities for technological competence and financial assessment are needed in a country's arms acquisition processes.

The past five decades of arms acquisition experience in India have revealed that even though decisionmakers want to indigenize weapon-building capabilities, they have generally ended up importing most of their frontline weapon systems, with some local production. This is mainly due to the fact that home grown systems are not technologically competitive by the time they enter service. Despite its large size, India's defense industrial base has not been able to build advanced technology competitiveness. This leads one to question why India has failed to develop its defense industrial capabilities base beyond those of a licensed weapon producer and why it has not been able to develop weapon design or co-development capabilities.

Because the cost of importing new weapon systems is rising prohibitively, the Indian Ministry of Defense currently has two choices: it can either keep seeking increases in its budget, which would cut into the government's social sector spending, or it can build globally competitive advanced technology capacities at home. Even though the Ministry of Defense has been trying to reform its arms procurement process for more than a decade, India's burgeoning arms import bill does not indicate success of its policies. Evidently, Indian decisionmakers pursuing arms procurement reforms have yet to reflect on the crucial question of whether a country's defense sector can become self-reliant when its research and development (R&D) sector lags behind other nations in advanced industrial technologies.

KEY CHALLENGES AND POSSIBLE OPPORTUNITIES

Among the conditions that contribute to a country's technological standing are sustained availability of research talent in advanced technology disciplines, high-end technology infrastructure for the design and development of internationally competitive industrial exports, and access to entrepreneurial finance. Conversely, conditions that stifle technology innovation are a lack of professional motivation in a monopolistic state-controlled R&D system, a lack of R&D alternatives for the user agencies that undermines competitiveness, state-regulated budgets unable to respond to market opportunities, and limitations in executive oversight to mentor and scrutinize complex technology projects. The Indian defense industrial base, to a great extent, exhibits a near absence of these enabling conditions and dominance of these limiting conditions.

Any analysis of the Indian defense sector takes place against the constraining backdrop of global changes that have been in motion over the past six decades: investment decisions that were earlier going into developments in military technology R&D are now shifting to fast-paced growth opportunities in R&D for industrial technologies. This is due to the unprecedented scale of global industrial growth and the increased rate of obsolescence compelled by commercial competition. Consequently, technology-savvy militaries are now increasingly integrating commercially developed components into their weapon development. In India, however, the state-led military R&D system resists opening itself up to competition, despite its inability to keep pace with the rapid obsolescence rate. As a result, the concept of self-reliance in weapon development has remained unfulfilled.

What can be done? A solution requires the bipartisan political will to implement policy initiatives that build global competitiveness in selected key advanced technologies pervasive in both industrial and military applications. India's aim should be to develop only critical systems that are internationally competitive, rather than its historical wont of making each and every weapon indigenously. The country would have to invest in setting up advanced technology infrastructure, train world-class human resources for research in key advanced technologies, and focus on developing its export standing in these selected technologies. Any new R&D system should be entrepreneurial, offer competitive alternatives to the state-owned R&D sector, incentivize advanced technology exports, and facilitate participation of innovative elements in the private sector in military R&D. If an enterprise-driven R&D system achieves economies of scale, it will reduce risks by integrating the needs of industrial and military markets, both within and outside the country. Such a new system should also inspire India's defense industrial base to liberalize and compete globally in the advanced technology market space.

WHAT IS MISSING AND WHAT PRIORITY STEPS CAN BE TAKEN?

The Ministry of Defense's focus has been to compensate for deficiencies in its weapon inventory. Even though India's generalist civil service benefits from insight into the country's broader priorities, it is difficult for a civil servant with frequent job rotations to develop enough expertise to scrutinize multifaceted, technology-related decisions. As the alternatives and complexities of advanced technology increase, the response of civil servants and military leaders often results in cautious handling of technologically unfamiliar questions, which slows decisionmaking and leads to cost and time overruns. A negative spiral of confidentiality and low accountability ensues, allowing waste and opportunities for fraud to creep into the arms procurement system. Consequently, to keep things under control, the Ministry of Defense continues to exert a monopoly—in the form of the uncompetitive Defense Research and Development Organization (DRDO)—over all military R&D conducted in India. Its often underperforming products are passed off as state-of-the-art systems to India's defense forces.[1]

A major reason for the DRDO's limitations is its triple-hatted R&D model, where a single person performs the roles of technology developer, scientific adviser, and executive manager. This method impairs checks and balances, verification of inputs, scrutiny of the stated technology objectives, and performance standards. The Ministry of Defense and the three armed services have yet to develop organic capabilities to verify technology development standards or actively participate in the DRDO's projects. As defense production entities, the research and development organization and the three armed forces function within rigidly defined vertical channels, handicapping innovation and cross-fertilization of ideas and thus impairing the mobility of skilled resources across military and industrial applications.

The Indian defense industrial base has thus not been able to deliver internationally competitive technology value. The country need not, however, remain hobbled by this limitation. India's defense industry can correct its deficiencies with a three-pronged strategy: (1) building capacity for sustained development of key advanced technologies; (2) fostering the convergence of advanced technology assets and needs to build economies of scale; and (3) encouraging conversions that prompt innovation in R&D, create space for entrepreneurial finance, and broaden market opportunities.

Policymakers and analysts ought to keep in mind Buckminster Fuller's observation: "You never change things by fighting the existing reality. To change something, build a new model that makes the existing model obsolete."

CAPACITY-BUILDING INITIATIVES

Arms procurement decisionmaking is not about merely replacing obsolete weapons with new systems. It requires institutions that can use a deeper knowledge of emerging technologies to develop new weapons competitively. In this regard, India needs to build both hard infrastructure capacities, such as high-end R&D labs, for the design, integration, and testing of advanced products, as well as soft infrastructure, the skilled resources to conduct research at these labs.

India needs to examine opportunities in advanced technology niche markets—particularly in states that are party to the Wassenaar export-control regime—to export competitive technology products. It should also focus on reforms that ensure nationwide compliance with international regulatory and patent rights regimes that safeguard enterprise and invention.

India also needs to redesign and implement a defense offset policy to incentivize investments in advanced technology capabilities in the country and in its technology exports. This inadequacy in India's defense offset policy is evident from the near absence of technology investments by the original equipment manufacturers (OEMs).

Institutional Capacities

India must enhance the capacity of its executive branch in technology contract management, particularly with respect to complex arms acquisition projects. This would require that the executive staff be trained in a diverse range of disciplines, such as operational research, decision sciences, systems analysis, systems engineering, contract management, international business law; financial risk management, and applied financial valuation. Thereafter, these basic decision skills would need to be enhanced through research in fields such as R&D risk assessment, technology forecasting, comparative defense industrial and R&D management, and financial probability and measure; as well as life-cycle cost analysis, technology export controls, and combinatorial optimization for weapon selection.

To improve professionalism in executive oversight capabilities, three kinds of national-level institutions are required. First, India needs an advanced technology management agency and service that would provide technology management specialists for staffing ministries that deal with technology-intensive decisions. Second, this capability should be supported by an advanced technology management institute and research service for comparative research in acquisition, production, financing, and delivery of complex technology projects. This research service would need to continuously deepen and widen its domain knowledge, evaluate domestic and international technology vendor capabilities, and examine cost efficiencies of defense projects.

Third, the government ought to establish a technology-proficient statutory audit authority that would independently evaluate technology designs, verify timelines and milestones achieved, and measure outputs and standards. The audit authority should have capabilities for online auditing of pre-production and post-induction parameters. It should be empowered to draw upon international as well as domestic expertise to map out India's comparative technology strengths and limitations.

Technocratization of Military Leadership

The growing sophistication of modern war fighting, commonly known as the Revolution in Military Affairs, requires that military officers refine their understanding of defense technology, just as their civilian counterparts in India's Ministry of Defense must do. The current standards for Indian officer education can be seen as a bare-bones minimal user concept; the next government should aim to turn this into a maximal user concept. This could enhance the battlefield utility of new systems. More importantly, it will also provide a boon for technology innovation by helping to bridge the gaps in understanding between developers and users.

The existing minimal user concept requires entry-level officers to have the education necessary to study maps; maintain basic financial accounts; and interpret training manuals, laws, and administrative rules. This concept was accepted at the time of India's independence, well over half a century ago. Since then, only the navy has made changes to the dated overall concept.

The necessary maximal user concept, conversely, requires military leaders to acquire tertiary-level engineering skills to maximize operational advantages through technology innovation. It should enable military leaders to combine their field experience and technical skills for the development of new weapons or to develop new countermeasures for weapons in the region. Instead of being trained merely to employ weapons, military leaders need to understand the science and engineering of developing such systems. Numerous other militaries in India's extended neighborhood, including those of Israel, Japan, Singapore, South Korea, and Taiwan, have adopted this approach with success.

In this context, it worth recalling Winston Churchill's observation that "unless the void that exists between the scientist or engineer and the war fighter is recognized, a hiatus will exist between the inventor who knows what they could invent if only they knew what was wanted, and the soldiers who know, or ought to know, what they want and would ask for it if they only knew how much science could do for them."[2]

CONVERGENCE STRATEGY AND ITS IMPLEMENTATION

India must shift its focus from its current R&D system, which is dependent on the Ministry of Defense for funds and contracts, to an entrepreneurial model. The new R&D model—known as a convergence strategy for its union of technology applications in defense and industry—should forecast technology growth opportunities in domestic and international markets and coordinate the defense sector's needs with other technology-intensive fields such as space, civil aviation, oil and gas, electronics, telecommunications, atomic energy, and shipbuilding. For example, it is estimated that by 2020, India will be importing $300 billion worth of telecom and electronics equipment, which would be more than India's oil import bill.[3] The approach that seeks broader investments in R&D projects would enable economies of scale, reduce financial risks in R&D, and generally encourage private sector participation.

Table 1 details some of the key advanced technologies that are required by the military sector, along with examples of industrial applications of these technologies.[4]

Several approaches are required to implement this convergence strategy.

First, India needs to build up sufficient capacities to provide a stock of skilled researchers in a sustained manner for R&D in these seventeen key advanced technology fields that have both military and industrial applications. This could be achieved by establishing seventeen consolidated research institutes of technological excellence dedicated to each of these technology fields to enhance the output of university and industrial R&D in these sectors. These research institutes should preferably be located in the vicinity of the Indian Institutes of Technology and other leading engineering research institutes to attract talented researchers with basic research experience. They should function in clusters of high concentration technology labs in easily accessible locations to attract technology and business

TABLE 1. PRIORITY TECHNOLOGY CONVERGENCE FIELDS

Technological Field	Potential Civilian Applications
Air-Breathing Propulsion	Aerospace, ship propulsion, and stationary power generation.
Semiconductors and Microelectronic Circuits	Automobiles, telecommunications, computer industries, and industrial robotics.
Passive Sensors	Firefighting; health care; pollution control; engine diagnostic tools; mining; industrial and chemical safety monitoring; and satellite-based imaging, communications, and weather forecasting.
Composite Materials	Aerospace, wind power, and construction.
Signal Processing	Neural network applications, security surveillance, medical diagnostics, and automatic machine tools.
Simulation and Modeling	Undersea geophysics and prospecting, petroleum exploration, virtual prototyping, and simultaneous design- and manufacturing-phase engineering.
Advanced Software	Air traffic control, ship design and construction, deep-sea mining, health care, computer security and cryptography, electrical power generation, and surface transport.
Radar	Robotics, automated manufacturing, traffic safety, and remote detection of chemical effluents.
Parallel Computer Architecture	Computer-aided design, engineering simulation, weather forecasting, petroleum and electronics research.
Photonics	Medical diagnostics, high-speed computing, laser detectors, local area networks, and transoceanic cabling.
Computational Fluid Dynamics	Aerospace; welding and soldering; and production of silicon wafers, circuit boards, machine tools, and gas turbine parts.
Machine Intelligence and Robotics	Industrial robotics, hazardous material handling, automated manufacturing, deep-sea exploration.
Data Fusion	Urban planning; pollution control monitoring; and climate, crop, and geological analysis.
Weapon System Environment	Pollution control; weather forecasting; and oceanographic, space, and geological research.
Pulsed Power	Electricity production and advanced medical equipment.
Hypervelocity Projectiles	Commercial space launch vehicles.
Superconductivity	Energy distribution, noninvasive diagnostic surgery, magnetic resonance imaging, and high-performance computing.

investors and foster linkages with other innovative technology enterprises in the country.

The research institutes should be supported by a corporate center for accessing entrepreneurial finance to help meet the cost of product development and incubation. The corporate center should also help in setting up joint ventures with the foreign OEMs and other Indian entities and should actively seek venture capital. R&D projects conducted at the research institutes should be flexible enough to choose appropriate manufacturing facilities in the private or public sector.

Second, India's private sector currently avoids investing in defense R&D projects because of inherent financial risks and delays in the government's decisionmaking process. The private sector companies could improve upon their R&D capabilities if they join consortiums of technology design houses, public sector labs, and original equipment manufacturers. While assessing their joint venture partners, the OEMs prefer to examine the commercial viability of business plans, technology value addition, or innovation capabilities that their potential partners can deliver. Indian companies are often found to be short on such abilities. The government could consider four areas of focus to develop specialization in Indian industry: product design; R&D, testing, and evaluation for prototypes and development models; manufacturing of assemblies as part of OEMs' global supply chains; and marketing and after-sales service support.

Third, because the key to military technology innovation is the integration of advanced engineering knowledge with combat experience, the three armed services should set up engineering labs and co-locate these with their doctrinal research centers. Convergence of the military's research and engineering labs staffed with technologists from the armed services will provide several advantages. It will help identify global developments in force multipliers, as well as exploit breakthrough technologies that may influence operational concepts. It will also enable the military to develop accurate estimates of comparative technology levels of the threats it faces and will align the battlefield user's operational needs with the R&D process and the manufacturers' production quality. Finally, such convergence will enable verification of equipment requirements with technical feasibilities, and build active participation of the user agency in the development of prototypes. Convergence processes would also help integrate the common user requirements of the three armed services, study the operational impact and opportunities offered by next-generation weapon systems, and verify technical thresholds claimed by the OEM suppliers for their systems.[5]

CONVERSION FOR COMPETITIVENESS

The Indian defense industry in the public sector, being closely bound in red tape, has to liberalize its R&D sector to make it competitive enough to be sought as a suitable collaborator by OEM suppliers and the private sector. To strengthen their R&D expertise, the research institutes should seek global partners for developing their advanced technology products. This could be done through consortiums of OEMs, venture capital investors, and global marketing companies to access global and domestic industrial and military markets for their advanced technology products. These consortiums should also seek offset contracts using the Pull Principle to develop common R&D requirements of defense and industrial sector products.[6] This approach will create R&D alternatives for the military, reduce the costs and risks of R&D, and help in improving the competitiveness of these labs.

A Model for Product Integration and Development Architecture

To complete R&D projects that may have commercial value, India requires a more robust systems integration architecture to ensure that the many complex components of a technology product interact properly with one another. At each stage of a product's development—from its proof of concept to the validation of its engineering model to its commercial rollout—specialized multidisciplinary teams would work toward this goal.

Technology Systems Integrators: These specialized technology development teams would be required to produce components and test subassemblies to make engineering or prototype models that are specific to their key technology fields. The systems integration entities should receive development funds from an autonomous financial commission.

Lead Systems Integrator: One of the research institute labs should be designated as the lead systems integrator on the basis of criticality of technology required by the specific product. The lead unit would complete the product prototype using components produced by the technology development teams or sourced globally. It should form joint ventures with manufacturing entities to develop a pre-production model ready for the marketing stage. Funding for this stage could be sought from financial institutions. Since risk levels are especially high during the R&D incubation stages, the lead systems integrator would need to demonstrate capabilities to produce the desired product within the target parameters of costs, performance, and production schedule.

Core Systems Integrator: The core systems integrator should bridge the gap between the user, the lab, and the larger market. It should have an overall coordinating function to identify and integrate the technology needs of the defense sector with those of other users in the country and from international markets. This integrator should facilitate the incorporation of components from global or Indian sources, setting up of joint ventures, and acquisition of new technologies through offset programs. It would coordinate assessment of technology applications with business planning to promote start-ups at the research institutes that have high commercial potential.

Technology-Transfer and Innovation Support Agency: This final technology integrator should support the core systems integrator in commercializing advanced technology R&D and facilitating patenting, export licensing, and global marketing. In this regard, the Foreign Ministry should be more proactive in facilitating technology exports. The technology-transfer integrator should link the research institutes and university research labs with financial backers and the market, serving as a one-stop shop for angel investors, venture capital investors, investment banks, and joint venture partners. It should facilitate start-ups and rapid entry of spin-offs into the technology market by managing their market and IP portfolio. In order to negotiate research, licensing, and marketing contracts, its staff should have scientific, industrial, and legal backgrounds, and expertise in diverse fields such as international business and patent law, technology export controls, financial risk management, applied financial valuation, and so on.

A Model for Entrepreneurial Finance

State funding would be required for establishing the seventeen research institutes of technological excellence, meeting personnel costs, and for leasing customized R&D infrastructure. To fund R&D operations, the government should set up an autonomous financial commission comprising experts from finance, marketing, and key advanced technologies. These experts would be best equipped to assess market opportunities for funding projects from different technology fields and to verify competence levels of technology developers at the labs. Funds needed by the financial commission should be drawn from technology-intensive ministries that are interested in the project, financial institutions, and the market.

To meet the costs for systems integration and risk capital, the government should consider establishing a dedicated advanced technology development bank, like the Industrial Development Bank of India. It should aim to encourage angel investor clubs, venture capital investors, and the rest of the private sector to support the manufacturing and marketing costs of technology products. In the long term, these research institutes should spawn scores of independent profit centers to become internationally competitive, globally recognized suppliers of advanced technology products. The advanced technology bank should organize seventeen multidisciplinary competence centers to incentivize innovative technology profit centers; conceive financial collaboration and early-stage financing; evaluate complex technology business models; and facilitate the creation of a stable yet vibrant market environment to generate demand for the country's advanced science and engineering disciplines.

Product development and the commercialization of advanced technologies depend upon financial support that should be available in a sustainable way. Because it is very difficult to raise funds from the market for high-risk and high-value R&D, state support has to continue for strategic systems whose components do not have commercial applications. In addition, business enterprise reforms are needed in defense R&D labs for seeking finance from the market.[7] However, R&D aimed at the development of common military and industrial components for wider markets should be able to raise finance from venture capital, angel investors, and other entrepreneurial sources.

CONCLUSION

Despite India's having experienced the benefits of the industrial liberalization of the early 1990s, the Ministry of Defense has neither liberalized nor de-bureaucratized its R&D system and manufacturing sectors. This is mainly because the ministry has an abiding preference for ownership and control.

The Indian military has to confront two strategic facts: the Chinese military will be bigger and will have more financial resources. India cannot offset those comparative disadvantages without developing advanced technology capabilities. The strategy requires building up a world-class technology infrastructure and improving the country's global exports in key advanced technologies. Without enhancing these capabilities, India cannot compete with weapons and technology suppliers from East Asia.

Technology acquisition capabilities require investing in people who can invent, create, or innovate new military products from emerging technologies. The OEMs investing in India have spent years developing these capabilities. Achieving this objective requires a coherent policy of advanced technology capacity building centered around upgrading the technological skill sets of the civil and military bureaucracies, through the research institutes and the infrastructure to support the development of seventeen pervasive key advanced technology fields in the country.

The Indian government needs to focus on creating competitive alternatives to the country's state-led monopoly R&D system. Several actionable initiatives for change—practices that are tried, tested, and followed in various countries—have been described. The recommended processes have been appropriately modified to address India's unique organizational limitations in building institutions and the change-resistant characteristics of its civil and military bureaucracies.

The political leadership's limitations include lack of knowledge of methods to implement changes that could lead to uncertain outcomes. The higher bureaucracy is more concerned with retaining its status in the policymaking order than with building up its specialization for mentoring advanced technology acquisitions in the country. The Ministry of Defense has to support the development of advanced technology clusters with the best operating conditions in special zones and provide attractive tax structures; liberal labor rules; sustained access to entrepreneurial finance; and a high quality, specialized workforce.

Because sufficient data are publicly available on good global practices in advanced technology acquisition, the new government should be able to present an advanced technology acquisition plan for parliamentary approval in its first year. This step will greatly facilitate partial implementation of all the recommendations within the next four to five years, though the benefits accruing from these changes will not begin to show up until five to fifteen years after implementation. The changes will also bring longer-term multiplier benefits to India's R&D system and value to the military's technological capacities.

For executive procedures, it is more efficient to bring about changes through professional legislative oversight processes. The parliamentary standing committees in India need to institutionalize procedures of and capacities for technical scrutiny, access independent experts to monitor implementation milestones, and review technology development plans periodically. Instead of changing their composition every year, the standing committees must institutionalize continuity in their membership for competence building and coherent scrutiny of the national R&D system.

If appointed, a task force composed of technical experts will be able to implement the paper's recommendations within five years of the new government's being voted to office in 2014.

NOTES

1   See Ravinder Pal Singh, "An Assessment of Indian S&T and Implications for Military R&D," *Economics and Political Weekly* 35, no. 31, July 29, 2000.

2   Winston Churchill, *The Great War*, vol. 4 (London: Home Library Edition, n.d.), Appendix 8, "Mechanical Power in the Offensive" (1916).

3   "India Needs to Develop Electronics, Telecommunication, Manmohan Singh Says," *Times of India*, December 5, 2013, http://timesofindia.indiatimes.com/business/india-business/India-needs-to-develop-electronics-telecommunication-Manmohan-Singh-says/articleshow/26889646.cms.

4   For a detailed discussion of these technological fields and their applications, see "Preparing for our Future: Developing a Common Strategy for Key Enabling Technologies," EU Commission Staff Working Document SEC(2009) 1257, September 30, 2009; and Ravinder Pal Singh, "Identifying Key Technologies in Major Weapon Systems," in *The Transfer of Sensitive Technologies and the Future of Control Regimes*, eds. P. Gasparini Alves and Kerstin Hoffman (New York and Geneva: United Nations Institute for Disarmament Research, 1997).

5   Convergence of operational experience and technological capacities has been used in innovative development of new weapon systems in Israel. Several Israeli military officers were engaged in the development of the Merkava tank, Uzi submachine gun, UAVs, the mobile telephony switching system, technology for non-invasive surgery, and other technologies. Innovation and value addition to military R&D comes from the exchange of cross-disciplinary experiences with specialists from different technologies and operational backgrounds. This concept has not yet developed in India.

6   Applying the Pull Principle to incentivize advanced technology investments by the OEMs would require creating conditions in India that are seen as commercially beneficial by the OEMs themselves to set up R&D resources and export facilities. The OEMs should select and decide on the advanced technologies that can be exported from India rather than Ministry of Defense civil servants deciding for them. The offsets should create desire in the OEM to use commercial and technological opportunities that are available in and from India.

7   India does not permit market finance for its R&D labs. China, by contrast, permits its defense sector to raise up to 22.5 percent of its budget in private equity. Since defense R&D has long gestation periods and uncertain outcomes, integration of these two sectors allows China to leverage advanced civilian R&D capabilities for its military. For China's Civil Military Integration strategy, see Tai Ming Cheung, "The Chinese Defense Economy's Long March From Imitation to Innovation," *Journal of Strategic Studies* 34, issue 3, June 2011; and Soumitra Dutta, ed., *The Global Innovation Index 2011, Accelerating Growth and Development* (Fontainebleau, France: INSEAD, 2011), 85.

CHAPTER 17

REJUVENATING FOREIGN POLICY

C. RAJA MOHAN

INTRODUCTION

The new government that takes charge in 2014 will face many difficult challenges across a broad front. Restoring the lost dynamism in India's vital strategic partnerships and regaining a firm handle on some of its traditionally difficult relationships will be at the top of the diplomatic agenda for the new government. India's very impressive foreign policy run since the nuclear tests of May 1998 petered out in the second term of Prime Minister Manmohan Singh. International condemnation of the tests quickly yielded to the improvement of India's relations with all the major powers. Thanks to purposeful and imaginative diplomacy on the part of Atal Bihari Vajpayee, India raised its profile in Asia's international relations and on the global stage. If Manmohan Singh inherited an India that was running forward full tilt, he leaves an India that is sputtering on all fronts.

In the first term of the United Progressive Alliance (UPA), Singh had the luxury of basking in the glory of economic growth generated by earlier reforms. While he was unwilling to push for second-generation reforms during 2004–2009, Singh seemed confident enough to take forward Vajpayee's many foreign policy initiatives—including those toward the United States, China, and Pakistan. Singh's second term, however, turned out to be disappointing on both the economic and diplomatic fronts. His government's missteps on economic policy were compounded by maladroit diplomacy and wishful strategic thinking. Together they undermined the narrative of India's rise that had gained so much traction in the earlier decade. The next government, then, must return to the basics. The successor to the UPA government must above all restore the authority of the prime minister and his leadership over the cabinet system of government so critical for the conduct of any national policy. On the foreign policy front, it must end the confusion injected by the UPA government into India's external goals, revive domestic political consensus on an effective strategy, and address the multiple structural constraints and institutional weaknesses that have hampered India's rise. This chapter is divided into three sections. The first offers an assessment of the UPA government's foreign policy record. The second section examines some of the long-term structural problems that must be addressed by the new government. The final section offers a set of recommendations for early action by the new government.

LOSING THE PLOT

The decade-long tenure of Manmohan Singh began with a bold determination to press ahead with the fundamental policy innovations launched by the Vajpayee government. Taken together, these innovations in five distinct areas helped transform India's geopolitical condition and secure India's rise in Asia and the world. The first was in the domain of nuclear diplomacy. In testing five nuclear weapons in May 1998 in defiance of global opinion, the Vajpayee government ended India's prolonged nuclear ambiguity and the many long-term costs that came with it. Nuclear ambiguity from 1974 put India at odds with the global nonproliferation regime, made it a major target of high-technology sanctions, complicated its relations with major powers, and prevented it from addressing the challenges of the regional nuclear environment. Pokhran II, then, was about cutting the Gordian knot, creating the space for a nuclear reconciliation with the United States that would eventually end India's prolonged alienation from the global nonproliferation regime. The second was in the area of neighborhood policy, where Vajpayee sought to limit India's extended conflicts with Pakistan and China and build more cooperative relations with its smaller neighbors.

Third, Vajpayee broadened the nation's foreign policy field of vision and defined India's interests as extending from Aden to Malacca. The new approach provided the basis for intensifying India's "Look East" policy and its engagement with the Middle East. While the first steps in this policy came from his predecessor, P. V. Narasimha Rao, Vajpayee expanded the scope of the Look East policy and looked beyond old shibboleths in the Middle East to reach out to Iran, Saudi Arabia, and Israel. Fourth was the transformation of relations with all the major powers, especially the United States. Discarding the old baggage of nonalignment, Vajpayee boldly reached out to the United States and declared to an initially skeptical American audience and a visibly nervous Indian one that New Delhi and Washington were natural allies. This new thinking broke decades of antipathy in the Indian political class and set the terms for a comprehensive restructuring of relations with the United States that would produce great dividends for India. Fifth and finally, Vajpayee began to discard the ideological baggage in the multilateral arena, where he broke loose from the canon in the nuclear domain, supported the United States on missile defense, and began to focus on India's interests rather than on ideological posturing at the United Nations and other multilateral forums. These five approaches broke the ideological rigidity that had taken hold of India's foreign policy and energized the Indian diplomacy in ways not seen since the 1950s under Jawaharlal Nehru.

In 2004, Manmohan Singh thus inherited a robust foreign policy agenda and an improved regional and global standing. Despite a constricting coalition with the Communist parties and his own Congress party's deep aversion to any political risk, Singh was eager to press ahead with Vajpayee's foreign policy innovations. During the first two years of his government, New Delhi clinched defense and nuclear deals with the United States, outlined the terms of a boundary settlement with China, initiated negotiations on the Kashmir dispute with Pakistan, and articulated a new vision for regional integration within the subcontinent. For the rest of the decade-long tenure, Singh had to struggle to sustain these early initiatives amid an internal political backlash and the lack of support from the Congress party.

With the United States, Singh quickly found himself fighting an unending battle on the implementation of the nuclear accord. On the face of it was the knee-jerk ideological opposition from the communists and the political opportunism of the post-Vajpayee Indian People's Party (BJP) leadership that put the nuclear deal in trouble. While the attitude of these two parties did create huge problems, the real sources of the trouble were within the government and the Congress party. In the government, key sections of the scientific bureaucracy, foreign office, and the security establishment were unwilling to recognize the extraordinary benefits of the civil nuclear initiative and raised concerns that were rooted in deep suspicion of the United States. The Congress party was even more uncomfortable with the new and unfamiliar terrain of India's relations with the United States and was concerned about the reactions of the Muslim and left-wing bases of support. Singh's inability to persuade the Congress party leadership of the nuclear imperative, his lack of authority over the cabinet colleagues, and his reluctance to discipline the bureaucracy prolonged a national nuclear debate on an agreement that was entirely in India's favor. It was only his threat of resignation three years after signing the nuclear accord that helped salvage it at the last moment.

The problems that Singh confronted in implementing the civil nuclear initiative were not limited to the United States. While Singh made progress in the negotiations with Pakistan and China, the Congress party was not willing to adopt a bold course or clinch the settlements that seemed within grasp. A visit by Pakistani President Pervez Musharraf to India in April 2005 set the terms for a new negotiation on Kashmir and provided the basis for agreements on the Siachen and Sir Creek disputes. But senior cabinet members from the Congress party were unwilling to move forward and were not even ready to support a visit by the prime minister to Pakistan. On the China front, too, the hopes raised by the 2005 agreement on boundary principles could not be translated into practical results. The boldness of the initial negotiation gave way to caution on the negotiation of the mutually acceptable territorial concessions in the second stage of the boundary settlement. China, concerned about the prospects for a new India-U.S. relationship, also seemed reluctant to move forward in resolving the boundary dispute. If relations with America, China, and Pakistan presented great strategic opportunities for India, the Congress party's ambivalence and Singh's reluctance to assert his authority stalled progress on the three major foreign policy accounts by the end of UPA's tenure.

The reelection of the Congress party in the 2009 elections with an increased number of seats raised hopes that the UPA-II would be bolder on the economic and foreign policy fronts. But in the second term, the prime minister seemed to have even less freedom than he had in the first term to advance a bold agenda of foreign policy, for the Congress party leadership began to impose even stronger constraints on Singh's room to maneuver politically. The mishandling of the liability legislation in 2010 completely undermined all the effort that went into ending India's prolonged atomic isolation. Excessive demands on suppliers put off not just the United States but also all of India's major partners that helped India regain access to the international nuclear commerce. Unreasonable liability burdens also imposed new constraints on domestic suppliers to the nuclear power industry and limited the prospects for significant expansion of atomic power generation in India. Singh's effort to revive the peace process with Pakistan faced resistance from the Congress party, but he did manage to negotiate a road map for normalization of trade relations and visa liberalization. Yet the prime minister remained hesitant to undertake a visit to Pakistan and, amid reports of violence on the border during 2013, Singh seemed to lose his nerve. The second term of the UPA-II also saw growing uncertainty in Sino-Indian ties thanks to the PLA's aggressive patrolling on the border and Beijing's reluctance to support India's international aspirations. In his second term, Singh devoted considerable energy to the transformation of bilateral relations with Bangladesh. When these agreements, for river water sharing and land boundary settlement, were ready to be signed, Singh encountered resistance from the chief minister of West Bengal, Mamata Banerjee, and lack of support from his own party to press ahead. The debacle on the Bangladesh front exposed the profound weakness of the government in bringing to a close major strategic initiatives and the Congress party's inability to construct a domestic consensus on vital national security issues. In the process, New Delhi let down Bangladeshi Prime Minister Sheikh Hasina, who went out of the way to address India's concerns on cross-border terrorism. Singh, then, ends his decade-long tenure with a whimper after having raised extraordinary expectations in the region and the world on leading India on its upward march in the global system.

STRUCTURAL CHALLENGES

In seeking to revive the momentum of India's foreign policy, the new government will have to address six important structural challenges. The first is the importance of rescuing the foreign policy from the old ideological demons, especially the idea of nonalignment, that have come to haunt New Delhi's mind. The UPA government, unfortunately, restored some of the Cold War–era baggage shed by Prime Ministers Rao and Vajpayee. If the ideological confusion of the first UPA term was driven in part by the pressures from one of its leading coalition partners, the Communist Party of India, the source of Indian ambivalence in the second term appeared to emerge from the Congress party itself.

The relative gains in India's economic and political weight in the international system over the past two decades and its prospects for emergence as a major power demand a very different way of defining the guiding principles of India's foreign policy. The concept of nonalignment, articulated in the early years of independence, was about retaining independence of judgment and action for a weak state with significant aspirations for a large role in world affairs. India today is a very different beast. As the world's tenth-largest economy (in real terms at the end of 2013) and the ninth-largest spender on defense, India has all the attributes of a major power in the making. While India's Cold War doctrine of strategic autonomy was about preventing external powers from limiting its choices, India's current objective must be to seek strategic influence over the evolution of the regional and international system in order to secure its interests. The quest for strategic influence is not a matter of choice, but an unavoidable imperative. With nearly 50 percent of its economy tied to imports and exports, India's ability to secure the growing levels of prosperity for its people depends upon its capacity to shape its regional security environment; contribute to stable great-power relations; become an indispensable element of the Asian balance of power; and ensure favorable international regimes on trade, climate change, and other pressing multilateral matters.

A second challenge for the new government lies in bringing clarity and dexterity to its engagement with great powers. Since the end of the Cold War and the launch of India's economic reforms, India's relations with all the major powers have been significantly improved. This was possible in part because of the absence of great-power rivalry in the past quarter century. That tranquil moment is beginning to break down, as relations among the world's three largest economies—the United States, China, and Japan—face unprecedented uncertainty, and Russia begins to assert itself with some vigor. India will perforce have to move from the omnidirectional engagement of the past to making some clear choices about its ties with major powers. Neither equidistance nor equal engagement will help India cope with the change in the distribution of power among the big nations of the world.

Rather than take a symmetric approach to relations with the United States and China, New Delhi has to deal with these two powers in very different ways. For decades now, and especially since the end of the Cold War, India agonized about American power during the unipolar moment and has sought to collaborate with other powers, including China, to construct a multipolar world. Paradoxically, though, it was a new relationship with the United States that allowed India to achieve greater flexibility vis-à-vis Pakistan and to gain a political accommodation with the global nuclear order from which it was isolated for decades. Further, it is the rise of Chinese power that is severely constricting India's room for maneuver in the subcontinent and the Indian Ocean. India now has reasons to worry about a precipitous decline in U.S. power and Washington's potential temptation to compromise with China on Asian and global issues. At the same time, India would not want to provoke a premature confrontation with Beijing by joining an alliance with the United States to contain China. As it guards against these potential pitfalls, New Delhi cannot avoid coming to terms with one important reality: India's core objective of expanding its comprehensive national power is more likely to be achieved in collaboration with the United States and the West than with China.

A third challenge, deepening India's regional engagement, presents itself in two different dimensions. One of the central vulnerabilities of India's geopolitical condition has been its perennial conflict with Pakistan and the increasing difficulty of asserting its primacy in the subcontinent. Therefore normalizing relations with Pakistan and ending the divisiveness within the subcontinent remain critical strategic objectives. Although successive Indian governments have sought to normalize relations with Pakistan, the persistence of cross-border terrorism has limited the political space at home for rapprochement with Islamabad. Yet at critical moments in the past decade, the UPA government has lost its nerve and abandoned opportunities—for example, in settling the disputes over Siachen and Sir Creek and instituting Kashmir-related confidence-building measures—for advancing its relationship with Pakistan. Since the end of the Cold War, India has also consistently sought to improve relations with smaller neighbors, but results have been mixed. While there is some progress in regional cooperation, India has not fully used its expanding economic weight to reintegrate the markets of the subcontinent. In the past two decades, India has also stepped up its engagement with East Asia, the Middle East, and Africa. While progress has been impressive, the effort has remained subcritical. Accelerating economic integration within the subcontinent and with the abutting regions, promoting connectivity, contributing to regional stability, and bolstering defense cooperation are all critical goals that need to be pursued with greater vigor by the new government in New Delhi.

Fourth, as the scale and scope of India's external engagement has dramatically increased, weak institutional capacity has prevented New Delhi from taking full advantage of the external opportunities that presented themselves. Responding to the widespread concerns that the size of its diplomatic corps is too small (currently at 600 officers), New Delhi has begun to expand entry-level recruitment and encourage the deputation of officers from other departments of the government. The pace of expansion, however, remains too slow to build a much-needed larger diplomatic corps. Inadequate manpower is only part of the problem. Raising the quality of the government personnel and supporting the development of strong policy and research institutions within and outside the government are others. India ought to promote synergies between the Ministry of External Affairs and other wings of the government, including the economic ministries and agencies dealing with the environment, science, and technology. While the Ministry of External Affairs is unlikely to regain its erstwhile leadership, New Delhi needs to ensure better coordination among the different agencies of the government and more effective delivery on agreements concluded with its international partners. Few countries are blessed with the kind of soft power resources—in arts, culture, and the media—that India enjoys. Yet, New Delhi has found it hard to leverage these in the conduct of its external relations. For example, its public broadcast systems remain ossified and unable to extend India's cultural footprint around the world. At the same time, New Delhi's restrictive visa policies have limited international exchanges between India and the world.

Fifth, the challenge of effective coordination cannot be met without restoring the prime minister's authority over the entire governmental structure. The nature of coalition governments tends to limit the prime minister's freedom of action on a range of issues. While stronger leaders such as Rao and Vajpayee managed to cope with this challenge, Manmohan Singh was constrained by the fact that he was not the leader of his own party. Under an unprecedented arrangement of power sharing between Congress party leader Sonia Gandhi and Prime Minister Singh in the decade-long tenure of the UPA government, Singh's influence over New Delhi's decision-making has been severely undermined. The prime minister's lack of authority over his cabinet translated into the weakening of the office of the cabinet secretary, the senior-most civil servant, in pushing through critical initiatives on foreign, commercial, and defense policies. Restoring the prime minister's authority and strengthening the position of the cabinet secretary are critical for effective delivery on agreements with other countries.

Sixth, Prime Minister Singh has had to face an unexpected difficulty in the form of opposition from state governments to engagement with important neighbors. From a purely legal perspective, of course, the making of foreign policy is an exclusive prerogative of the union government in India. Yet, from a political point of view, New Delhi always has had to take into account the sensitivities of states in crafting its foreign policy—Tamil sentiments, for example, in dealing with Colombo. Under UPA-II, though, New Delhi seemed paralyzed by state government protests. For example, the opposition of West Bengal Chief Minister Banerjee unraveled one of the major foreign policy initiatives toward Bangladesh. While Banerjee's obstreperousness has been substantial, the inability of New Delhi to manage the political dynamic with Kolkata has been equally responsible for the undermining of a major diplomatic outreach to Dhaka. Similarly, in the case of Sri Lanka, the UPA-II has failed to handle the Tamil politics in Chennai in coping with the challenges in Sri Lanka. Yielding to pressures from Chennai, the prime minister chose not to attend the Commonwealth Summit in Colombo at the end of 2013.

But not all states have had a negative effect on India's regional diplomacy. For example, in Punjab, where the ruling Akali Dal supported the normalization of relations with Pakistan and demanded greater transborder cooperation in the divided state, New Delhi seemed unable to take full advantage of this opportunity. Any new government will have to focus on ways to reclaim the central government's prerogative to conduct foreign policy while being more sophisticated in managing the concerns of the states. It must also explore possibilities for turning its border states into partners for transforming relations with neighbors.

PRIORITY STEPS

The most important priority for the new government is undoubtedly the revival of India's economic growth. An emphasis on "economy first" by the new government will have significant benefits in the conduct of foreign policy. It will open spaces for the expansion of cooperation with India's strategic partners, provide a basis for limiting some of the conflicts with its adversaries, and help raise India's influence in the subcontinent and beyond.

Central to this strategy must be greater political commitment to trade liberalization at the regional and global levels. The political urges for protecting the Indian market are understandable; those impulses are not limited to the left in India but have long animated the two centrist parties, the Congress party and the BJP. The new government will have to overcome this ambivalence, articulate the importance of gaining access to world markets, and construct a new domestic coalition for economic regionalism and globalization. If New Delhi does not act quickly, it will be left out in the cold as trade liberalization gains traction in the Asia-Pacific and the Atlantic through the Trans-Pacific Partnership and Transatlantic Trade and Investment Partnership negotiations. Concluding India's free trade negotiations with Europe, actively contributing to the construction of an Asian economic community through the Regional Comprehensive Economic Partnership, and initiating negotiations on free trade with the United States should be at the top of India's foreign economic agenda. India's political objective of sustaining its primacy in the subcontinent depends critically on promoting regional economic integration. Although the UPA government talked the talk on improving India's physical connectivity with the subcontinent and beyond and giving better market access to its neighbors, it has not walked the walk. A positive approach to multilateralism at the global and regional levels is necessary to strengthen India's role, as a responsible power, in shaping the emerging regimes on such issues as climate change and Internet governance.

Second, revitalizing the strategic partnership with the United States must be the foundation on which the new government pursues its great-power relationships. Relations between New Delhi and Washington have plateaued over the past few years amid American disappointments on a range of fronts. These include the constraints, stemming from India's nuclear liability legislation, on American companies' participation in India's nuclear power program; apparent Indian reluctance to pursue defense cooperation; and the difficulties of accessing the Indian market. Regional developments in the Middle East and Southwest Asia and a variety of multilateral issues have also exposed considerable divergences. While India and the United States are unlikely to be allies in the traditional sense and differences will remain on a range of issues, more intensive political cooperation with the United States is critical for India in coping with turbulence in the Middle East, uncertainty in Afghanistan after the United States withdraws most of its forces, and prospects of a non-peaceful Chinese rise in East Asia. A strong partnership with the United States will expand India's economic and political leverage with the other major powers, including Europe, China, Japan, and Russia. India cannot let any tactical considerations cloud this fundamental strategic objective vis-à-vis the United States.

The third priority is the management of the China challenge. The past few years have shown that distancing itself from the United States does not in any way improve New Delhi's ability to resolve its manifold problems with China. A strategic partnership with the United States is in fact critical for India in coping with the economic, political, and military consequences of the widening gap in the material capabilities with China. China's GDP and defense expenditures are now four times those of India. Beyond the partnership with the United States, India will have to do much of its own internal balancing vis-à-vis China, including upgrading its border infrastructure, modernizing its military, and expanding its comprehensive national power. Even as it seeks to balance China, India must necessarily expand economic cooperation with China and press Beijing for better market access for India's manufactured goods and services. India must also shed its reluctance to work with China on the integration of the subcontinent to the markets around it. If China is a challenge as well as an opportunity, New Delhi must learn to walk on two legs—productive bilateral cooperation and effective competition.

Strengthening India's ability to shape the future of Asia is the fourth objective. In the East, New Delhi must respond more effectively to the demand for greater economic, security, and military cooperation with India. In the West, it must end the neglect of the Middle East in recent years and build strong ties to all the key nations in the region—including Egypt, Iran, Iraq, Israel, Saudi Arabia, and Turkey—and reclaim India's once-critical role there. New Delhi must also end the continuing neglect of vital regions in the world—including Central Asia, Eastern Europe, Latin America, and Oceania—that will increasingly matter for India's national interests.

Fifth, India must find ways to quickly respond to the growing demands for defense cooperation with India in different parts of the world, especially in the Indo-Pacific littoral. To be sure, India has expanded its defense diplomacy in recent years, especially in the field of exchanges, joint exercises, and military training. While the Foreign Office and armed forces see immense prospects for defense diplomacy, however, the Ministry of Defense remains politically inhibited and institutionally underequipped to address the opportunities knocking at India's door. The new government must make defense diplomacy a high priority and create a framework of more intensive military cooperation with major powers as well as regional partners. Equally important is the need to create a strong domestic defense industrial base through policies that promote the production of weapons at home and facilitate export of defense hardware and services.

Sixth, India must lead the promotion of peace, prosperity, and stability in the subcontinent. On the economic front, India must open its markets to smaller neighbors, promote greater transborder connectivity, and modernize its infrastructure to facilitate trade. Unlike Manmohan Singh, who rarely traveled to neighboring capitals, the next prime minister must make such travel routine and intensify the high-level political engagement with neighbors. New Delhi must seek to become the most important trade partner, external investor, and assistance provider to most of its smaller neighbors. Although India has stepped up its economic assistance to many of its neighbors, it has had big problems in implementing strategic economic projects in the region. Creating an effective framework for project exports in the neighborhood is an important priority for the new government.

Seventh, India must resolutely confront the challenges of extremism and terrorism that not only seek to destabilize India but also to undermine state structures in Afghanistan, Pakistan, and Bangladesh. These challenges are likely to become more acute after the withdrawal of U.S. forces from Afghanistan and the impact on the subcontinent of the sectarian rivalry in the Middle East that has gained traction in recent years. Although Pakistan has been a difficult partner, the new government, like the previous ones, must persist in its engagement with Pakistan and seek improvements wherever possible while keeping one long-term objective in mind: promoting internal change in Pakistan in favor of those who seek a normalization of relations with India. Failure to manage the relationship with Pakistan would enormously complicate the pursuit of India's larger goals in the region and beyond.

Finally, India can no longer waste its natural strengths in the domain of soft power. Whether it is promotion of tourism or cultural diplomacy, expanding the global footprint of Indian media, or cultivating political constituencies around the world, New Delhi has performed far below its potential. While Indian electronic and print media have become a powerful force at home, they have little presence abroad. This could change with a conscious policy to promote a strong public-private partnership to promote India's rich culture and its political perspectives around the world. New Delhi must also build on its unique religious heritage—Zoroastrian, Hindu, Buddhist, Islamic, Sikh, Jain, Christian—to promote greater engagement with the world and initiate a sustainable interfaith dialogue.

RECOMMENDED READING

Center for Policy Research, *Nonalignment 2.0: A Foreign and Strategic Policy for India in the Twenty-First Century* (New Delhi, 2012); for a critique, see Ashley J. Tellis, *Nonalignment Redux: The Perils of Old Wine in New Skins* (Washington, D.C.: Carnegie Endowment for International Peace, 2012).

Satish Kumar et al., *India's Strategic Partners: A Comparative Assessment* (New Delhi: Foundation for National Security Research, 2011).

Kishan S. Rana and Bipul Chatterjee, eds., *Economic Diplomacy: India's Experience* (New Delhi: CUTS International, 2011).

INDEX

informal sector, low productivity in, 11
informal sector producers, presence of, 76
infrastructure: banks not able to finance investment, 30; deficit, 79; development through PPPs, 141; government underinvested in, 139; inadequate becoming a drag on the economy, 137; investment in, 141; modernizing to facilitate trade, 308; projects, 137
Inner-State Council, 236, 274
institutional capacities, 285–286, 304
institutional mechanisms, governing delivery of educational services, 109–110
institutional structure, governing education delivery, 104–107
Insurance Regulatory and Development Authority, 98
investment, ratio to gross domestic product (GDP), 42
investment projects, problems of approvals and legal bottlenecks, 30
investment sources in agriculture, 61
Irrigation Service Fees (ISF), 187, 188
Israel, 295n5

J

Jain Commission, 249
Jala Yagnam (water worship), 204n3
Jawaharlal Nehru National Urban Renewal Mission (JNNURM), 166–167, 168, 169, 202
jobs: creating in the manufacturing sector, 219; extra needed, 95; losses dominating headlines, 91–93
Judicial Appointments Commission Bill, 2013, 259

Judicial Standards and Accountability Bill, 259
judiciary, 248, 266
justice system, 251, 256
Jyotigram scheme, 194, 202

L

labor (skilled and unskilled), cost of procedures and processes on, 82
labor conditions, 79, 84
labor deployment, 78–79, 84
labor force participation rate, 96, 102n8
labor laws, 84, 101
land: agricultural, 175; centrality of, 171–172; cost of, 82; cost of securing, 101; fragmented, 176; price of determined by its use, 175; restrictive rules on for new urban uses, 158; unlocking the capitalization potential of, 174
Land Acquisition Act, 1894, 159, 177
Land Acquisition, Rehabilitation, and Resettlement (LARR) Bill, 76, 82, 83–84, 85, 159, 178, 179
land acquisition system, reform of, 172
land costs, keeping at acceptable levels, 83–84
land market: broken, 171; facilitating an efficient, 174; gulf between supply and demand, 172; institutions needed to facilitate functioning of, 159; issue of regularizing, 182; overregulated, 153
land records, 176, 180–182
Land Titling Bill, 181
land-ocean interfaces, 233
LARR. *See* Land Acquisition, Rehabilitation, and Resettlement (LARR) Bill

T

Tariff Authority for Major Ports, 142–143
technocratization of military leadership, 286–287
telecommunications industry, 98
Tendulkar poverty line, 47
Terrorism, 309
tertiary education, 106, 116–118
transaction costs, regarding land, 172–175
transport infrastructure: fundamental issues facing, 136–139; modal mix, 148; modernizing, 135–149
Transport Ministry, 148
tribal populations, 178, 241
trickle-down growth, 46
Twelfth Five Year Plan (2012–2017) document, 127

U

Union List, 109, 229, 273
United Progressive Alliance (UPA), 42–45, 53, 91, 209, 266, 270–271, 297–299, 301–306
United States, 299, 300, 303
universal franchise, 4, 5
universal health coverage, 122, 129–132
University Grants Commission, 109
urban densities, 162–163
urbanization: coordinated response for managing, 166–169; increasing demand for commercial fuels, 219; managing, 151–169; overview, 152–158; stylized facts on, 153

V

Vajpayee, Atal Bihari, 297, 298, 299
visa policies, 305

W

wastewater, 192, 193, 237
Water and Land Management Institutes, 187
water economy, 186–187
welfare state: dismantling, 41–53; expenditures of, 49
Western Ghats Expert Ecology Panel, 242
White Revolution, in milk, 58, 64
wind energy, 216
worker population ratio (WPR), 93, 102n8

Z

zoning and regulations, 175–177

CONTRIBUTORS

Ritu Anand is an economist with expertise in macroeconomics and public policy. She has extensive experience working with financial institutions, multilaterals, government, and regulators in the areas of economics and policy. She retired from the Infrastructure Development Finance Company (IDFC) as a group head and chief economist at the end of 2013. Before joining the IDFC, she held the position of deputy managing director and chief economic adviser at the State Bank of India; lead economist at the World Bank; adviser at the Reserve Bank of India; and various positions with the Finance Commission, Planning Commission, Bureau of Industrial Costs and Prices, government of India, and Tata Consultancy Services. Anand holds an MSc in Economics from the London School of Economics and a BA from Wellesley College and one from St. Xavier's College, Mumbai.

Surjit S. Bhalla is chairman of Oxus Investments, a New Delhi-based economic research, asset management, and emerging-markets advisory firm. He has taught at the Delhi School of Economics and held positions at the RAND Corporation, the Brookings Institution, and the research and treasury departments of the World Bank. He has also worked at Goldman Sachs (1992–1994) and Deutsche Bank (1994–1996). He is the author of *Devaluing to Prosperity: Misaligned Currencies and Their Growth Consequences* (2012) and *Imagine There's No Country: Poverty, Inequality,*

and Growth in the Era of Globalization (2002). His present research interests include the study of the middle class, male preference, and skewed sex
ratios, and the effect of economic performance on electoral outcomes. He
has been a member of several government committees on economic policy,
most recently the committee on capital account convertibility. He is on
the board of the National Council of Applied Economic Research, India's
largest think tank, and was an appointed member of the National
Statistical Commission of India. He is also a regular contributor to news-
papers and magazines on economics, politics, and cricket.

Laveesh Bhandari leads Indicus Anlytics, India's premier economics
research firm. He works on issues related to the measurement and analysis
of socioeconomic deprivation, access to education and health, and the performance of markets. He has done extensive work on inequality and socioeconomic performance at the level of states, districts, and cities of India.
After receiving a PhD in economics from Boston University, he worked at
the National Council of Applied Economic Research in New Delhi before
founding Indicus Analytics. He has also taught at the Indian Institute of
Technology Delhi and is the former managing editor of the *Journal of
Emerging Market Finance.*

Bibek Debroy is a professor at the Center for Policy Research, New Delhi.
He has worked in academia, industry chambers, and for the government,
including in leadership positions in the Legal Adjustments and Reforms
for Globalizing the Economy project and the Commission on Legal
Empowerment of the Poor. Debroy is the author of several books, papers,
and articles. He holds degrees from Presidency College in Kolkata, the
Delhi School of Economics, and Trinity College in Cambridge.

Omkar Goswami, an economist, is the chairman of CERG Advisory,
which specializes in economic research and corporate consulting. He
received his DPhil from Oxford University in 1982 and taught at several
leading universities in India and abroad from 1982 to 1996. He served as
the editor of *Business India*, a well-known fortnightly publication, and was
the chief economist of the Confederation of Indian Industry from 1998 to
2004 before founding CERG. He also serves as an independent director
on the boards of some of India's best known companies.

Ashok Gulati has held the post of Chair Professor for Agriculture at the Indian Council for Research on International Economic Relations (ICRIER) since March 2014. From 2011 to February 2014 he was Chairman of the Commission for Agricultural Costs and Prices (CACP), a body responsible for recommending Minimum Support Prices (MSPs) of 23 important agri-commodities to the government of India. Prior to this, Gulati was the director of the International Food Policy Research Institute (IFPRI) for more than ten years. Before joining IFPRI, he also served as the NABARD Chair Professor at the Institute of Economic Growth, and Chief Economist at the National Council of Applied Economic Research. He holds an MA and a PhD in Economics from the Delhi School of Economics. Gulati has been a member of the Prime Minister's Economic Advisory Council, the State Planning Board of Karnataka, and the Economic Advisory Committee of the Chief Minister of Andhra Pradesh. He is the author of more than ten books on issues related to Asian agriculture with a focus on India, as well as several research articles in major international and Indian journals.

Sunjoy Joshi is the director of the Observer Research Foundation in New Delhi. He previously served in the Indian Administrative Service for over twenty-five years before he sought early retirement in 2009 to pursue his primary interests in energy and the environment. He has been writing and speaking about India's energy needs and how they are expected to interact with and affect global narratives on development and climate change.

Devesh Kapur was appointed director of the Center for the Advanced Study of India at the University of Pennsylvania in 2006 and is the Madan Lal Sobti Associate Professor for the Study of Contemporary India. Kapur was previously associate professor of government at the University of Texas at Austin, and before that the Frederick Danziger Associate Professor of Government at Harvard. His research focuses on human capital, national and international public institutions, and the ways in which local-global linkages, especially international migration and international institutions, affect political and economic change in developing countries, especially India. His latest book, *Diaspora, Democracy and Development: The Impact of International Migration From India on India*, was published by Princeton

University Press in August 2010, and earned him the 2012 ENMISA (Ethnicity, Nationalism, and Migration Section of the International Studies Association) Distinguished Book Award. Kapur holds a BTech in chemical engineering from the Institute of Technology, Banaras Hindu University, an MS in chemical engineering from the University of Minnesota, and a PhD from the Woodrow Wilson School at Princeton.

Rajiv Kumar, a well-known Indian economist, is the author of several books on the Indian economy and India's national security and one of the country's leading columnists. He is presently a senior fellow at the Center for Policy Research, New Delhi, and a senior fellow with the Wadhwani Foundation, New Delhi. He was secretary general of the Federation of Indian Chambers of Commerce and Industry (2010–2012); director and chief executive of the Indian Council for Research on International Economic Relations (ICRIER, 2006–2010); and chief economist of the Confederation of India Industries (2004–2006). He worked in the Asian Development Bank, Manila, from 1995 to 2005. Kumar is presently an international board member of the King Abdullah Petroleum Studies and Research Center, Riyadh, and the Economic Research Institute for Asia (ERIA), Jakarta. In India he is a member of the Central Board of the State Bank of India, India's largest commercial bank, the Governing Board of the Gokhale Institute of Economics and Politics, Pune, and the board of directors of the Indian Institute of Foreign Trade, Delhi. He was a member of the government of India's National Security Advisory Board for 2006–2008. He holds a DPhil in economics from Oxford University and a PhD from Lucknow University.

Rajiv Lall is the executive chairman of the Infrastructure Development Finance Company (IDFC). He has three decades of experience with leading global investment banks, in multilateral agencies, and in academia. His areas of expertise include project finance, private equity and venture capital, international capital markets, trade, infrastructure, and macroeconomic policy issues. Lall is an avid commentator on issues related to public policy. He writes a regular column for the *Business Standard*, a leading financial daily in India. He was India's representative to the Group of 20 Workgroup on Infrastructure and has chaired the Global Agenda

Council on Infrastructure at the World Economic Forum. He is a member of the City of London's Advisory Council on India and chairs the Confederation of Indian Industry's National Committee on Infrastructure. Lall is a member of the Managing Committee of ASSOCHAM. He was also a member of the Planning Commission's Steering Committee on Urban Development Management set up to help formulate India's Twelfth Five Year Plan, the prime minister's Committees on Infrastructure Finance and Transport Sector Development, and the Expert Group on Modernization of Indian Railways. He holds a BA in Politics, Philosophy, and Economics from Oxford University and a PhD in Economics from Columbia University.

Somik V. Lall is a lead economist for urban development at the World Bank. He was a core team member of the *World Development Report 2009: Reshaping Economic Geography*, and recently senior economic counselor to the Indian Prime Minister's National Transport Development Policy Committee. He currently leads a World Bank program on the Urbanization Reviews, which provides diagnostic tools and a policy framework for policymakers to manage rapid urbanization and city development. His research interests span urban and spatial economics, infrastructure development, and public finance, with more than 40 publications featured in peer-reviewed journals, edited volumes, and working papers. He was a coauthor of the World Bank report *Urbanization Beyond Municipal Boundaries: Nurturing Metropolitan Economies and Connecting Peri-Urban Areas in India*, published in 2013, which forms the basis for the contributed paper in this volume.

Barun S. Mitra is a commentator on current affairs on a range of issues from economic development to wildlife conservation. His articles have appeared in Indian and international publications. His current interest is the interface between political context and public policy and its effect on the viability of policy proposals. Mitra is the founder and director of the Liberty Institute, a nonprofit, independent public policy research and advocacy organization based in New Dehi that was recognized with the Templeton Prize for Social Entrepreneurship in 2003. He also directed the award-winning Empowering India initiative of Liberty Institute, which seeks to make democracy more meaningful and encourages active citizenship. In 2011, he conceptualized the Right to Property initiative, in collaboration with Action Research in Community Health and Development (ARCH) in Gujarat, to help indigenous communities living in and around forest areas claim their land rights and rights over local resources. Mitra was trained as an electrical and marine engineer.

Madhumita D. Mitra is an independent legal consultant. She has worked with the Indian government, advised corporate clients, and consulted for nongovernmental and international organizations on regulatory issues. She is interested in transparency and anticorruption, employment and business ethics, property rights and public interest law. Mitra holds an LLM from the Washington College of Law, American University, a BA in Law from the Faculty of Law, University of Delhi, and a BA and MA in English from the University of Madras.

C. Raja Mohan heads the Strategic Studies Program at the Observer Research Foundation in New Delhi and is the foreign affairs columnist for the *Indian Express*, a leading English language newspaper published from multiple centers in India. He was professor of South Asian studies at the Jawaharlal Nehru University, New Delhi, and the Nanyang Technological University, Singapore. He is a nonresident senior associate at the Carnegie Endowment for International Peace in Washington, DC, a nonresident fellow at the Lowy Institute for International Policy in Sydney, and a visiting research professor at the Institute of South Asian Studies in Singapore. His latest book is *Samudra Manthan: Sino-Indian Rivalry in the Indo-Pacific.*

Ligia Noronha is executive director (research coordination) at the Energy and Resources Institute (TERI) and serves as the director of the Resources, Regulation and Global Security Division, leading research on resources, environment, trade, and sustainable development. She currently serves on the National Security Advisory Board of the government of India; is a member of the Global Agenda Council on Responsible Management of Natural Resources, World Economic Forum; and is a member of the "Good Governance of Extractive and Land Resources" thematic group of the United Nations Sustainable Development Solutions Network.

Ila Patnaik is a nonresident senior associate in the Carnegie Endowment's South Asia Program. She is also a professor at the National Institute of Public Finance and Policy (NIPFP) in New Delhi. Her main area of interest is the study of India as an opening economy, and her research includes issues related to capital flows, business cycles, the financial sector, and Indian firms as India opens up its capital account. She writes regular columns in the *Indian Express* and the *Financial Express*. Before joining NIPFP in 2006, Patnaik served as economics editor of the *Indian Express* (2004–2006); senior economist at the National Council of Applied Economic Research (NCAER), New Delhi (1996–2002); and senior fellow at the Indian Council for Research in International Economic Relations (ICRIER) (2002–2004). Patnaik was a visiting scholar at the International Monetary Fund in 2003, 2010, and 2013.

Tushaar Shah is a senior fellow with the Colombo-based International Water Management Institute (IWMI) and works out of Anand, Gujarat. Over the past thirty-five years, Shah has published extensively on water and agricultural policies in South Asia and comparative analyses of water governance in South Asia, China, Mexico, and Sub-Saharan Africa. In 2002, Shah was honored with the Outstanding Scientist award of the Consultative Group of International Agricultural Research (CGIAR). Shah led the IWMI-Tata Water Policy Program for several years. His recent work includes *Taming the Anarchy: Groundwater Governance in South Asia*. Shah serves on the boards of several academic institutions and NGOs and is a director on the board of the ICICI Bank.

A. K. Shiva Kumar, a development economist, is a visiting professor at the Indian School of Business in Hyderabad and teaches economics and public policy at Harvard University's Kennedy School of Government. He is also policy adviser to UNICEF India. He has been a regular contributor to the United Nations Development Program's Human Development Reports and is currently a senior adviser to the Human Development Report Office. Shiva Kumar has served on the Indian government's Mission Steering Group of the National Rural Health Mission and was a member of the High Level Expert Group on Universal Health Coverage. He also serves on the boards of several nongovernmental organizations including the Public Health Foundation of India, the International Center for Research on Women, the Institute for Human Development, and the Center for Science and Environment.

Ravinder Pal Singh was formerly a senior fellow at the Institute for Defense Studies and Analyses, New Delhi, and later a Ford Fellow at the University of Maryland. He led the research project on arms procurement decision-making in China, India, Israel, Japan, South Korea, and Thailand at the Stockholm International Peace Research Institute. Subsequently, this project went on to conduct studies in Chile, Greece, Malaysia, Poland, South Africa, and Taiwan. As senior fellow at the Geneva Center for Democratic Control of the Armed Forces, he was engaged in the NATO Parliamentary Assembly's work on security sector reforms in the former Warsaw Pact countries. After the end of the Balkan conflict in 2001, he led the United Nations Development Program Mission for Security Sector Reforms in the Former Republic of Yugoslavia. His current work is on security sector governance and civil-military relations in transitioning democracies.

Ashley J. Tellis is a senior associate at the Carnegie Endowment for International Peace specializing in international security, defense, and Asian strategic issues. While on assignment to the U.S. Department of State as senior adviser to the undersecretary of state for political affairs, he was intimately involved in negotiating the civil nuclear agreement with India. Previously, he was commissioned into the Foreign Service and served as senior adviser to the ambassador at the U.S. embassy in New Delhi. He also served on the National Security Council staff as special assistant to the president and senior director for strategic planning and Southwest Asia.

Reece Trevor is a research assistant in the South Asia Program at the Carnegie Endowment for International Peace, where he was previously a junior fellow focusing on South Asian security and U.S. grand strategy. Prior to joining Carnegie, he served as a congressional aide in the U.S. House of Representatives. He completed his BA with honors at the University of Chicago.

Milan Vaishnav is an associate in the South Asia Program at the Carnegie Endowment for International Peace in Washington, DC, where he coordinates Carnegie's India Decides 2014 initiative. He has previously worked at the Center for Strategic and International Studies, the Council on Foreign Relations, and as a postdoctoral research fellow at the Center for Global Development. He has also taught at Columbia, Georgetown, and the George Washington University. His primary research focus is the political economy of India, and he is currently writing a book on the interplay between corruption, democracy, and economic reform in India. He holds a PhD in Political Science from Columbia University.

Shilp Verma is an independent researcher and doctoral fellow with the Integrated Water Systems and Governance Group at UNESCO-IHE in Delft, the Netherlands. Verma graduated with honors in economics from the University of Delhi in 1998 and completed his postgraduate program in Rural Management in 2001 at the Institute of Rural Management, Anand (IRMA), before joining the International Water Management Institute (IWMI). In 2005, Verma received an IWMI fellowship to undertake an MSc in Water Resources Management at UNESCO-IHE. The main areas of his research include groundwater governance, the energy-irrigation nexus, river basin management, community management of water resources, water-food-trade policies, and smallholder farming in South Asia and Sub-Saharan Africa.

Tara Vishwanath is currently a lead economist at the World Bank, Middle East and North Africa region. Before joining the Bank, she was a professor in the economics department at Northwestern University and has published widely in leading international economics journals. At the Bank, she has led the work on poverty, gender, and impact evaluation focusing on countries in South Asia and the Middle East. She also led the work on the report *Urbanization Beyond Municipal Boundaries: Nurturing Metropolitan Economies and Connecting Peri-Urban Areas in India*, published in 2013, which forms the basis for the contributed paper in this volume.

CARNEGIE ENDOWMENT FOR INTERNATIONAL PEACE

The Carnegie Endowment for International Peace is a unique global network of policy research centers in Russia, China, Europe, the Middle East, and the United States. Our mission, dating back more than a century, is to advance the cause of peace through analysis and development of fresh policy ideas and direct engagement and collaboration with decisionmakers in government, business, and civil society. Working together, our centers bring the inestimable benefit of multiple national viewpoints to bilateral, regional, and global issues.